Racial Conflict and Healing

An Asian-American Theological Perspective

ANDREW SUNG PARK

ORBIS BOOKS

Maryknoll, New York 10545

The Catholic Foreign Mission Society of America (Maryknoll) recruits and trains people for overseas missionary service. Through Orbis Books, Maryknoll aims to foster the international dialogue that is essential to mission. The books published, however, reflect the opinions of their authors and are not meant to represent the official position of the society.

*In memory of my mother, Chong Hui Kim,
who gave me her unconditional care and love,
and my father, Chae Ki Park,
who taught me his unreserved faith in God*

Contents

PART III

METHODOLOGY

PART IV

AN EMERGING THEOLOGY

Preface

I asked my ten-year-old son, Amos, "Do you enjoy living this life?" Puzzled, he responded, "What do you mean?" I explained, "You weren't here ten years ago. Compared with the time before you were born, do you like this life?" He answered, "I don't remember that time, so I can't compare it with now." Then he asked, "Where was I before my birth, and why am I here?" I could not answer his questions.

No one volunteers for his or her present life. Amos did not choose his parents, gender, race, or nationality. Even a bird or an insect does not select its own species. This means that there is no basis upon which to claim superiority to any other person—or any other creature.

We are all here to live the lives that have been given to us. There is nothing to boast of or to feel shameful about concerning our intrinsic being. There is nothing we can despise or disrespect in the world. All the animals and all the races, all people of the two genders, must be respected as they are. Everything has a divine right to be here. The one thing that is required is that we live our life faithfully and truthfully.

So, why is there so much racism in this society? Recently the Los Angeles eruptions and the O. J. Simpson trial have divided us sharply along racial lines and have raised racial tensions. It seems almost impossible to bridge the profound gap between races.

Will racial conflict endlessly swell, or is racial healing possible? Who will bring about reconciliation and healing? What is the role of the church in a racially divided society?

I believe that the primary task of the church in the United States is to elicit racial justice and healing. All other accomplishments of the church (such as growth in church membership, increase in the church budget, construction of new church buildings, even the zeal of the church for Bible study) can be superficial and hypocritical if the church neglects the pressing issue of racial justice.

I believe it is possible to change the situation of racial conflict by changing our deep images of each other and by transforming the structure of racial discrimination. As a Christian, I dare to undertake this difficult problem from a Korean-American perspective. Korean-Americans were victims of the Los Angeles eruptions, with over twenty-five hundred Korean-American shops attacked, looted, and burned. We are the "oppressed of the oppressed," without political or social protection.

I believe that true reconciliation can take place only when an oppressed group initiates it; only the oppressed can generate a racially harmonious society. Using a Korean and Christian spiritual ethos, I attempt in this book to bring basic healing to a racially wounded society.

In completing this book, I am deeply indebted to the following individuals. Editor Susan Perry devotedly carried out her work despite the fact that she had barely recuperated from her automobile accident. Publisher Robert Gormley of Orbis Books has strongly supported this project from the beginning. I am also grateful to Production Coordinator Catherine Costello for her helpful work. Newell Wert, former dean of United Theological Seminary, read the whole manuscript and made many valuable comments. Susan Brooks Thistlethwaite of Chicago Theological Seminary suggested some inspiring titles for the book. Stuart McLean of Phillips University and Seminary and Robert McAfee Brown of Pacific School of Religion helped and encouraged me in many ways. My former colleague Cornish Rogers provided helpful resources. Through my colleague Marsha Foster-Boyd, Warren Lee of San Francisco Theological Seminary sent his autobiography to me. Kwang Chung Kim of Western Illinois University and Sang Yil Kim of Hanshin University suggested useful resources. Young Chan Ro of George Mason University shared his insight. My colleagues at United Theological Seminary have been very supportive of this project. Barry Gannon, Patricia Wagner, Suzanne Smailes, and Ritter Warner were very helpful in improving the manuscript. Martha Anderson assisted me in preparing the bibliography.

Finally, I deeply appreciate my spouse, Sun-Ok Jane Myong, for her steady support and love. I also thank my two sons, Amos (10) and Thomas (7), for their direct and indirect contributions to the book. During the lonely period of the writing, the time to play with them was my joy.

Introduction

One sunny afternoon my son Amos, then eight years old, ran to the house, saying that some children had taken his bicycle. I rushed out with him, got into my car, drove two blocks and found about nine boys riding bicycles. One of the youngest—about five years old—sped away from me on Amos's bike. I shouted aloud, "Stop! Come here." The tallest and oldest boy, the ring leader of the group, was shouting, "Run away! Run away!" The little boy was scared, however, and came back to me. We got back the bicycle with Amos's wrist watch hanging on it. "Are you going to report us to the police?" asked one of the boys. I replied, "I will report the incident, but I will not turn you in to the police." They had a girl's bicycle with them, too. Therefore, I began to moralize with them for a few minutes, and then I confronted the oldest boy (who said he was fourteen years old), demanding that they not do such a thing again. He did not like my reproof and he reviled me. He even threatened me by showing me part of something metal in his back pocket. I was scared, but I asked, "What's that, a gun?" (Ril Beatty, Sr., a civil rights leader, was killed by a seventeen-year-old boy two weeks before this incident—September 24, 1994—when he tried to quiet three rowdy youths in front of his house. He was the father of one of our seminarians.) The other kids said, "No." In fact, it was a pair of pliers. In the end, all the boys except the oldest apologized and promised that they would not do such a thing again. However, I felt humiliated by this fourteen-year-old boy and experienced hurt.

I came back home depressed. My mood lasted for several long days. During this time my yearning for a just and peaceful society in the United States became real. It gradually dawned on me that the incident of the bicycle theft brought back memories of the Los Angeles eruptions (I was a resident of the Los Angeles area at that time and witnessed the eruptions). Beyond the problem of racial division, these two incidents revealed the problems of the socio-economic and political structures that result in class division and racial conflict. When Amos's bike was stolen, we lived near the seminary in Dayton, in a predominantly middle-class African-American neighborhood, whereas these children came from west Dayton, a poor neighborhood where, not long ago, one child killed another in order to steal his expensive jacket.

The United States has faced racial and ethnic strife and economic disparity for a long time. It may not collapse suddenly, as the Soviet Union did in 1992, but it can disintegrate slowly. How this country deals with these matters will determine its final destiny.

To provide a portrait of a harmonious ethnic America sociologists have come up with different theories. Amalgamation theories envision a melting-pot America, where all different racial and ethnic groups intermingle and integrate together, finding their new American identity. Assimilation views stress the consolidation of diverse cultures into the dominant culture. On the other hand, cultural pluralism theories project a society where various groups keep their cultural identities, celebrating their diversities. The ideal is unity in diversity and diversity in unity.

In the early part of the twentieth century, melting-pot theories and assimilation theories predominated. The policy of the government, favoring European immigration, made such theories possible. Presently, with more non-European immigrants, the view of cultural pluralism prevails in our social arena. Although racial and ethnic diversity is stressed, we have experienced little unity. These sociological models are insufficient to advance our society to a new plane of racial and ethnic relations. By focusing on racial and ethnic relations, these theories have endeavored to improve them. This focus, however, is the precise reason that they have not accomplished their purposes, for they overlooked the significance of socio-economic and spiritual factors. The nine African-American children did not steal my son's bicycle because he was a Korean-American. The Los Angeles eruptions did not start from South Central Los Angeles, the poor neighborhood of African-Americans and Hispanic-Americans, without reason. Even if ethnic and racial harmony is achieved today in Los Angeles, more racial eruptions will occur tomorrow unless we change the inner-city economy and its socio-spiritual structure and ethos. This book is an effort to prevent such destructive events and to improve ethnic relations.

I would like to address this issue of racial and ethnic relations from an Asian-American perspective. Very little work has been done in this area from either theological or Asian-American perspectives. Most churches, except for some ethnic churches, have been relatively silent on the issue. Few theological models have been suggested on this pivotal matter. There was no map I could depend on to find my way out of the mire of racial and ethnic relations. This project is the result of my own struggle to create such a theological and Asian-American model.

We need a strategy to change our social conditions. By changing the way we see, I believe that we can turn our society into a community of care and equity. To do so, not only a paradigm shift in our thinking but a vision shift is needed. When our inmost vision is shifted, action will come naturally.

To change our social problems, cultural diversity and unity are not enough. Economic and political changes must take place. Simultaneously, we need to change our religion, which is the soul of our culture. Without changing the spirit of the culture, a deep change is unlikely. That is, in order to change our society it is necessary to change our cultural "unconsciousness" and "superconsciousness," as well as the consciousness of the society.

In shifting our images of the self, others, and society, we move from the society (*Gesellschaft*) of oppression, repression, injustice, violence, and mammonism into a community (*Gemeinschaft*) of equity, fairness, and consideration for others.[1] We need, therefore, some theological models for our racial and ethnic relations. The basic motif of this book is *han* (a Korean term describing the ineffable pain of the unjustly oppressed). A deep *han* of this society is its individualistic ideology, which underlies corporate America, its media, culture, and Christianity.

This book suggests a model of *transmutation* as an alternative vision. This theological model surpasses the view of the melting-pot community (assimilation to the one dominant culture) and the view of a culturally pluralistic society, where either unity or diversity is stressed. The vision of transmutation underscores economic, socio-political, and cultural *conversion* as well as their diversity and unity. This model espouses the shared enhancement of various racial and ethnic groups. To change others means recognizing that they have their own bases from which they carry out their dialogue and transforming work. Through strengthening one another, various groups move toward unity. Through finding their own bases, they come to find their own uniqueness (diversity).

The impetus of reciprocal enhancement does not arise from simple theories or models. It emerges from the indispensable and inmost visions that diverse groups share. These visions draw us near and empower all of us to become ourselves.

The methodologies we employ are crucial in our struggle for treating the *han* and the sin of our society. The process of healing is as important as healing itself. Such transformation does not begin with good intentions only. First and foremost, we must *see* each other. Seeing is the power of mutual transmutation. It changes both the seeing and the seen. If we truly see, the seeing will guide us into the next steps to resolve our social *han*. We are here to see each other. Seeing presupposes *being*, causes *understanding*, and elicits *change*.

We can engender a society in which we truly see each other and enjoy each other's company. In this seeing, people's *han* begins to melt. By seeing each other's strength, our capacity comes to its full blossoming. By seeing others' shortcomings with supportive eyes, we help each other to complete our incompleteness.

Augustine set a theological model for his own time in *De Civitate Dei* (*The City of God*). This work was his defense of Christianity against accusations that neglect of the old Roman gods was the cause of the downfall of Rome. Augustine posited two cities, each founded on love. The *earthly city* is built on love of self, even to the contempt of God; the *city of God* is founded on the love of God. Although these two cities are intermingled at the present, only the city of God will last in the end. Built on self-love, all the powerful earthly kingdoms and cities will wither and fade away in spite of their transitory glories, as Babylon and Rome did. Constructed on God's will and salvation, the city of God will stand tall and endure.

The present work treats the current socio-economic and cultural issues against the backdrop of the Los Angeles eruptions of 1992. Analyzing the root causes of the eruptions, I make distinctions between sin and *han*. Discussing and treating the problem of sin as traditional churches have done does not fully address certain issues that our society is facing. To make our society sounder, we must distinguish sin from *han* and provide some relevant prescriptions for their dissolution. Korean-Americans as well as many other ethnic people suffer more from *han* than sin.[2] Accordingly, Korean-American churches must address the issue of actual *han* more, although they should not neglect the matters of sin. For example, few Korean-Americans kill others; more are killed by others. It is perhaps unnecessary to stress not killing to the victims of violence. We need to keep a balance between *han* and sin, but in the past we have unilaterally emphasized the matter of sin; for the oppressed, we need to put more weight on *han* for their healing and new visions for social change.[3]

This project consists of three parts. Part I is a diagnosis of social problems from a Korean-American perspective. Chapter 1 describes *han*, sharing tales of *han* as related to the Asian-American experience. Chapter 2 analyzes the *han* of the Korean-American community in the setting of the 1992 Los Angeles eruptions. Their root causes are diagnosed as the expansion of transnational corporations, racial discrimination, redlining, discrimination against entrepreneurs, and classism. Since the *han* of our society is more decisive than its sin in our daily struggle, it is discussed first. We need, however, to be concerned about the issue of sin as well. Chapter 3 treats the sins of the Korean-American community, such as labor exploitation, racial prejudice, and a sexist culture.

Part II suggests some answers to the problems we investigated in Part I. Chapter 4 suggests developing some visions that can lead our society to becoming a community of unity. I mean here vital visions that no group can achieve by itself but can only accomplish in cooperation with other racial and ethnic groups. Without such visions, our society will balkanize further and further—and will suffer more racial and ethnic conflict. Furthermore, we need some inmost visions that transcend the category of indispensability and reach an intrinsic appreciation of "otherness." When these deep-seated visions grasp us, we are bound to change our world.

Chapter 5 treats an innermost vision of the self in order to surmount American rugged individualism through suggesting the trinitarian self of Asian thinking. No self can exist by itself; the trinitarian self is formed from the relationship between a person and his or her parents. This understanding of the trinitarian self supports *parens, ergo sum* ("I am interconnected to parents, therefore I am") rather than *cogito, ergo sum* ("I think, therefore I am").

Chapter 6 deals with a Christian understanding of *parousia*, an innermost vision of the future Christian society. Many Christians, particularly Korean-American Christians, are preoccupied with the wrong image of the second coming of Christ. As most Jewish people have waited for the first coming of a glorious messiah, so many Christians await the second coming of a magnificent Christ. Here *parousia* is reinterpreted as the coming of the *han*-suffering.

Part III discusses how to achieve the goals of the solutions. Chapter 7 treats major sociological theories for the racial and ethnic relations of America: the amalgamation theory, the assimilation theory, cultural pluralism, the triple melting-pot theory, and the new ethnic identity theory. Most dominant sociological theories are lacking in the dimension of societal reformation in their striving to bring about a harmonious society; they lack socio-economic analyses and solutions.

Chapter 8 looks into three Korean-American models: a withdrawal model, an assimilation model, and a paradoxical model. On the one hand, in light of the Korean-American models it can be seen that most sociological theories neglect the presence of non-European groups in society. On the other, this chapter indicates the need to develop a relevant Korean-American model for a creative society.

Chapter 9 suggests a transmutation model, a Korean-American model. Instead of espousing sociological theories, this view challenges the horizontal emphases of racial and ethnic relations and treats the communal repentance of each ethnic group as well as the healing of its *han*, an approach the three sociological models lack.

Chapter 10 quests for some insights of Korean thought that might contribute to the wholeness of society. Such concepts as *hahn* (divine greatness and acceptance), *jung* (affection and endearment), and *mut* (harmonious beauty, the zestful art of life) are introduced to express Koreanness and enrich the meaning of cross-cultural transformation.

Chapter 11 illustrates a way of healing *han* at the basic level of the social unit: the family. Presently, we are approaching a post-nuclear-family era. The nuclear family is gradually disintegrating in many sectors of society. We cannot go back to the nuclear family, but we should move forward to a modified form of the extended family in order to heal the brokenness of the lonely.

Part IV reaches toward an emerging theology of seeing. Seeing is the best gateway of transmuting *han* into the creative strength of *hahn, jung*, and *mut*. Chapter 12 discusses the significance of seeing in the Bible. The biblical revelation means nothing without our seeing. The good news is good news when we not only hear it, but also see it. Without seeing, revelation cannot be revelation.

Chapter 13 develops a theology of seeing through which we try to resolve the problems of *han* and sin. Genuine seeing triggers oppressors to repent of their sins and the oppressed to resolve their *han*. This book focuses on the disintegration of *han* and the vision of a new world order. Through what we have in our mind, we see others. Our creative seeing toward others changes their thinking and behavior. Seeing is *under*standing for the oppressors and *up*standing for the oppressed. It is also transmuting.

Chapter 14 treats the four perspectives of seeing for resolving *han*: visual seeing, intellectual seeing, spiritual seeing, and soul seeing. Through all four types of seeing we transmute *han* into the vision of *hahn, jung*, and *mut*. Visual seeing uses an imagery hermeneutics of questioning to unmask the *han*-ridden world. Our senses and perception comprise visual seeing. Intellectual seeing corresponds to an imagery hermeneutics of construction, which transmutes our *han* into the vision of *hahn* at a conscious level. Spiritual seeing engages an imagery hermeneutics of affection, which turns our *han* into the heart of *jung* at an unconscious level. Soul seeing utilizes an imagery hermeneutics of celebration, which changes our *han* into the art of *mut* at a superconscious level. *Mut* arises when the mind of *hahn* and the heart of *jung* are united. It is the zestful art of life in the midst of sorrow and suffering.

Part I

PROBLEMS IN THE KOREAN-AMERICAN COMMUNITY

1

Han-Talk

THE PORTRAIT OF *HAN*

When a person puts up with long suffering or a sharp intense pang of injustice, he or she develops a "node" of pain inside—a visceral, psychological, and pneumatic reaction to the unbearable pain. This phenomenon is called *han* in Korean. *Han* is the inexpressibly entangled experience of pain and bitterness imposed by the injustice of oppressors.

The term *han* is too intricate to define completely. Korean *minjung* theologian Young-Hak Hyun, however, describes it as follows:

> *Han* is a sense of unresolved resentment against injustice suffered, a sense of helplessness because of the overwhelming odds against, a feeling of acute pain of sorrow in one's guts and bowels making the whole body writhe and wriggle, and an obstinate urge to take "revenge" and to right the wrong all these combined.[1]

Han is the void of grief that the suffering innocent experiences. When grief surpasses its sensibility line, it becomes a void. This void is not a mere hollowness, but an abyss filled with agony. *Han* is the abyss of the dark night of grief. As a long or sharp agony turns into a dark void, the void swallows all the other agendas of life, intensifying its hollowness. *Han* is the experience of the powerless, the marginalized, the voiceless of our society. Women, particularly, have experienced the long suffering of dehumanization. Thus, their *han* is deeper than men's.

Social injustice, political repression, economic exploitation, cultural contempt, and war, all of which affect the downtrodden as a whole, raise the collective *han*. When the oppressed undergo suffering over several generations without release, they develop collective unconscious *han* and transmit it to their posterity. In Jungian terms, this is something similar to the "collective unconscious."[2] Collective uncon-

9

scious *han* is, however, different from Jung's. For Jung, the collective unconscious is "more like an atmosphere in which we live than something that is found in us."[3] Jung's collective conscious is universal, whereas the collective unconscious *han* is particular to certain persons or groups. Furthermore, for Jung, "the self is not only the centre, but also the whole circumference which embraces both conscious and unconscious; it is the centre of this totality, just as the ego is the centre of consciousness."[4] Individual unconscious *han* is not only embedded in the substratum of the self but also in the bottom of a racial ethos. This *han* deepens and hardens generation after generation in the history of the downtrodden.[5]

As an inexpressible feeling, *han* cannot be neatly analyzed. Neither can it be bifurcated, but, for purposes of illustrating its depth, we can distinguish four categories within it. It has two dimensions: personal and collective.[6] Each dimension has two levels: conscious and unconscious.

At the personal conscious level *han* is expressed as the will to revenge and resignation. At its personal unconscious level, *han* is buried in bitterness and helplessness.

At its collective conscious level, *han* is demonstrated through the corporate will to revolt and corporate despair. At its collective unconscious level, it is submerged under racial, sexual, and religious resentment and the ethos of composite lamentation. Nature has global *han*, expressed through anomalies of climate and natural disasters.[7]

Han was originally a shamanistic term used to describe the unresolved entanglement of the dead, the bereft, and the down-and-out. Shamanism was the religion of the downtrodden, and its goal was to resolve their *han*. It was revived by *minjung* theologians in the 1970s. How to resolve *han* has been a major issue of Korean sociology, anthropology, history, literature, arts, and particularly theology since then.

The term *han* exists in other Asian countries. In Chinese, *hen*, which has the same ideograph as *han*, means "to hate" and "to dislike."[8] It enfolds extreme passion for vengeance, abhorrence, and cursing. *Hen* holds a much stronger and more negative meaning than *han*. In speaking of remorse, Chinese *hen* contains more intensive meaning than that of Korean *han*. A story in the *Shih Ching* or "Classic of Songs" characterizes the Chinese concept of *hen*: King Fu-Tzu of Wu swore his vengeance against King Kou-Tzu of Yueh, and he slept painfully on top of brush wood in order not to rest his heart of revenge. In turn, King Kou-Tzu engraved revenge in his heart by chewing the dry gall bladder of an animal in order not to forget his original intention of vengeance.[9]

In Japanese, *han* is pronounced *kon*. *Kon* means "to bear a grudge" and "show resentment."[10] The term *kon* is not used by itself, however. People use it in *enkon* to express a deep revengeful mind. *Enkon* or *urami* characterizes the unplacated spirit of the deceased.[11] It also signifies a vengeful mind like the Chinese *hen*. The popular story of the forty-seven samurai in the tradition of the Bushido spirit epitomizes the Japanese *enkon*. The story goes like this: A certain feudal lord was trapped into drawing his sword in the Edo castle and was unfairly forced to commit suicide. His forty-seven samurai vowed vengeance against the enemy lord. One snowy night when half the enemy castle guard was sent away, they stormed the castle and caught the enemy lord. They required him to commit suicide. When he could not do it, they decapitated him. After this vengeance, they quietly waited until the government required their suicide. All Japan chanted their praises, and ever since they have been the unrivalled exemplars of Bushido.[12] This real event took place in 1702 and epitomized the Japanese notion of *han* and its way of resolution.

In Vietnamese, *han* is *han*. Its meaning is similar to the Korean, probably due to their similar geopolitical situations. The *han* of Koreans coincides with the *han* of the Vietnamese. Luat Trong Tran, a Vietnamese-American pastor, summarized the tragic results of the thirty-year war (1945-1975) with the term *han*. Children were born under the thunder of bombers, grew up in battle fields, and experienced a life of destruction. Almost every Vietnamese has experienced the loss of a family member, relative, or friend in the war, which killed two million Vietnamese, injured four million, and left 57 percent of the population homeless.[13] No other word can better describe their experience of bitterness than *han*.

Korean Buddhist Ko Eun explored the meaning of *han* in other Asian countries. In Mongolian, *han* is *horosul*, and it denotes melancholy and sorrowfulness. In Manchurian, *han* is equivalent to *korsocuka*. Its meaning has two phases: before the fall of the Ching Dynasty, *korsocuka* meant anger and hatred; after its fall, it has changed to mean sadness and grief over tragedy.[14]

In ancient Hindi, *han* is expressed as *upanaha*. It consists of two words: *upa* ("near to") and *naha* ("sitting or lying down") and originally meant "being close to me." Later, it evolved into "being attached to something," and then into "malevolence," "loathing," and "rancor." While Korean *han* features its passive character, Indian *upanaha* underscores its active nature.[15]

These expressions of *han* in different Asian countries have different emphases. The Korean notion of *han* stresses the more sad, melancholy, and passive aspect of *han* in its meaning and perception of human suffering. Each country's concept of *han* reflects its own geopolitical, sociocultural, economic, and historical background.

The following narratives are stories of *han* limited to Asian-Americans, particularly to Korean-Americans. They are here because of *han*, and their living in a new land is a *han*-laden life. The stories will explain their *han*ful backgrounds.

THE *HAN* OF WAR AND THE DIVIDED KOREA

When Germany lost the war in 1945, it was divided because of its potential threat to future world peace. When Japan lost the war in 1945, *Korea* was divided, with its south occupied by the United States and its north by the Soviet Union. Why was Korea divided, when it was Japan that started the war and was a potential threat to future world peace? Let us review briefly the *han* of the division of Korea.

In 1882 the United States signed a treat of amity with Korea, which stipulated mutual protection. After defeating China in 1894, Japan waited for the right opportunity to annex Korea. In July 1905 Japanese Prime Minister Taro Katsura and American Secretary of War William Howard Taft secretly met in Tokyo. Their meeting produced the Taft-Katsura Agreement, in which the United States sanctioned Japan's annexation of Korea; in return, Japan pledged not to object to American rule in the Philippines.[16] According to Tyler Dennett, President Theodore Roosevelt wrote to Russia that "Korea must be under the protectorate of Japan."[17] Not knowing of the agreement between Japan and the United States, King Kojong of Korea sent an emissary to President Roosevelt to beg for help based on the treaty of amity. Roosevelt refused even to see Homer Herbert, the emissary, an American missionary and educator.[18]

In 1905 Japan forced Korea to sign the Protective Treaty, which empowered Japan to interfere with Korea's governing. In 1910 Japan annexed Korea. For the next thirty-six years Korea suffered under the iron rule of Japan. Such a disgrace as the loss of its national sovereignty had never happened before in the five-thousand-year history of Korea. The deep pain and disgrace of the Koreans were increased when the Japanese imperialists forced them to use Japanese rather than their own language and to change their names into Japanese. For Koreans, their language and the act of naming were the core of their soul.

During the Second World War, Japan attacked the United States. The United States fought back furiously. Struck with nuclear bombs, Japan unconditionally surrendered to the United States in 1945. Patrick Blackett, the 1948 Nobel Prize laureate in physics, claimed that the United States did not need the atomic bombs to win the war against Japan. The all-out air attack on Japan was already accomplishing this. Yet the United States devastated Japan with the two nuclear bombs, slaughtering numerous, innocent civilians. Although many believed that the bombing was necessary to save American lives, Blackett believed that was only a partial reason. The major reason for dropping the bombs was that the long-demanded Soviet offensive was supposed to take its planned course on August 8, 1945. At that time the Soviet armies were moving from the Western front to the Eastern. The United

States feared that Stalin might claim a part of Japan by participating in the winding-down war against Japan. The United States wanted to force Japan to surrender to American forces alone. Therefore the United States dropped the first nuclear bomb on Japan on August 6, just two days before the Soviet Union formally declared war on Japan.[19]

On August 14, 1945, the United States received the unconditional surrender of Japan. Just before the war ended, on August 10-11, 1945, the decision to divide Korea was made. During a night session of the State-War-Navy Coordinating Committee in Washington, D.C., Assistant Secretary of War John J. McCloy asked two young colonels, Dean Rusk and Charles Bonesteel, to withdraw to an adjacent room and within thirty minutes to locate a place to draw a line across Korea. They chose the thirty-eighth parallel, because it included Seoul in the United States zone.[20] Dean Rusk later acknowledged that this line was "further north than could be realistically reached . . . in the event of Soviet disagreement," since the Soviets had already engaged the Japanese in Korea.[21] When the Soviets complied with the proposed partition, Rusk was "somewhat surprised." This decision on division "has been attributed both to that confusion and to a simple U.S. desire to find a line to demarcate Soviet and U.S. responsibilities in accepting the Japanese surrender."[22] Dean Acheson, then the Secretary of State, admitted that "the United States was an initiator, planner, and author of the division of Korea; if it does not bear the whole responsibility, it bears the major responsibility."[23]

Korea, a non-threatening country, was divided against its will after thirty-six years of oppression by Japan. What irony! Korea was free from Japan only to be divided instead of Japan being divided. Korea became a historical sacrificial lamb in place of a Japan that had ruthlessly oppressed it for thirty-six years. Even worse was the fact that the division caused the Korean War, an outcome of the Cold War between the communist and capitalist camps. It cost millions of lives and the devastation of a barely liberated country.

In addition, the division has burdened both North and South Korea with heavy military spending. They have spent 30 to 40 percent of their national budgets and 6 to 10 percent of their GNP for national defense. For fifty years both Koreas have lost blood from their own defenses, perpetuating military cultures in both states. The year of 1995 is the year of *Jubilee* (the year of liberty, Lv 25:28), in which rest for soil, reversion of landed property, and emancipation from slavery take place. The blood-drenched soil of Korea should rest, separated families (a hundred thousand) should be reunited, the barbed wire of a divided land should be removed, and refugees should be allowed to have their homes back. The division, the root of many evils in Korea, is the main cause of *han* in Korea, and it is partially responsible for the emigration of Koreans. A large number of Korean women married to U.S. soldiers, their families, some students, and many refugees from North Korea have immigrated to the United States.

God sent us to the country that liberated Korea and yet had a heavy hand in the division of Korea. Why are we here? What should we do in this country? There must be some missions for Korean-Americans in this country. I believe that one such mission is to be a voice of conscience over the national interests of the United States so that there will not be another Korea. Influencing this country from within to make honorable decisions is the best way for us to contribute to the true national interests of this country. However difficult our task may be, we should raise a voice for those whose voices are ignored in this country. We are not here just to live comfortably or complacently. God calls us to live justly, responsibly, and truthfully. We should not forget our experience in Korea but should use it for converting this nation to make foreign policy decisions that are just and conscientious before God and before humans.

"COMFORT WOMEN"

About two hundred thousand Korean young women and wives were tricked, conscripted, forcibly taken from their homes, or kidnapped on the streets by the Japanese military government from 1941 to 1945. Called "comfort women," they were raped daily by Japanese soldiers.[24]

Song Ji Kim (alias) recollects, "I was returning home one day when Japanese and Korean men forced me onto a ship headed for Southeast Asia. There I spent four unbearable years."[25] Even now, fifty years later, she wakes up every morning with severe pain all over her weary body. Besides persistent migraines, she suffers from intense stomach cramps that are the outcome of a harsh beating by a Japanese soldier during a sexual assault. Compared with her psychological agony, however, her physical sufferings are minor. The memories of her past continue to haunt and torment her.

Although the Japanese conscripted women from several Asian countries, 80 percent of the comfort women were Koreans. They were scattered around the Asia-Pacific region, wherever Japanese soldiers were based. Some were sent to live in rundown buildings in Hiroshima and Nagasaki, others to remote rural regions of Burma (Myanmar), Thailand, Malaysia, and Papua New Guinea.

Since the Japanese usually provided these women with only small amounts of rice and radishes twice a day, the women were constantly on the border of starvation. Confined to partitioned rooms in stables, storage areas, schools, and temples, these women were coerced to have sex with an average of twenty to thirty and up to seventy soldiers a day.[26]

Those who refused were punished with physical violence, torture, and brutal rape. Many women suffered from venereal diseases, tuberculosis, and other physical ailments, but no medical care was provided.

Kidnapped at the age of twelve while she was playing with a doll house with friends in her village, Oak Boon Lee testified, "On weekends, soldiers waited in a long line of a few hundred meters. . . . A woman from Bo-Joo contracted venereal disease, was beaten every day and died eventually."[27] When these women had free time, they were compelled to do kitchen work. Their conditions were inhuman; they were used for sex, and some were discarded or killed when they became sick. Most "comfort quarters" were quarantined, making escape or suicide almost impossible. When caught trying to escape, some were brought back and ruthlessly beaten or killed. Sung Ja Lee (alias), a survivor, states, "I remember the Japanese soldiers cutting off one of a woman's breasts when they caught a group of us attempting to escape. This atrocity was meant to horrify us."[28]

Many Korean women committed suicide rather than be forced to have sex with Japanese soldiers. In Japan there is a cliff from which hundreds of Korean women plunged into the sea on the way to comfort quarters. The Japanese call it Tazimazmiski Cliff.[29]

Since the Japanese government destroyed the documents concerning comfort women, it is hard to obtain detailed historical information. Documents recently found in Korea reveal that the Japanese government conscripted even elementary school students.[30]

Yoshida Seigi, a former "mobilizer" of Korean women for the Japanese, confessed in an interview that most comfort women from Korea were not recruited but were abducted as slaves. He and his collaborators from the police or military surrounded a village with military trucks and captured young women. By 1943 few single women were available, so they took young married women.

At the end of the war most of these women were left behind to die in isolated areas or were exterminated to conceal evidence of these atrocious crimes.[31] The soldiers had comfort women stand in front of open graves and then opened fire on them. Sometimes they bombed trenches and caves holding comfort women. There is even an account of some two hundred Korean women forced into a submarine that was later torpedoed.[32] Seigi contends that the act of exterminating comfort women was as vicious as the Jewish Holocaust in Germany.

There are still survivors from among the comfort women, and in the early 1990s their story was picked up by news media around the world. In 1992, after forty-seven years of denial, the Japanese government reluctantly acknowledged the existence of comfort women. The Japanese government, however, offered no compensation to the survivors. The women suffer shame, nightmares, physical and mental sicknesses, hopelessness, darkness, and miserable self-esteem. They did not do anything wrong, but they have borne the shame and false guilt of being comfort women. They were the victims of an atrocity, but they have buried themselves under history. This is their *han*, the unspeakable agony that continues to reverberate in the remote comfort quarters of various parts in Asia.

What can Korean-Americans do for these women? First, we must hear their groaning. Second, we must try to understand the voices of their *han*. Third, we can be amplifiers of their small voices. Fourth, we can work toward the resolution of their *han* through revealing the facts, bringing Japan to justice, and stopping sexual exploitation now happening in the world.

There are 800,000 Koreans in Japan today. Eighty percent of them are second and third generation Korean-Japanese, survivors or descendants of the 2,400,000 conscripted Koreans in Japan in 1945.[33] They are severely discriminated against in Japan. Even after losing the unjust war, the Japanese have continued to oppress the very people they once criminally conscripted and illegally exploited, now by despising them and legally discriminating against them.

The more than one million Korean-Americans are not in the United States for personal reasons alone, but also to help oppressed and maltreated Koreans and other groups in the world. One possible task of Korean-Americans is to be in solidarity with Koreans in Japan and cooperate with their efforts for liberation from oppression and exploitation.

Our loyalty should not be given to any particular country but to the establishment of the society of God. I believe that loyalty to God alone is the true way of caring for this country. God's Kingdom comes through building the society of justice in the United States and our ancestral country. We are here to tell the stories of our original country and also to tell the stories of the United States to our original country. We call ourselves *kyo-po* (bridging people). We build an arch between the United States and our original country through fairness, peace, and truth.

VINCENT CHIN

Vincent Chin's death, an extreme case of ethno-violence, speaks to racism against Asian-Americans. He was a victim of his time. In June 1982 he was bludgeoned to death with a baseball bat in Detroit, where Orientals and "Toyotas" are often rejected. It happened in a bar:

> The victim, drafter Vincent Chin, 27, a Chinese American, was at his bachelor party; he was to be married in nine days. His attackers, a father who was a Chrysler foreman and his stepson,

were angry and addled: Ronald Ebens and Michael Nitz blamed Japanese carmakers for Detroit's problems, and Chin—Chinese or Japanese, it made no difference to them—was a convenient target. "It's because of you we're out of work," screamed Ebens, who was in fact employed full time. The pair got a baseball bat and beat Chin to death. Said he as he lost consciousness: "It isn't fair."

When Ebens, 44, and Nitz, 23, were sentenced last March after confessing to the murder, Chin's dying complaint seemed all the more apt: Wayne County Circuit Judge Charles Kaufman gave the killers three years of probation and fines of $3,780 each. He said that the men, who had no prior criminal records, were "not the kind of people you send to prison."

The light sentences enraged newspaper editorialists across the country and prompted Asians to mount a protest campaign. "I love America," said Chin's mother Lily, 63, a naturalized citizen. "I don't understand how this could happen in America."[34]

Facing strong protests, the Justice Department launched an investigation into Chin's murder in the summer of 1982. Finally, a grand jury in Detroit indicted Ebens and Nitz on new federal charges for conspiring to deprive Chin of his civil rights and killing him on account of his race. The new trial, however, ended in acquittal. The killers have never spent a single day in prison. No more energy was left to protest the verdict. The silence and tears of Chin's mother and Asian-Americans turned into *han* in this country.

This incident was not isolated. The resentment felt in Detroit was directed against the Japanese. New York real-estate tycoon Donald Trump declared on the Donahue television show: "The Japanese are taking advantage of us and ripping us off." He was applauded. "The Japanese are coming in. While we're trying to deal with things in the front yard, they're in the back yard taking over the country," Chrysler Chairman Lee Iacocca told a group of House Democrats in 1985. Bennett Bidwell, Chrysler official and former president of the Hertz Corporation, went further when he remarked that the best way to deal with the trade imbalance would be to charter the *Enola Gay*, the B-29 that dropped the atomic bomb on Hiroshima.[35] Such comments revealed not only arrogant discrimination against Japanese but also the mood in society to despise all Asians. Bidwell would not dare to suggest massacring six million Jewish people, even if he detested Jews.

Some unemployed auto workers taking a sledgehammer to a Japanese auto received media attention. Following the footage of laid-off auto workers, Representative Helen Bentley of Maryland with nine of her fellow Republicans jointly smashed a Toshiba boom box on the Capitol lawn on a summer day. The photographers recorded the smiles of the wrecking party members at the historic moment. Bentley told reporters that the boom-box bashing was not an anti-Asian or even an anti-Japanese gesture, but a simple way to send a message to Toshiba, which sold "highly sensitive technology to the KGB." But none of the products of Kongsberg, a Norwegian firm which sold a related high-tech system to the Soviet Union, was smashed along with the boom box.[36] Such a climate murdered Vincent Chin.

Chin's last words, "It's not fair," speak for his own death, the unjust trial, and the widespread animosity against Asian-Americans. It is impossible to imagine that in Detroit two Asian-Americans could bludgeon a white to death with a baseball bat and go free, with only three years of probation and fines of $3,780. People and the news media would not downplay the incident as they did in Chin's case. They would make sure that such a criminal ruling would not leave a bad precedent for any other case.

These words must have been the last words of Abel to his brother Cain: "It's not fair." These are the words of *han*, reverberating in the hollow space of Asian-Americans' hearts. The many victims of racism barely whisper these words.

THE ABANDONED WOMAN

A Korean-American woman in her thirties walked into the Korean-American Community Center in Atlanta about the time of its closing. "It is all over. I want to die. Before my death, however, I'd like to share my *han*-ridden story to fellow Korean-Americans," said the woman to a counselor.[37]

She trod the stony road of *han* in Korea as well as in this country. A stepmother who had become a widow during the Korean War raised her. In order to escape poverty, she married an American soldier. She yearned for and worked hard to create a warm and happy home. For eighteen years she was married to him. They had two sons, currently seventeen and thirteen years old.

When they moved to the States, their marriage began to crumble. Her husband frequently had extramarital affairs and harassed her, repeatedly saying that he regretted marrying a Korean woman. Finally, he filed divorce papers. Incited by their father, her children openly persecuted her for her poor English and her Korean background. The older son said, "Mom, get out of this house as soon as possible."

Through hard negotiation, however, she and her husband agreed that she should stay home until the younger son would become eighteen. After making the agreement, however, her husband disappeared, leaving word that he was going to Korea on business. It has been a year since he deserted them.

Because of the hardship of raising two sons by herself, she moved to a big city where there was a Korean-American community and had her children learn *Tae-Kwon-Do*, a Korean martial art. She became acquainted with her children's martial-arts master, who was quite nice to her at first but later showed his prejudice against her because of the interracial marriage in her background. His rudeness escalated to the point where he insulted her before her two sons. One day his abusiveness toward her was so extreme that the police arrested him. His church pastor came to see her in order to vindicate the master, advising her not to victimize him as a scapegoat and to help him get out of prison. Later a disgraceful rumor about her spread in her own church, and her pastor asked her to transfer her membership to another church or not to attend church services for a while.

The woman was rejected by her Caucasian husband because of her Korean background and was maltreated by the martial-arts master because of the stigma of her interracial marriage.[38] Even her own church disdained her as a sinner. She could turn to no one and was despondent.

This woman represents many victims of the Korean War caused by the division of the country, the agony of unequal interracial marriages, the Korean social stigma against American soldiers' spouses, the patriarchy of the Korean-American community, and the self-righteous attitude of some Korean-American churches. Her existence was full of *han* from being born in Korea as poor, female, and parentless. By bearing the *han* of Korea imposed by the Cold War of the superpowers, which caused the Korean War, she carried the sin of the world as its sacrificial lamb.

BIASED WRITER FOR FILM PRODUCTION

The media reflect, and sometimes foster, social racism. The film "It Could Happen to You," for example, characterizes a Korean-American grocer couple as unfriendly, overcharging workaholics.

Walking into Mr. Sun's store, the extremely principled New York cop (Nicholas Cage) sarcastically asks, "How are things in the mysterious Far East?" and "You aren't artificially inflating prices, are you?" Under the counter a robber is holding a gun to Mrs. Sun's head. Outside, Cage figures out that a robbery is going on inside because of two clues: Mr. Sun was unusually kind and generous to him (giving him free coffee), and Mr. Sun told him that his wife missed work because of sickness.

Bo, Cage's African-American partner (Wendell Pierce) rejoined, "That bitch would work even if she was dead!" This particular line upset MANAA (the Media Action Network for Asian Americans). MANAA president Guy Aoki protested: "This line lessens the seriousness of the situation and what real-life Korean-American grocers face on a daily basis. It also adds a tone of hostility not found in any other scene—even with the more hateful Rosie Perez character (Cage's wife)—and is therefore incongruous with the rest of the film."[39] And that is not to mention the sexism toward Mrs. Sun ("that bitch"). Such a remark dampens the morale of hard-working immigrants and proliferates the distorted stereotype of Korean immigrant workers, ignoring hundreds of kind, earnest, and generous Korean-American shopkeepers.

Ironically, this film shows sensitivity toward African-Americans, particularly in a scene where Pierce tells Cage of his outrage at a fellow officer's stereotypical image of African-Americans. Pierce represents the present situation of our society; on the one hand, some African-Americans protest discrimination, and on the other, they discriminate against other ethnic groups. Such a double standard will hurt the genuine fight against racism.

Aoki asked the studio to edit out the word "bitch" from future prints in a telephone conversation with Kevin Misher (Tristar Senior Vice President of Production) and Ed Russell (Senior Vice President of Publicity). Russell promised to convey MANAA's concerns to both writer and director but did not believe that the deletion would be made.[40]

The film's writer (Jane Anderson) and director (Andrew Bergman) show what they think exists in our society. They see what they want to see. If they intend to fight against racism, however, they should be consistent in avoiding stereotypes. Instead, they elevate the position of African-Americans by demeaning Korean-Americans. They criticize the diligence of Korean-Americans. We should not apologize for this! Diligence and perseverance should be acknowledged and valued rather than mocked.

Despite such denigration of Korean-Americans, we have been relatively silent. We do not have the strength to counter such injustice. We cannot speak out strongly, but only groan under insult, attack, and maltreatment. This is the *han* of Korean-Americans in this society. No one represents the many Korean-Americans who are hospitable, sincere, and caring, respecting African-Americans and other peoples.

WHITE CHRISTIANITY

Dr. Warren Lee is professor of Asian-American ministry at San Francisco Theological Seminary in San Anselmo, California. In his autobiography he shares two shocking events in his life. The first happened when he was a first-year student at the University of California Los Angeles. One day he was sitting on campus with his two close friends Rick Fries and Leroy Knouse. He grew up with them in an African-American neighborhood in Los Angeles and graduated with them from Manual Arts High School, a predominantly African-American school, in the early 1960s. Rick and Leroy are Caucasians. Then their mutual friend Steve walked up and started chatting with them. While talking, Steve impetuously invited Rick and Leroy to apply for membership in his fraternity. Aware of Warren's presence, Steve turned and said to him, "I'm sorry, Warren, but our fraternity is for white Christians only."[41] Those three words—"white Christians only"—shattered his Christian identity. For the first time he faced Christian racism.

The second incident occurred when he was a first-year student at the Princeton seminary. One of his classmates invited him to lead a winter youth retreat for his church in Pennsylvania. While he was leading the retreat, the pastor of the church came to see the progress of the program. He was quite impressed by Warren's leadership.

After dinner the pastor took him aside and advised him, warning that what he was about to say would hurt him: "Warren, I like you and it is clear that you are a gifted person. It would be a shame to see so much talent go to waste. You know that the Presbyterian church is 99 and 44/100% white so there's no place in it for you. You should withdraw from Princeton immediately, transfer to law school, and move to Hawaii."[42] This piece of advice threw him into the pit of depression again.

Christianity in general has been white in this society. In the name of Christ, white Christianity has seduced and deprived the souls of colored peoples. The name of Christ has been used to propagate the subtle message of white superiority. For such white Christians the cross of Jesus Christ symbolizes not their suffering with others but the suffering of others for them.

In spite of the pastor's advice, Warren Lee became an ordained minister and a professor at one of the finest Presbyterian seminaries, instructing seminarians in the true meaning of Christianity. Nothing can prevail over the strength of truth. He was ordained despite the bias of people who tried to place him "where he belonged."

Still, racial discrimination within the church is serious. A visible example is the sharing of church buildings. Along with other Korean-American churches, a number of Korean United Methodist churches have a hard time finding United Methodist churches that are willing to share their facilities with their fellow ethnic Methodist churches. Although Korean-American and Euro-American pastors are appointed by the same bishop of a conference, many Korean-American pastors who start new congregations have to beg fellow Euro-American pastors to rent their buildings to their congregations. They are treated as second-class pastors.

POLICE DISCRIMINATION

Korean-Americans are a politically unprotected, vulnerable group. During the Los Angeles eruptions of 1992, Korean shopkeepers called the Los Angeles Police Department (LAPD) and other officials for protection from the mobs invading Koreatown. There was no response from the LAPD! Over twenty-five hundred Korean-American stores were burned. The LAPD consciously opted to exclude Koreatown from its protection perimeter.

On the other hand, as looters began to invade major shopping malls, such as the Fox Hills Mall in Culver City, the police stopped them, and business people and residents praised police efforts.[43] The downtown businesses were also protected, and the predominantly Euro-American communities of West Hollywood, Beverly Hills, and Santa Monica "emerged remarkably unscathed by the riots" on account of the police forces, lauded the westside edition of the *Los Angeles Times*.[44]

In Chicago a similar pattern of police racism was practiced in the early 1990s. After the National Basketball Association championship victory by the Chicago Bulls in 1991, seven Korean-American-owned stores were looted. In June 1992, after the Bulls' second championship victory, the mob damaged and destroyed a total of 350 stores, most owned by Arabs and African-Americans (forty were owned by Korean-Americans). Foreseeing a violent reaction to a victory by the Bulls, the Korean Merchants Association had urged the police department and the mayor to provide some plans to protect them. No response was received from either. On the night of June 14, thirteen hundred police were deployed throughout Chicago. Seven hundred were dispatched to the small northside area to patrol the Euro-American-owned businesses; three hundred were sent to the area around the Bulls' stadium; and three hundred were dispersed in the south and west side, where the small businesses of Arabs, African-Americans, and Korean-Americans were. While the south and west sides were being smashed, 450 state police were standing by, waiting for a call from the police superintendent, who never called them.[45] These are a couple of conspicuous examples of racist police acts. The racist police attitude itself triggered the wrath of African-Americans and then the police failed to prevent the 1992 riots. The LAPD policy generated the *han* of Korean-Americans. To the LAPD, Koreatown was a waste land, and West Hollywood and Beverly Hills holy lands. Koreatown was a marginalized land; no one came when it cried out for help.

VICTIMS OF MEDIA RACISM

The media of this country also have conjured up an image of a model Asian-American minority, praising these immigrants for having fulfilled the so-called American dream. They have depicted such immigrants as a hard-working, law-abiding, and self-sufficient people. This stereotypical picture of Asian-Americans is dangerous when it is used for chiding other groups. The subliminal message says to other ethnic minority groups, especially to African-Americans, "This country is not racist. Look at *this* minority group. Why can't you make it in this great country of equal opportunity like this group? You are basically lazy and inferior to the model minority. You deserve your miserable lot."

Sometimes the mass media use inter-ethnic tension to deflect attention from white racism. For instance, in the summer of 1990, when the tension between African-Americans and Euro-Americans was intensified following an African-American youth's death at the hands of Euro-American racists in Bensonhurst, New York, the news media shifted its focus to the conflict between a Trinidad woman and a Korean immigrant storekeeper in Brooklyn, New York. The African-American community in Brooklyn boycotted two greengrocer stores owned by Korean immigrants, and the media, sympathetic to the Korean immigrant-owned Red Apple grocery store, immediately branded the boycott as the act of racism on the part of the African-American community. As the media focused on the tension between African-Americans and Korean-Americans in Brooklyn, the Bensonhurst case slowly faded away. The Brooklyn case was scrutinized for six months.

In 1992 the media concentrated on the Rodney King incident and slowly juxtaposed it with Korean grocer Soon Ja Du's shooting of fifteen-year-old Latasha Harlins. In the Los Angeles area the media contributed to diverting the acute tension between African-Americans and Euro-Americans over the Rodney King incident to tension between African-Americans and Korean-Americans. Many Korean-Americans in Los Angeles believed that Soon Ja Du's killing of Latasha Harlins was wrong. The media, however, depicted Soon Ja Du as a "typical" Korean-American.

The sentence that Judge Karlin assigned Du—community service with a $500 fine—was unfair. The sentence implied that taking an African-American girl's life is less serious than beating an intoxicated African-American man. Furthermore, this unjust verdict set the stage for an inevitable inter-ethnic explosion.[46] Personally, I was outraged by the verdict. Du's killing of Latasha Harlins was definitely wrong, and Karlin's verdict was too light. If she had sentenced Du to imprisonment, the results of the Los Angeles eruptions may have been different.

Moreover, the yellow journalism of the media fanned the furious reaction of the African-American community. Headlines in the *Los Angeles Times* and the *San Francisco Examiner* on November 16, 1991, trumpeted: "Korean Shop Owner Freed" and "Korean Grocer Receives Probation." In criminal cases such proclamations of ethnic identification violate standard journalistic practices. No headline dares to announce "Jewish Shopkeeper Convicted" or "Black Man Freed."[47] Since there had been many incidents between shop owners and customers, the case could have been treated as a case between a store owner and a customer rather than a racial conflict between African-Americans and

Korean-Americans.[48] The news media, as in the Rodney King case, chose to report it instead as a racial issue. The unfair verdict by an Euro-American judge and the unfair, sensational reports of the major California newspapers contributed to the destruction of Koreatown after the Rodney King verdict.

The *han* of Korean-Americans was that we did not have control over the verdict of the Soon Ja Du case or the bias of the news media. Our destiny was in the hands of the powerful. The media misguided the public, and the police force did not protect us; we were trapped in between. According to Edna Bonacich and Ivan Light, the economy of Los Angeles was revived by Korean immigrant entrepreneurs in the 1970s.[49] We have worked for the revival of the inner-city economy, but have received undeserved mistreatment.

Major U.S. mass media are controlled by powerful corporations. Eight business and financial corporations own the three major networks (NBC, CBS, ABC), some forty subsidiary television stations, over two hundred cable TV systems, over sixty radio stations, fifty-nine magazines (including *Time* and *Newsweek*), chains of newspapers (including the *Los Angeles Times*, the *New York Times*, the *Washington Post*, the *Wall Street Journal*), forty-one book publishers, and various motion picture companies.[50] They are preoccupied with their own profit. Past events show that they have manipulated public information for their own benefits.[51] The media corporations in Los Angeles certainly would not like to see arson and looting spill over into the Hollywood area. Their media must have worked hard to prevent such a happening in Los Angeles.

We are not struggling against a visible adversary but against invisible foes who control the power of the air. St. Paul shows us the universal dimension of this struggle: "For our struggle is not against enemies of blood and flesh, but against the rulers, against the authorities, against the cosmic powers of this present darkness, against the spiritual forces of evil in the heavenly places" (Eph 6:12[52]). The media corporations serve only one god. The name of their god is Profit, and in its name they do all kinds of malicious acts. They inform and misinform society; they shape its culture, misguiding its direction.

By merely overcoming our sin in society, we cannot complete cosmic salvation. "The cosmic powers of this present darkness," the forces of evil, produce the structure of *han* in which we are caught. Even after the solution of the sin problem, we need the resolution of *han* to experience a holistic healing and salvation in our society. Jesus Christ represents the strength of truth, which unmasks the injustice of the world. His voice on the cross was not heard by many, but his voice has prevailed over history, because it is the voice of truth. The power of truth, the invincibility of the cross, will overcome the cosmic powers of the

present darkness. The cross of Jesus Christ exhibits the power of evil
and the *han* of its innocent victims. With the power of the cross, we
should expose the evil structures in our society and heal the wounds of
the *han*-ridden.

2

The *Han* of the Korean-American Community

While most oppressed groups grapple more with the problem of *han*, most oppressor groups in society struggle more with the problem of sin. This does not mean, of course, that the oppressed commit no sin or that the oppressors suffer no *han*. Both of them experience both sin and *han*.

In the United States most ethnic groups have been preoccupied with repenting their sins, following the lead of the dominant theologies. American Christianity has focused on the problems of the oppressors, while scarcely treating the issues of ethnic communities. A few sources of *han* in the Korean-American community are racial conflict, transnational corporations, redlining, the "middle-agent minority" phenomenon, classism, and a crisis of identity. It is time for all ethnic groups, including Korean-Americans, to address the issue of *han* theologically.

RACIAL CONFLICT

The face of racism in the United States varies depending on the ethnic minority in question. Korean-Americans face two expressions of racism. One is racial discrimination because of their being Asian-American. The other is because of their being Korean-American. As economic hardship in this country increases, anti-Asian Americanism intensifies. As the inner-city economy hollows out, anti-Korean-American attitudes sharpen. First, we will look into discrimination against Asian Americans. Second, we will examine racism directed specifically toward Korean-Americans.

Prejudice against Asian-Americans

Anti-Asian-Americanism has its root in the nineteenth century. Chinese immigrants were welcomed in this country because they would

26

work hard in undesirable jobs for low pay. Yet they were also rejected because they brought a "strange" culture. Euro-Americans disliked Chinese immigrants so much that Samuel Gompers, founder of the American Federation of Labor (AFL), continually objected to helping Chinese laborers and rejected a union of Chinese restaurant employees within the AFL.[1] In 1882 Congress legislated the Chinese Exclusion Act, which prohibited Chinese immigration for ten years and specifically refused citizenship to Chinese immigrants. In 1886 the Statue of Liberty was dedicated along with the poem by Emma Lazarus welcoming "the tired, the poor, and the huddled masses." This was a mockery to the Chinese.[2] Congress extended the Exclusion Act for another ten years in 1892 and renewed the Act after the turn of the century. Two decades later the Exclusion Act was extended again, this time applying to other groups.[3] The Exclusion Act lasted until 1943.

Encouraged by the Exclusion Act, the Theodore Roosevelt administration confirmed the so-called Gentlemen's Agreement with Japan in 1908. According to the agreement, Japan would discontinue further immigration to the United States, and the United States would terminate its discrimination against Japanese already in this country. The Japanese immigration stopped, but anti-Japanese feelings endured.

Laws on citizenship underlined the pervasive anti-Asianism. At first non-whites were prohibited by federal law from becoming citizens. This was modified to extend citizenship to persons of African descent in 1868 and to some Native-Americans in 1887. No modifications were made for persons of Asian descent. The Supreme Court repeatedly interpreted this silence as a constitutional directive against them. In 1943 federal law finally included the Chinese, and first-generation Japanese in 1952.

With Japan's attack on Pearl Harbor on December 7, 1941, anti-Japanese feelings flared. Racism fanned by rumors spread widely. On February 13, 1942, President Franklin Roosevelt endorsed Executive Order 9066, which ratified removal of any people considered menaces from designated strategic military areas. Over a hundred thousand people of Japanese ancestry (one-eighth was sufficient) on the West Coast were taken to concentration camps; two-thirds of them were citizens.[4] They were not allowed to take their household belongings but only personal luggage. They had to liquidate their possessions very quickly. For instance, one woman sold a thirty-seven-room hotel for three hundred dollars. The evacuees lost from 350 to 500 million dollars, averaging nearly ten thousand dollars per family.[5] In this country, the *yellow peril* has never disappeared; it has only fluctuated with international situations.

Even now, antagonism against Asian-Americans has not dissipated. In 1993, according to the National Asian Pacific Advocate Legal Center (NAPALC), crimes against Asian-Americans numbered 335, and there were at least thirty murder cases considered hate crimes in the United States. The NAPALC reported that 28 percent of the crimes occurred in homes and 10 percent at businesses, and most of them were perpetrated by Caucasians.[6]

Prejudice against Korean-Americans

Korean-Americans suffer their own unique *han* of racism. Their immigration to this country started with the recruitment of 7,226 Koreans (637 of them women) by the Hawaii Sugar Planters' Association between 1903 and 1905. Of these, 1,999 moved to the mainland to work building the railroads. They were the minority of the minorities among the Chinese and the Japanese and suffered more than these two groups.[7]

Koreans replaced the Chinese laborers who were excluded by the 1882 Chinese Exclusion Act. In 1905 Korea became the protectorate of Japan, which stopped emigration. However, between 1907 and 1924 several thousand more Koreans immigrated into this country, most of whom were "picture brides," political activists against the Japanese occupation, or students. With the Refugee Relief Act of 1953 many Koreans came to the United States as refugees or as war brides. The 1965 Immigration Act liberalized eligibility rules, and Koreans could join family members in the United States. The chain migration pattern that resulted led to a fivefold population increase within ten years (from 70,000 in 1970 to 355,000 in 1980).[8]

Korean-Americans occupy a low rung on the ethnic ladder. According to the social distance[9] ranking developed by Emory Bogardus (based on a predominantly Euro-American sample), Koreans ranked no higher than twenty-seventh (of thirty) during the five periods from 1926 to 1977.[10] From an African-American sample, however, Korean-Americans were nineteenth of thirty-one groups.[11]

As newcomers, Korean-Americans undergo direct and indirect racism from various groups. Many Korean-American small business people in particular are affected by anti-Asian-American sentiment. For example, in August 1993 a man shot a Korean-American grocer in Washington, D.C., took a potato chip package, and walked out slowly. It was surmised that the motive was not robbery but racial hatred. In the same month someone broke into a Korean-American's house at Rowland Heights, California, and left a burned swastika and racially insulting graffiti on a rug and a wall inside. About the same time, a New York policeman hurled racial epithets at a young Korean-American woman and then hit her. Her "crime" was a parking violation. In September 1993 a liquor store owner and his son in Lake Forest, New York, were beaten by six youths shouting racial epithets. In February 1992 a Korean-American youth, fourteen years old, was chased by twenty youths in the Bronx and was beaten with a baseball bat. In January 1991

Caucasian golfers in Milpitas, California, beat Korean-American golfers, shouting, "Get lost, Orientals!"[12]

STRUCTURAL PROBLEMS

For Korean-Americans the racism of the dominant group is one thing and ethnic racial tension is another. We feel inter-ethnic tension particularly in the business world. This tension does not derive simply from cultural and social differences. Some problems Korean-Americans face stem from international economic and political factors. The Korean-Americans in the Los Angeles area, for example, experience interracial conflict with African-Americans and Hispanic-Americans because of economic and political contention among the groups. The 1992 Los Angeles eruptions focused national consciousness on racial and ethnic tension. The events started with the unjust acquittal of the policemen in the Rodney King case but ended with the burning of Korean-American businesses. All these incidents arise from structural problems that cause *han* for Korean-Americans and others. These deep-seated systemic problems of our society need urgent attention and change.

Redlining

The policy of redlining contributed to the Los Angeles eruptions. Redlining is the unethical practice by financial institutions and insurance companies of withholding home-loan funds or insurance from poor ethnic neighborhoods considered economic risks (originally marking these areas off on maps with red lines). In 1974 the Federal Home Loan Bank requested 127 of 180 savings and loan associations in the Chicago area to reveal the geographic locations of their home mortgages and savings deposits; it found that older neighborhoods were receiving far less home loan money than suburban areas. The predominantly white areas in the newer southwestern and northwestern parts of Chicago obtained 4.5 times more in new home loans than the areas of the city where the economically depressed African-Americans lived.[13]

The Community Reinvestment Act (CRA) of 1977 bans redlining and empowers regulators to control a bank's requests to expand or merge according to its efforts to meet the credit needs of its diverse constituencies—poor and rich, minorities and majority. Unfortunately, CRA has produced a regulatory mess with large loop holes. Although more than 85 percent of all banks receive satisfactory or outstanding ratings from regulators on the CRA reviews, available data show that CRA has been far from fruitful in eradicating redlining of poor minority neighborhoods or racial discrimination in lending.[14] Recently the Northern Trust Company of Chicago and three of its affiliates, indicted by the Justice Department, agreed to settle scores of loan discrimination claims by compensating over sixty African-Americans and Hispanic-Americans whose mortgage loan applications were rejected.[15]

There are phases of redlining in home loans. The first phase involves increasing the difficulty of securing a home mortgage by imposing high interest rates and terms of under twenty years. The second phase involves cutting off conventional mortgages to a community. Home buyers then need to find financial institutions that will approve FHA-guaranteed mortgage loans. As conventional mortgages disappear, home improvement loans also decline, for some bankers who handle FHA loans do not cover home-improvement loans in areas redlined from conventional mortgages. Consequently, property in redlined neighborhoods falls further into disrepair. Opening businesses in these areas is exhausting because of the difficulty in obtaining bank loans and various kinds of business insurance. Only small mom-and-pop grocery stores exist in these areas. Since immigrants can start their businesses with relatively small amounts of money, they purchase inexpensive stores in these depressed neighborhoods.

A federal law, designed as a step toward abolishing redlining, requires all lenders to show that they are following affirmative-action programs by providing home loans to low-income neighborhoods.[16] In spite of this law, redlining by banks and mortgage companies is conspicuous in African-American ghettos such as Harlem in New York or South Central Los Angeles.

In 1988 the Department of Housing and Urban Development (HUD) conducted a second national study of housing market discrimination.[17] This study comprises thirty-eight thousand paired tests completed in twenty-five metropolitan areas during the late spring and early summer of 1989. HUD data reveal that real-estate agents provide substantially different information for minority customers about potential sources of financing and are more likely to provide assistance to Euro-Americans in obtaining financing. In more than 20 percent of the audits, an offer to assist in securing financing was provided to Euro-Americans only. Minorities were less likely to be informed about conventional and adjustable-rate mortgages than were Euro-American home buyers and were more frequently told about FHA and VA financing than were their Euro-American counterparts. These government-based financing sources cost more, require more processing time, and have fewer financial institutions participating as loan originators. In addition, there is a ceiling amount that these loans can offer.[18]

The 1990 Home Mortgage Disclosure Act data inform us that the rate of loan denial increases as the proportion of minority residents increases. And according to Federal Reserve data on mortgages, low- to moderate-income Euro-American applicants had a higher rate of securing loans in 1990 than high-income African-Americans.[19]

It is apparent that Euro-American landlords, apartment managers, suburban developers, and real-estate agents have obstructed ethnic minorities, especially African-Americans, in their access to housing in Euro-American areas. The lending policies of various financial institutions segregate ethnic peoples. Local governments have furthered segregation through zoning codes, building codes, and development regulations, as have the FHA and VA regulations of the federal government.[20] The passage of the Civil Rights Act of 1968 (which bans discrimination in the sale or rental of most housing), CRA, and a few important decisions of the Federal courts, have had little impact on exclusionary tactics.[21] Various subtle tactics have defeated the purposes of the anti-discrimination policies.

In some cases, governmental policies against redlining are triggered by banks or other financial institutions. A good example is the case of Chevy Chase Federal Savings Bank and its subsidiary, B. F. Saul Mortgage Co. The Justice Department's civil-rights division filed a charge in U.S. District Court that from 1976 to 1992 these two institutions underwrote 97 percent of their loans in chiefly Euro-American areas. The bank and mortgage company had ninety-two offices but had opened no offices in any census tracts that had an African-American majority in the District of Columbia or in neighboring Prince Georges County, Maryland. The government charged that they engaged in illegal redlining by not opening offices in African-American neighborhoods. On August 24, 1994, they agreed to invest $11 million in African-American neighborhoods to resolve the Justice Department's charges of mortgage discrimination.[22] "To shun an entire community because of its racial makeup is just as wrong as to reject an application because they are African-American," said Attorney General Janet Reno.[23]

After the investigation began in 1993, the bank opened seven bank or mortgage company offices in African-American areas. The bank denied any discriminatory intention on its part and did not admit breaking the Fair Housing Act, the Equal Credit Opportunity Act or other laws. Nevertheless, it agreed to open offices in African-American neighborhoods, to consider inaugurating others, to advertise its loans in African-American areas, and actively to recruit African-American loan officers.[24]

Insurance companies practice redlining too. Since a number of insurance companies do not insure businesses in redlined areas, in 1992 most Korean-American small businesses in Los Angeles had no insurance, were underinsured, or held policies with "non-admitted carriers," whose credibility was low. Business owners who held policies with non-admitted carriers assumed that they held valid policies. In spite of their claims of damages of over $8 million from the eruptions, Korean-American shop owners were compensated only about $3 million.

Some owners settled for drastically lower compensation because of their immediate need of funds; others are still waiting for promises from their insurance agencies to be met. Litigation against fourteen non-admitted insurance carriers is being conducted by the Asian Pacific American Legal Center (APALC), Public Counsel's Urban Recovery Legal Assistance, and Brobeck, Phleger & Harrison.[25]

These practices are common in cities throughout the United States. Many small businesses in Boston's inner city are not insured because most insurance companies refuse to insure stores located in poorer neighborhoods or put their premiums out of reach.[26] Accused of these practices, five insurance companies began a drive to provide more coverage to small business owners in Roxbury, Mattapan, and Dorchester.

Despite the redlining occurring in cities across the country, legislation that contained revised CRA regulations was introduced in both the House and Senate on March 30, 1995, that would relieve banks with less than $250 million in assets—almost 88 percent of U.S. banks—from in-depth scrutiny under the Community Reinvestment Act. The original twelve-factor review was replaced with a streamlined review of only three areas: lending, service, and investment. These regulations became effective January 1, 1996.[27]

Redlining is an economic, social, moral, and spiritual issue. Regulations alone are not enough to deter the various ways to practice redlining. All ethnic groups should cooperate to resist any kind of redlining practices. They should raise their voices against these practices, stressing the social responsibility of financial institutions. It is necessary to have prevention programs as well, such as requiring social ethics courses in MBA degree programs. Meanwhile, churches need to teach members, particularly youth, the anti-Christian nature of redlining.

Transnational Corporations

The looters of the Los Angeles eruptions represented various ethnic groups. Contrary to common understanding, the issue probably was not African-Americans *vs.* Korean-Americans. It was more likely lower class *vs.* lower-middle class.

The gap between the rich and the poor has widened over the years. The Los Angeles eruptions tell us that race matters are intimately connected with class matters, in part through transnational corporations. Let us examine the eruptions from a global economic perspective.

The capitalist global economy controlled by transnational corporations is responsible directly and indirectly for the eruptions. According to Peter Drucker, the world economy has changed from international to *transnational* since the mid-1970s.[28] A transnational corporation does not have clear loyalty to any nation but only to its own profits. For

U.S.-based transnational corporations, this country, as well as other countries, is a target, a potential market.

In the *Wall Street Journal* Blant Hurt depicts Arkansas as a third-world country with a ruling oligarchy, a small and powerless middle class, and a disenfranchised leaderless people. He believes that this can be applied coast to coast.[29] Bernard Sanders in the *Los Angeles Times* concurs with Hurt by pointing out three issues: the United States is rapidly moving toward an oligarchy; the United States is becoming a third-world economy; the United States is fast becoming a non-democratic country.[30]

Transnational companies ravage U.S. cities and countryside as they have third-world countries. Compared with the Japanese economic model, U.S. capitalism is destructive for inner cities. In *Beyond Capitalism*, Eisuke Sakakibara, a senior official in Japan's Ministry of Finance, describes Japan as a "noncapitalist market economy," one that strives to maximize production and employment, as opposed to the U.S. capitalist economy that stresses consumption and return to investors.[31] U.S. capitalism should learn to keep the balance between profit-making and people's employment.

Ivan Light and Edna Bonacich explain how U.S. investment stimulated Korean immigration in the 1960s, bringing forth labor conflict in U.S. inner-cities. U.S. conglomerates invested in major cities in Korea, attracting farmers and laborers into the cities. The more farmers and laborers concentrated in cities, the cheaper labor became. Meanwhile, farming in Korea declined. The authors contend that the surplus laborers of the working class were absorbed in the United States through U.S. immigration policy.[32]

Immigration is a traumatic experience. Living in a strange land itself is stressful. Nevertheless, Koreans immigrate to this country for better living conditions. As Korean immigrants arrive, they look for jobs. Because of the language barrier and cultural differences, they find no jobs commensurate with their skills and training. Thus, they are forced to work in Korean immigrants' stores where they need only minimal English to survive. Eventually they tend to open their own businesses and hire newly arrived Korean immigrants or Hispanic-Americans. In the United States, the basic struggle between employers and employees has been over the issue of compensation for labor. As new immigrants enter the job market, Korean-American immigrant employers prefer hiring cheaper immigrant workers to local workers. Because Korean immigrant shopkeepers pay low wages and offer no benefits package to newly arrived immigrants, they can survive in a tough competitive market, contributing to maintaining cheap labor. Such a hiring pattern among Korean immigrant shopkeepers elicits a conflict between immigrants and African-Americans (local workers). The mu-

tual misinformation on customs, culture, and language, as well as ethnocentrism, escalates the inter-ethnic conflict.

The above shows that the conflict between African-Americans and
Korean-American shopkeepers is inherent in the structure of U.S. capitalism. Any immigrant store owners will have some tension and conflict with local groups. They are in inner cities and ghettos to distribute
the goods of transnational corporations. Immigrants and local workers compete over little crumbs of the corporations' wealth. Transnational and financial corporations occupy some 40 percent of U.S.
trade, including international trade.

Meanwhile, transnational corporations and financial institutions in
the United States have caused real wages to fall to the level of the mid-
1960s. Economic Policy Institute economists Lawrence Mishel and Jared
Bernstein report that more than seventeen million workers were unemployed or underemployed by mid-1992, with an increase of eight
million during the Bush administration. About 75 percent of those job
positions are permanently lost.[33] In the 1980s, of the limited increase
in total wealth "70% accrued to the top 1% of income earners, while
the bottom lost absolutely," says M.I.T. economist Rudiger Dornbusch.[34]

In the entire globe, approximately 900 million of the world's 5.5 billion people are unemployed. Free-market capitalism created such mas-
sive unemployment through its contemporary servants—automation
and modern communications. While some leaders worry about their
national unemployment state, business people cash in on the global
oversupply of workers. They spread the corporate culture.[35]

Furthermore, transnational corporations control international financial institutions. The International Monetary Fund (IMF), the World
Bank, the General Agreement on Tariffs and Trade (GATT), the Group
of Seven industrial nations are designed to serve the interests of
transnational corporations and financial institutions. These institutions
reap the harvest of international trade. The World Bank reports that
protectionist practices by the industrialized countries slim down the
income of third-world countries by nearly twice the sum of official aid
to them. With the help of the programs imposed by the International
Monetary Fund and the World Bank, these protectionist measures have
doubled the gap between rich and poor countries since 1960. Most of
the rich countries in the past decade have increased protectionism,
with the Reaganites waging wars against economic liberalism. Resource
transfers from the poor to the rich countries added up to more than
$400 billion from 1982 to 1990. For the savings and loan associations
and transnational corporations "free-market capitalism" means "risk
free."[36]

GATT and NAFTA (the North American Free Trade Agreement)
should be understood within this frame of self-interest. The primary
objective of the United States in these treaties is to protect the interest

of its "national" corporations. The U.S. International Trade Commission estimates that U.S.-based companies will collect $61 billion a year from third-world countries, provided that U.S. protectionist measures are accepted at GATT.[37]

The Labor Advisory Committee, instituted by the Trade Act of 1974 to advise the executive branch on trade agreements, concluded that NAFTA, an executive agreement on August 12, 1992, would be beneficial for investors but harm workers in the United States and probably in Mexico. NAFTA will help U.S. agribusinesses wipe out Mexican corn farming and drive farmers from rural to urban areas, depressing already low labor wages even further. According to economist David Barkin, labor's share of personal income in Mexico plummeted from 36 percent in the mid-1970s to 23 percent by 1992.[38] Senator Ernest Hollings argues that the direct effect of NAFTA is to underpin Mexico's one-party state and the corrupt oligarchy that regulates its politics and economy.[39] In the United States, after twenty-two months of NAFTA, nearly fifty thousand Americans have lost their jobs. This prompted a bipartisan group of lawmakers to drive for a renegotiation of the free trade pact.[40]

In international trade transnational corporations reap enormous harvests. They undermine the infrastructures of the national as well as the foreign economy, shattering local communities through relocations, creating friction between immigrant workers and local workers, and driving out local industries and businesses through competition.

The "Middle-agent Minority" Phenomenon

There is another factor that contributed to the Los Angeles eruptions and increases the *han* of Korean-American business people: the "middle-agent minority" phenomenon. This theory was developed by observing minority groups in the world: Jews of the diaspora; the Chinese in Southeast Asia; East Indians in Burma, Uganda, and South Africa. According to this theory, the middle-agent minority group acts as a buffer between dominant and oppressed groups of society. In times of socio-economic stress, the middle-agent minority provides a target for the anger of the exploited yet is itself socially isolated and politically unprotected. The buyer-seller relationship is inherently one of conflict, and this situation becomes worse when the buyers are poorer than the sellers and the sellers are immigrants or foreigners. Sociologist Herbert Blalock reasons that middle-agent minorities easily become a target of attack by the angry downtrodden in times of crisis because (1) immigrants and foreigners are visible; (2) they have economic power but no political power, thus no political protection; and (3) they are the symbolic representatives of the dominant group in the eyes of the oppressed.[41]

Sociologists Bonacich and Light decided, however, that the middle-agent minority theory was too restrictive to describe Korean immigrant business people in the United States. They widened their terminology from "middleman minorities" to "immigrant entrepreneurs."[42] The first reason they broadened the term was that Korean immigrant entrepreneurship takes place in a developed society, whereas the middle-agent minority theory arose from third-world contexts. The second reason was that while traditional societies disparage commercial roles and the minorities that fill them, U.S. society treats small business owners as cultural heroes. The third reason was that while the middle-agent minority theory features sojourning minorities—such as Chinese, Jews, and Gypsies—whose historic status is that of pariahs in society, Korean entrepreneurs have no tradition of wandering through the world as commercial middle-agents.[43]

Despite this new term developed by Bonacich and Light, I will keep using the term *middle-agent minorities* because the theory runs parallel with the situation of Korean-American business people in the Los Angeles area. Indeed, the economy of the South Central area of Los Angeles is turning into that of a developing country.

Korean-American shops in the Los Angeles area became the targets of looting and arson during the Los Angeles eruptions in part because they represented the face of the dominant group. But in addition they were identified as the oppressors who exploited African-Americans and despised them. The New York boycott of the Red Apple Grocery and the Latasha Harlins cases stoked anti-Korean-American feelings in the African-American communities.[44] So Korean-American storekeepers effectively functioned as a buffer between Euro-Americans and the oppressed and poorer groups of society. When the verdict of the Rodney King case was announced, Korean-American store owners became the target of the anger of the outraged African-Americans. Located between the South Central Los Angeles of the suppressed and the Hollywood of the dominant group, the Korean-American community was severely attacked and damaged.

Because of unemployment or underemployment many highly educated Korean immigrants have been driven to open their own businesses (Korean immigrants' self-employment rate is higher than that of any other ethnic group in the United States[45]). With the help of relatives, friends, or *kye* (a small rotating credit group that allows its members money on a rotating basis to gain access to even more additional capital), they purchase small mom-and-pop grocery stores in rather inexpensive areas. A 1984 Chicago survey showed that 34 percent relied on a *kye* for their businesses.[46]

In South Central Los Angeles a number of Korean immigrants bought their grocery and liquor stores from African-American owners. Many of these stores had been owned by Jewish people before the Watts eruptions of 1965. One aftermath of the Watts event was the exodus of the Jewish people from that area. In the mid 1960s African-American entrepreneurs obtained these stores for low prices (around $80,000, or twice monthly gross sales), assisted by the easing of government-backed loans. But in the late 1970s and early 1980s the deregulation of liquor pricing (in 1978) and subsequent price wars, combined with the high-risk nature of the job, elicited a sell-off of the stores to Korean immigrants who were looking for such opportunities. It was a good time for African-American entrepreneurs to sell; selling prices had risen to about five times monthly gross sales or $300,000.[47]

After purchasing the stores, Korean-American owners worked to establish their businesses, often without considering their neighborhood problems. This contributed to the conflict between Korean-Americans and African-Americans. It would be ideal for more African-Americans to purchase back businesses from Korean-Americans in their own neighborhoods.

Clearly redlining, the capitalist global economy, and the middle-agent minority phenomenon lie behind the eruptions that occurred in Los Angeles on April 29. These are not only immediate causes of the eruptions, however, but symptoms of an unjust social structure. To prevent such eruptions, we should collaborate to abolish covert and overt redlining policies of financial institutions and insurance companies. Further, small business ownership in South Central Los Angeles and other ethnic enclaves must shift. Until ethnic groups own most of the businesses in their own communities, racial unrest will recur. Korean-American businesses need to move slowly out from these communities, with local people taking over most businesses in their own areas.

Classism

The extensive participation of various ethnic groups in the looting following the Los Angeles eruptions indicates that class factors as well as racial ones played a significant role in the eruptions. The verdict of the Rodney King case ignited not only racial outrage but also became a channel to release the pent-up indignation of the low-income class. The Los Angeles eruptions were not an accident but rather the consequence of the poverty experienced by the oppressed for the past few decades.

Since the 1965 Watts riot politicians have not kept their promises to improve conditions in the area. Few of the recommendations of the McCone Commission report were carried out, and Caucasians moved to the western part of the city or to the suburbs. In 1976 the Euro-American middle class succeeded in a tax revolt—Proposition 13—to dump the burden of the urban poor whom they left behind. It was a bad divorce with no alimony for the urban poor.[48] For example, no public investment was made in the education of inner-city youths.

The economic gap between Caucasians and African-Americans has widened since 1965. In 1992 the poverty rate in South Central Los Angeles was more than two times higher than the national average (30.3%); dropouts from the labor force made up close to half (41.8%) of the adult population; about one-quarter (24.9%) were on welfare.[49]

It was estimated that in 1993, 39.3 million Americans (15.1%) were below the official government poverty level. In 1983, 32.4 million (13.1%) were poor. Median household income, adjusted for inflation, dwindled from $33,585 to $31,241 over the period.[50] According to a 1994 report, about twenty-two million people, 10 percent of the total population, are hungry or depend on soup kitchens or food stamps. The Internal Revenue Service reveals that the richest 1 percent of U.S. households possessed 36 percent of the nation's wealth in 1989 (up from 31 percent in 1983).[51] The Congressional Budget Office reports that between 1977 and 1989 the wealthiest 1 percent of American families hoarded 60 percent of the growth in after-tax income, while the poorest 40 percent of families experienced declines in income with the bottom 20 percent of poor families suffering a 9 percent income loss. In the same period CEO (chief executive officer) salaries rose from 35 to 120 times the average worker's salary.[52] Economic historians document that the concentration of wealth at the top, begun in the 1960s, accelerated in the 1980s. This reflects the national income disparities that marked the late 1800s and early 1900s and were halted only by the Great Depression.[53] The recent phenomenon has a tie with the unbridled capitalism and political and bureaucratic corruption in the 1980s: corporate mergers, junk bonds, and financial mismanagement plagued by deregulation and the multi-billion dollar Savings and Loan crisis.

Further, in 1994, federal expenditure for national defense was $279.9 billion, in contrast with an expenditure for education of $50.8 billion.[54] In other words, the federal government spent over five times more for national defense than for education. In the present system many young urban dwellers feel deep frustration and despair. They have little education, no jobs, and no future. For them, the only solution they see may be to bring down the present system of society.

Identity Crisis

First-generation Korean-Americans who have lived in this country for a long time usually undergo an identity crisis, especially if they return to visit Korea. They realize that they are neither fully Koreans nor fully Americans. And most second-generation Korean-Americans experience role-confusion at home, in schools, and in society.

I am well acquainted with the family of a teenage girl named Julie (not her real name). Julie is undergoing a serious identity crisis. A senior in high school, tall (5'9"), and "thin," she is a beautiful girl and a good student. However, because her fellow students have mocked her as a "flat nose," "flat face," and "Chink" for a long time, Julie has lost her sense of identity and self-esteem. Indeed, she has become seriously depressed. Although Julie was born in the United States, she feels estranged from this country; she does not have a sense of belonging. At home she feels not quite Korean; at school she is not fully accepted as an American. Caught in between the two cultures, she has been torn apart and has even considered committing suicide. Why in the world should such a fine young woman think of ending her life? It is *han* that she has to undergo such a struggle of identity because of her Korean heritage. Such a struggle is very common among Korean-American and other ethnic youths.

Another young woman disclosed the *han*-ridden life of her immigrant home:

> I am a high school girl. Because my parents always work, I don't have enough time to share something with them. My mom works as janitor during the day and as a tailor at night. My father works at a gas station during the week and at a hotel on weekends. Frankly speaking, my sister and I are very disappointed that we don't have enough time with our parents. Is there any way to persuade them that we need parents more than money?[55]

This girl endured the emptiness of immigrant life. In the absence of her parents, any economic success would be meaningless. Her letter shows that many immigrant families tend to lose the meaning of life in busyness. For what do they have to survive and for whom do they bring financial success? A parentless home is no home. They live a life without content.

A third-generation Japanese-American articulates his identity-confusion in a poem. He thinks that he is an American. But people who see his Asian appearance constantly question his nationality.

> Who am I?
>   I sometimes wonder.
> Am I Japanese?
> Am I American
>   or just both?
>
> I am me, a human being.[56]

Erik Erickson pointed out that a healthy identity includes "the accrued confidence that the inner sameness and continuity prepared in the past are matched by the sameness and continuity of one's meaning for others."[57] He pointed out that adolescents can be strongly clannish and cruel in their exclusion of those who are unlike them in skin color, cultural background, tastes, and habits.[58] Thus many Korean-American and other ethnic youths suffer feelings of exclusion and the loss of self-identity. Their heart is broken in *han*—the feeling of helplessness.

To Erickson, it is important to have the double requirement for ego-identity: a sense of historical and cultural connectedness with one's past, present, and future; and a sense of belonging in a community. When people lack these elements, they feel marginal and may withdraw into self. The loss of self-identity results in role-confusion, a sense of inauthenticity and feelings of shame and worthlessness. This disconnectedness between the past and the present is experienced by many Korean-Americans, particularly the young.

RESULTS OF STRUCTURAL PROBLEMS

Korean-Americans and other ethnic people live as second-class citizens in their own country. The dominant groups in this country often remind them of their "inferiority." They do not treat Korean-Americans as fully equal with them; something is missing in the Korean-American and Asian-American face, appearance, speech, behavior, thinking, and working.

Even though Korean-Americans succeed in their careers or businesses, they feel left out of society and thus feel failure. By internalizing the negative projection of the dominant group toward them, they feel a certain gap between their own values, behavior, and identity and the dominant group's values, behavior, and identity. When they realize that the dominant group will never fully accept them, they experience marginality. Their marginal situation creates anxiety, confusion, and insecurity.

We have discussed the *han* of Korean-American communities, centering on the Los Angeles eruptions in 1992. Some of the *han* results from racial and ethnic conflict, redlining, the work of transnational corporations, scapegoating, classism, role-confusion, police discrimination, and media bias. One of the deepest causes of *han* is that the world has shaped us, and we are unable to determine our own destiny. We have worked hard to develop our latency, but our efforts have been thwarted by outside forces. We cannot give up, however, for we are called from above to use our *han* as an opportunity to change the world.

3

The Sin of Korean-American Communities

One of the major problems for Korean-Americans is fear. Out of insecurity, many Korean-Americans withdraw into their own enclave and tend to be exclusive, losing the opportunity to know other groups. Instead of enhancing respect for other groups, such isolation produces indifference toward other groups or fosters prejudice and misunderstanding. Within the Korean-American community the tendency to withdraw nurses the sins of racial prejudice, sexism, and the practice of labor exploitation.

RACISM

Korean-Americans have been discriminated against by Euro-Americans since Korean immigration started. Racism is original sin, according to Jim Wallis, editor of *Sojourners*. Racism consists of prejudice and discrimination. Discrimination is an outward act, which is criminal; prejudice is an attitude, which is intangible. It is an anti-Christian attitude. Although they may not overtly discriminate against others, many Korean-Americans have prejudice against other ethnic groups, particularly African-Americans. The pejorative depiction of African-Americans in the U.S. news media prevails throughout the world. It is no accident that then Japanese prime minister Yasuhiro Nakasone bluntly remarked in 1986: "The level of intelligence in the United States is lowered by the large number of Blacks, Puerto Ricans, and Mexicans who live there."[1] Nakasone did not know that nurture (as well as nature) is the decisive factor in human development. I.Q. tests were given to all children over four years of age in 101 transracial adoptive families when the adopted children were seven years old (on average) and once more when they averaged seventeen years of age. The findings suggest that the influences on intellectual development in the sample of African-American adoptees raised in Caucasian families are similar to those for children in the ma-

41

jority population of the United States and Western Europe.[2] This indicates that IQ test scores also reflect education and environment.

Like Nakasone, Koreans have believed in the inferior IQs of African-Americans. It is much easier to learn prejudice against African-Americans than to understand their history of suffering and courageous survival. Many Korean immigrants have adapted the unfair hierarchical, racist values of U.S. society, consequently holding African-Americans in low esteem. Their understanding of African-Americans is as distorted as their naive expectations of the United States as a utopia.

Korean-American prejudice toward African-Americans is reinforced by business experiences in high-crime areas. It is necessary for Korean-Americans to make a distinction between racial issues and class issues. What they have experienced in high-crime areas is not a racial matter but a class matter. They need to see how African-Americans have had to compete in society, often without wealth and education, and how many of them have been denied job opportunities and have been forced into fatalism.

Some Korean-Americans call African-Americans *Gumdoong-yi*, which means "darkies." This title is derogatory. There is a positive term for African-Americans—*Hwoock-in*, "black people." I have quite often heard the term *Gumdoong-yi* from respectable Korean-Americans and been disappointed at their racist remarks. We are mocked as "Gooks," yet we mock others with *Gumdoong-yi*. We see the speck in our neighbor's eye, but do not notice the log in our own (Mt 7:3). As long as we have racism within, we cannot fight racism without.

Korean-Americans even discriminate against one another. Most Koreans are prejudiced against people from the Chollah provinces. This is a serious problem in Korea, affecting electoral votes and employment. Korean immigrants have brought this provincialism into this country, extending it to African-Americans and Hispanic-Americans. In this new land, Korean-Americans must remove provincialism and racism in order to participate in the new history of this society.

When Euro-Americans have prejudice against us, we are resentful, but when we are biased against African-Americans and others, we are indifferent. When shall we learn from our own experience not to prejudge others? It is the teaching of the Lord's prayer on forgiveness: "And forgive our debts, as we also have forgiven our debtors" (Mt 6:12). Until we stop prejudging others, we will be unable to ask for the cessation of prejudice against us.

People sometimes transfer their *han* to others by inflicting the same pain upon them. Korean-Americans are the victims of racism, but in turn we become racists toward others. The act of hurting others is sin. Such sin and *han* is broken with the act of true seeing. When we truly partake in the pain of others, we will repent of the sin of prejudice against our victims.

It is undeniable that racism against African-Americans and Hispanic-Americans is extensive among Korean-Americans. Since more than 70 percent of Korean-Americans are Christians,[3] Korean-American churches should educate their congregations on race matters. Korean-American churches must start the movement to repent of racism. If the churches are silent on this acute sin, their silence seems to sanction the community's prejudice. However hard the task may be, Korean-American churches must grapple with this important issue.

SEXISM

Sociologist Won H. Chang in his research of Korean-Americans in Los Angeles observes that the hierarchical order between husband and wife stabilizes their immigrant life. Because of the economic pressure of immigrant living in the United States, increasing numbers of Korean immigrant women have sought employment. Proportionally, more Korean married women are employed than Euro-American and African-American married women in this country.[4] Their economic independence subsequently has weakened the traditional authority of husbands, who are likely to feel threatened and attempt to resume their undisputed authority over the family. While they have adjusted to the two-income structure of the American lifestyle, they still adhere to the old value system of Korean life in their ethnic customs. "The traditional authoritarianism and more dominant values and the new values embedded in the egalitarian orientation of American society have not found a constructive synthesis within the family. Conflict often leads to family break down."[5] An Korean-American enclave is a protective shield for the authoritarian lifestyle of Korean-American husbands. Out of the 483 married respondents, 261 respondents (54 percent) were employed. Only one-third of the respondents indicated the employment of husbands only.[6] Even when both husband and wife work outside the home, the wife usually does most of the housework, including cooking, childrearing, grocery shopping, housekeeping, laundry, and dishwashing. The survey reports that Korean husbands evenly share the household task of managing the family budget and disposing of garbage.[7] Korean immigrant husbands, whether they work long hours or not, generally are not much involved in household tasks. So their wives must basically carry out all the housework in addition to their jobs. The wives are not only worn out physically, but also suffer emotionally whenever their husbands exercise sole final authority, disregarding their opinions.

Furthermore, Korean immigrant women suffer from the sexism of the society. As women, they are humiliated in various ways. They are harassed by superiors who expect them to behave in a certain way. Their salaries are lower than those of Korean-American men and much lower than those of Euro-American men. Further, people in general impose stereotypical images on them. A second-generation Korean-American woman who made several requests at a fancy California restaurant was asked, "Why can't you act like an Oriental?"[8] This kind of abuse derives not only from sexism but also from racism. It is hard to separate these two in the experience of oppression of Korean-American women.

Moreover, employed Korean-American women are discriminated against even by women of European descent. The disgrace of being passed over for promotion humiliates Korean-American women. These women suffer from all these dimensions of social and family life. They have borne a heavier burden than married women in Korea and most married women in the United States.[9]

Most Korean Christian women dedicate time for church work.[10] Many Korean-American churches demand that they attend weekday meetings, such as daily dawn prayer meetings, Wednesday evening services, Friday Bible study meetings, and seasonal revival meetings, as well as Sunday morning services and Sunday evening services. At the church, women are willingly or unwillingly relegated to secondary positions, doing all kinds of manual jobs such as preparing for fellowship, receptions, meals, washing dishes, and cleaning the church. Although many women have the qualities needed to be church elders, it is rare to promote women laity to this position even in Korean-American United Methodist churches.[11] Most Korean-American Presbyterian churches, except the Presbyterian Church (USA), do not allow woman elders. Korean-American churches strongly reflect their cultural background.

As women's group members, women organize and sponsor all kinds of church activities. They are the backbone of the Korean-American churches. For many of them, churches are not places where they experience liberation but rather mental and physical exhaustion and repression. Yet the church was the symbol of the women's liberation in the beginning. The Bible was translated into Korean (urn-moon), the despised language of women and children, at the turn of the twentieth century. At that time the learned used Chinese (han-moon). But as the church established itself in society, many men joined the movement and established their hegemony. It has reverted to its patriarchal culture.

At least seven Korean-American Presbyterian churches in Southern California withdrew their memberships from the Christian Reformed Church in 1993 because of the denomination's move toward ordaining women.[12] Such action was anachronistic and repressive. These churches expect women to work harder than men, yet do not recognize women's leadership in their churches. This act is religious exploitation.

Korean-American women have been overburdened and burned out by housework, employment, church work, and discrimination against them. Sexism, racism, and the hardship of immigration life have engendered their *han*-laden agony.

LABOR EXPLOITATION

As reported by the Korean Chamber of Commerce of Southern California, there were approximately seven thousand Korean-American businesses in Los Angeles County in 1984.[13] It is remarkable that Korean immigrants have achieved so much within a short period. There are various reasons for this success in business. A major one is the cheap labor of immigrants. Light and Bonacich are certain that the labor standards under which the typical Korean immigrant entrepreneur operate have been low compared with the average U.S. situation.[14] Korean-American immigrant small-business owners work hard and long hours. Operation of their businesses is regarded as a form of "dirty work," an undesirable job by U.S. labor standards.[15]

Korean immigrant business owners sometimes hire non-family members. These employees serve the business with extraordinary dedication and loyalty, laboring long hours with their bosses under unfavorable working conditions at cheap wages. These workers establish somewhat strong bonds with their employers because of their intimate personal knowledge of their bosses. The loyalty on the part of the employees creates an obligation on the part of employers to secure the jobs of employees, a benefit in the tight job market.

Light and Bonacich describe the cause of cheap Korean labor in the United States this way:

> First, conditions in their homeland led the immigrants to leave with certain customs and expectations that conditioned their attitudes toward work. Second, the immigrant situation played a part in shaping their choices. Third, the concentration in ethnic small business itself acted as a depressant on immigrant labor, helping to maintain its cheapness.[16]

The second and the third points are more fundamental than the first, which focuses on low labor standards in South Korea. These low standards predispose immigrants to accept the substandard working conditions of small Korean-immigrant businesses. Light and Bonacich, however, disregard the fact that most Korean immigrants constitute a middle class, not a Korean labor class. Many of these middle-class entrepreneurs avoid doing manual work by hiring low-wage laborers, concentrating their energy on management.

Their second point is that the language barrier and job discrimination have limited Korean immigrants' job opportunities to a highly competitive Korean-American job market. Korean business owners survive on the cheap labor of newly arrived immigrants, and the immigrants have little with which to bargain.

The third point is that "cheap labor is both the cause and effect of Korean concentration in small business."[17] The concentrated form of small Korean business functions as a depressant to Korean immigrants for longer than one might expect. Small Korean businesses in Koreatown attract and entrap new immigrants and retard the process of their acculturation and assimilation. For new immigrants, obtaining jobs outside the ghetto is a catch-22 situation: to get outside jobs, they need to speak good English; to speak good English requires work experience beyond the Korean immigrant communities. Caught in this predicament, they stay in the communities and earn low wages.

Besides Light and Bonacich's points, there are at least two more reasons why Korean immigrant labor is cheap and is exploited. One derives from *che-myun* ("saving the face") of the reference person. Korean immigrants usually find jobs through friends or intermediaries.[18] Korean immigrant laborers try to "save the face" of their friends or the intermediaries who introduce them to their employers by working long and hard and not actively seeking increases in their wages. Because of *che-myun* these workers do not change their jobs quickly, even though better ones might appear.

The other factor contributing to maintaining cheap labor is the aspiration of employees to start their own businesses someday. Thus they learn how to run a business thoroughly, persevering through all the exploitation. Their hope to have their own businesses helps keep wages low in the communities.

It is commendable that Korean immigrants work hard and become successful entrepreneurs. However, if they thrive at the expense of exploiting others with long hours of labor and an inadequate compensation package, by endangering their own health, and by neglecting their own children's well-being, they fail in achieving their "American dream." This type of success is an act of idolatry, of worshiping business success while caring little for their family or their laborers. Exploiting defenseless immigrants should be stopped. Korean-American business people need to compensate workers' labor at an adequate level. It is time for the Korean-American communities to hear the words of Deuteronomy: "You shall not withhold the wages of poor and needy laborers, whether other Israelites or aliens who reside in your land in one of your towns" (Dt 24:14).

Though we Koreans might be victims of racism, sexism, and economic exploitation in this society, we in turn victimize fellow Korean-Americans and others with the same sins. From the perspective of Korean-American women, newly arrived immigrants, and the victims of provincialism and racism, these are not sins but *hans*. This reality of *han* and sin is interwoven in the structure of our Korean-American existence. From the thickness of this jungle of sin and *han* we must find a way to transcend our cyclical return to hopelessness by our quiet contemplation of life and the world.

Part II

TOWARD SOLUTIONS

4

A Vision for Society

We need to examine the sin and *han* of Korean-American communities in a larger social context in order to understand them better.
Korean-Americans' *hans* and sins are the symptoms of the nation's *hans*
and sins. Racism, corporate greed, patriarchy, and economic exploitation flourish. The Bible declares, "Where there is no vision, the people
perish" (Prv 29:18, *KJV*). But, in fact, there are too many visions in our
society. People have been bombarded with many confusing images that
have been advanced by the advantaged in order to increase their economic and political control over others (racial mercantilism), but we
have had few visions that encourage a full life of social relationship.

How does a vision transform the *han* and sin of our world? Thomas
Kuhn maintains that a *paradigm* is key to changing the reality of the
world. In *The Structure of Scientific Revolutions* he writes that "the suc-
cessive transition from one paradigm to another via revolution is the
usual developmental pattern of mature science."[1] When an old paradigm fails in a new situation, a new paradigm emerges as an alternative explanation. Thus scientific environments shift. When paradigms
change, the world changes with them. And, theologian Sallie McFague
contends that when our metaphors and models change, theology
changes.[2]

I believe that paradigms, metaphors, and models point to images. It
is not until we change our images that we change. When our images
shift, the reality of our society shifts. Unity will come only from changing the deep images we hold of one another. No knowledge, concept,
or idea can change our consciousness, our community, and our society better than images; knowledge that is not translated into image remains an abstract.

Three things are needed for true unity in a nation: a common vision, an indispensable vision, and an inmost vision. When people find
a common aim, they can work together. A common objective can bind
people as they cooperate to achieve their goal. To achieve a durable

51

unity among people, it is necessary for them to share something beyond a common goal.

An indispensable vision values the contribution of diverse groups and breaks through the recalcitrant conflict of racial and ethnic groups. A society of diverse groups needs still more than a respect for diversity, though, because such a respect for diversity does not fully recognize the innate value of other groups; its focus is on their instrumental value.

An inmost vision points to an *intrinsic value* in each group *beyond* its usefulness in realizing a desired goal. In a religious setting it can denote the actualization of the community of God, for which every person is essential. It refers to a deep-seated vision that God has buried in us.

On the one hand, an inmost vision can heal the *han* of the oppressed by turning it into fuel to materialize the image. On the other, the inmost vision enables the oppressors to see their sin, the sin that prevents other groups from actualizing their potential. Oppressors begin to see that the unrealized gifts of the oppressed are a great loss in pursuing a shared inmost vision.

A COMMON VISION

During the Cold War era external enemies created feelings of unity in this nation. Now that common cause has faded. We need to replace it with a vital vision that will shape our thinking and attitudes. This nation has found certain common ground for all groups in the freedom of religion, speech, the press, assembly, and right of petition. These values, however, have not been sufficient to provide a genuine relationship among diverse groups. Something beyond the present social and political values is required. Finding a common goal brings a certain unity in society. A common goal derives from the common interest of individuals or groups to preserve and maximize their own potential. It provides the temporary unity of society until the goal is achieved. Without a common vision, a community hardly exists. However, the unity this common goal provides might not be strong enough to meet the needs of this nation at the present time. We need to examine the roles of indispensable and inmost visions.

AN INDISPENSABLE VISION

Beyond a common goal we need to find an end that is fundamental for all the different groups in the country. An indispensable vision provides such a fundamental unity of community. It emerges from the realization that we cannot achieve a goal by ourselves and that others are indispensable for accomplishing it. The mutual actualization of potential is a key to understanding an indispensable vision. A good example that illustrates mutual indispensability is the so-called Robbers' Cave experiment.

The Robbers' Cave Experiment

To observe how group dynamics work, social psychologists Muzafer and Carolyn Sherif and their collaborators organized summer camps for boys in upstate New York, Connecticut, and Robbers' Cave, Oklahoma. The outcomes were indistinguishable, so we will describe only the Robbers' Cave group.

A group of boys aged eleven and twelve from middle-class families were selected from different schools, supposedly to attend a typical summer camp. Upon arrival at camp, they were escorted to a cabin. There were two cabins, but each group was unaware of the existence of the other. Each had time to plan group activities and develop its group identity as reflected in its name, regulations, and jokes. One named itself the Eagles, the other the Rattlers.

When the time came to induce intergroup conflict, the two groups were introduced and set to compete for group rewards. As rivalry and the level of frustration grew, name calling, physical aggression, and camp raids followed. The increasing hostility consolidated group identity and group unity *within* each group but exacerbated the mutual mistrust and lack of respect *between* the groups. The two groups standardized for themselves derogatory attitudes and stereotypes toward one another.[3]

The next phase investigated how to reduce the conflict between the two groups. The researchers provided some opportunities for contact between the two groups without any common goals. First, the researchers tried to stress the higher values of brotherly love and cooperation through religious services, but these bore little fruit. Second, they introduced a third party to be a common enemy. This effort temporarily reduced the conflict. Third, they provided for conferences between group leaders. When the leaders agreed to end hostilities, their group members threw apples at them. Fourth, the researchers tried common activities, such as special meals, desserts, fireworks on the Fourth of July, and movies. These did not work but rather provided further opportunities to express enmity.[4]

The researchers finally succeeded in reducing the mutual bitterness only through a common task that required the cooperation of both groups. They called this a "superordinate goal." When attaining the goal "is compelling but . . . cannot be achieved by the efforts of one group alone, they will tend to cooperate toward the common goal."[5] The superordinate goal is different from an ordinary common goal in terms of its emphasis on the inescapable aspect of *joint* effort. A goal can be "superordinate" when involved groups see it as compelling and understand it as attainable *only* through their joint endeavor. A superordinate goal requires a genuine need for the cooperation of involved groups. Mere verbal persuasion cannot create it.

The researchers presented various superordinate goal situations. First, the water supply line was "mysteriously" cut off. The groups joined efforts to locate the broken spot. This temporarily helped them reduce their hostility. A series of such joint ventures eventually thawed their mutual hostility: they collected money to rent their favorite movie, pulled a food supply truck to start it, and prepared food together instead of alternating meal preparation. Through these common projects group members came to appreciate the other group and develop friendships beyond their own group. Most of the boys even opted to return home on the same bus.[6]

The effects of superordinate goals have been confirmed by other research using adults from various ethnic groups.[7] This research shows that any form of competition between ethnic groups will bring forth conflict, not cooperation. Only a "win-win" game will bring out collaboration between them. In the United States, social, geo-political, and economic structures are quite competitive. To have true unity, we need to identify some superordinate goals in order to develop a respect for our diverse groups. Such goals will empower people to be themselves and also to be united in moving toward joint goals. Following are some concrete examples.

David and David against Goliath

David Rogers, a star graduate of Harvard Medical School, was building a career in genetics and pediatrics.[8] On his father's birthday,[9] David picked up a birthday cake and was driving on the freeway when a wheel and axle from a truck in front of his car flew off and crashed through his car roof. The wheel changed his life permanently. He became a quadriplegic at 29.

David Kaplan, a retarded man, spent fourteen years in a sheltered workshop. He developed sufficient skills to live independently, yet he wanted to get involved in more meaningful work. David Rogers owned a clinic in the city, and someone connected the two. Now David Kaplan answers the phone, stamps a signature, turns pages, writes, and pushes David Rogers's wheelchair. "He is my hands. He does everything for me, from delivering and getting records to making phone calls. . . . He remembers phone numbers, people I saw or spoke to two months ago. He's invaluable."[10] These two persons with disabilities actualize their potential through each other, serving their community together. "Weak David plus weak David, the paraplegic and the sheltered one, together carry on a medical career and serve people. They are strong."[11] They became a team to serve their community as healing agents. As these two men have shown, through cooperation they surmount the impossible and uplift their community. Instead of being burdens, the wounded have become the healers.

David and David could cooperate because both had a strong desire to serve the weak and the sick. This goal united them and made them able to serve their community. An African-American quadriplegic and a mentally challenged Jewish-American recognized and respected each other's very different gifts and now use joint ability for helping the needy. Instead of being defeated and helpless, David and David *together* have defeated their Goliaths.

America can be robust when its ethnic groups realize their vulnerabilities and embrace complementarity. When groups unite with respect for their diversity and seek a superordinate goal, they become vigorous and potent. It is essential for ethnic groups to find a higher common goal that they can reach only by working together and recognizing each other's gifts.

The Bloods and Crips

One of the positive effects of the 1992 Los Angeles eruptions was the Bloods-Crips truce. The gangs had been enemies for many years. But when they saw their very community at stake, they could not stand its further destruction and the mutual killing any more. They buried their old vendettas and promised to cooperate to rebuild the community. The number of gang-related homicides plummeted. Further, the gangs came up with concrete suggestions for reorganizing their neighborhoods. In the South Central Los Angeles area, nihilism and fatalism were rampant. Without jobs and with drugs, young residents brooded in an atmosphere of hopelessness and despondency. The fact that the gangs came up with concrete visions for their neighborhoods was a marvelous event in itself.

The two gangs saw something very crucial and important beyond their own agendas—the survival of their community. They abandoned their individual goals and committed themselves to building up their community instead of tearing it down, a task neither group alone could achieve. They needed each other in order to stop the killing and to revitalize their neighborhoods. In 1993, they even got together to record an album, "Bangin' on Wax," which was intended to convince gang members to do battle with words rather than with bullets.[12] Furthermore, on October 30, 1994, gang leaders Juan Longino of the Crips and Twilight Bay of the Bloods spoke in London as part of their United Kingdom tour to urge aspiring British gang members to stop killing and make peace as they did.[13]

This event shows that to change our streets we need not more force but more superordinate goals for which we can live and strive—and thrive—together. Groups in conflict should be guided to meet each other more often and visualize together a common goal that requires their mutual cooperation.

In "Strong Institutions, Good City," Robert Bellah and Christopher Freeman Adams emphasize the need of community in America.[14] For them, "community requires members to be constantly engaged in discussion about goals and purposes."[15] Engendered in part by an American ideology of individualism, the lack of authentic community spawns all kinds of moral problems such as alcoholism, substance abuse, family breakdown, proliferation of gangs, street violence, and ethnic tensions. Authentic inter-ethnic and larger community building is, therefore, the best prevention of these crimes and immoralities around us. Authentic inter-ethnic community can be established only in the context of larger community building. No group can be healthy without the health of larger community. The church and other community organizations can foster such indispensable goals.

AN INMOST VISION

In the parable of the Lost Sheep we find a shepherd leaving ninety-nine sheep in the fold to look for one lost sheep (Mt 18:12-14). It doesn't seem that the lost one is needed for the survival of the rest of the sheep. Christ, however, does regard the lost one as indispensable for the rest, redefining the meaning of indispensability. Without the one, the ninety-nine are lost as far as Jesus is concerned. The parable teaches us a new view of indispensability in a world of pragmatic values. The view that Christ takes—that "useless" human beings are indispensable for his community—is inmost for the salvation of humanity.

Our true hope is that we realize that we are indispensable for one another. In our childhood we see that some people are necessary for our survival. As we mature we realize that most people are valuable for our community. At the maturity of our Christian life we see that each and every person is indispensable for God's community, regardless of his or her apparent usefulness. In this stage our inmost or deeply felt image shifts to the divine and the divine community.

Such an inmost image leads people to transcend their self-centered interpretation of a relationship in order to reach a community-conscious interpretation of relationships. At this turning-point from ego-centered to divine-centered life, we affirm our unity with all and voluntarily commit to a vision of unity in community.

In this society we need common and indispensable goals, but to reach genuine unity we need an inmost vision that values each and every person regardless of group or "functional value." We need to realize that each group—each person—is irreplaceable in our life journey. The deeply felt vision will gradually ripen our understanding of interracial relationships to the point that each group is innately a blessing to the social life of all and a precious companion for building the community of God. The following story illustrates an inmost vision.

Jack Sunwoo

On February 3, 1994, Los Angeles Councilman Mark Ridley-Thomas, an African-American, introduced a motion to the members of the Los Angeles City Council to pay tribute to Jack Sunwoo, the slain owner of Sun Moon Market. All council members stood in tribute and reverence and adjourned in his memory.[16]

Sunwoo, who had owned the market since 1975, was shot to death on December 17, 1993. He was fifty-five years old. Four African-American gang members, aged seventeen and eighteen, killed him and robbed his wife.

Over the years, Sunwoo had made many friends with people who lived in the predominantly African-American and Hispanic-American area where his store was located. He used portions of his income for the benefit of his poor neighbors, including the payment of funeral costs for some neighbors.

Jack Sunwoo refused to have a gun to protect himself. He had the conviction that he should not hurt others with a gun even if that meant his own death. His wife, Seung-ja Sunwoo, said that he had an angelic heart. She intends to dedicate her life to spreading the compassion of God and promoting gun control.

The Sunwoo family immigrated to this country in 1974. Before his immigration Jack Sunwoo, who had graduated from Seoul National University, worked as a high-ranking official in the Agriculture Department. Like other immigrants, in the beginning his family struggled to survive in a strange land. Later, his family purchased a small grocery market in South Central Los Angeles. Without any other help, Sunwoo and his wife worked from 7 A.M. till 9 P.M. daily.

During the last twenty years they had faced a number of thefts, robberies, and other trials. In 1985 their business was burned by unknown gang members. Their whole dream turned into ashes. For two years Sunwoo worked for another small store. Despite these hardships, he stayed in South Central. He could have left that business for a better one in a much safer area, but he decided to stay, although his friends and his children entreated him to leave the dangerous neighborhood. He and his wife saw their mission in the South Central area and refused to leave. Their primary purpose in running the market was not for financial gain but for alleviating racial tension and sharing God's good news through helping their poor neighbors whenever they could. To them, their clients were as precious as Jesus Christ; their neighbors' joys and sorrows were their own.

Many stories epitomize his life in the neighborhood. For example, at first the Filipino owner of the building containing Jack's store took advantage of Sunwoo for his own gain. After dealing with Sunwoo for a long time, the owner was deeply inspired by his words and deeds. His influence was so profound that the owner was converted to Christianity and later became an ordained minister.[17]

During the 1992 Los Angeles eruptions thousands of stores were looted and gutted. Sunwoo's market, however, remained untouched. As the eruptions started, his neighborhood friends came to help, saying, "Jack, please close your market and go home. We will protect your market for you."[18] He left the store and his African-American friends guarded his business, stationing themselves in the front, in the back, and on the roof.

After his death, his neighbors, from ages five to eighty, continually visited the store and mourned for him, placing flowers, candles, and bibles in front of the store. Isabel Sanchez, aged twenty-six, said tearfully, "He was a missionary rather than a businessman."[19] Parents leading their children paid tribute, expressing their grief. The overwhelming response of his neighbors was uncommon in a time of frequent robberies and murders in small shops.

Sunwoo saw something many business people fail to see. To him, his clients and neighbors were not mere means of his financial support (instrumental indispensability) but were *intrinsically indispensable* for his business. His mission in life was to care for and improve the neighborhood. Every day he risked his life, but he lived joyfully to serve his poor neighbors. He saw his needy neighbors and understood their agony. His *seeing* was that of understanding, participating in and transforming their hardship. At the end, he quietly laid down his life to fulfill his mission. His *seeing* his neighbors was an *inmost vision* of valuing them as people.

An inmost goal is a vision of the ontological indispensability of others in the process of building the community of God. We need others, not to achieve our goals, but because they are the end of the mission of our lives. This vision points to the people we serve, not to our goal of achieving.

The United States consists of peoples from all over the world. In spite of such efforts as affirmative action, this nation has suffered great racial and ethnic conflicts. As it was in the old Soviet Union, racial and ethnic tension in this country is one of the most pressing issues, one on which this nation might stand or fall. It is essential for us to live harmoniously in unity.

Even though common goals, indispensable vision, and inmost vision are distinguished above, it is difficult to separate them. Our common goals, for example, can grow into an inmost vision. To gain more perspective on the necessary unity of ethnic groups, we focus below on two possible indispensable visions: eco-social justice and media justice.

A VISION OF ECO-SOCIAL JUSTICE

Urban Environment

Establishing a racially just society is perceived as the primary issue for ethnic groups, while promoting an ecologically sound society is seen as the urgent issue for Caucasians. In fact, these two issues are inseparable, intertwined in the texture of profit-driven capitalism. Many instances of racial injustice and environmental crisis derive from the same source—economic misuse and abuse.

Jesse Jackson proposes diverting the investment of transnational corporations from third-world countries to urban areas. In principle this could improve the economic situation of the inner cities, but it could also trigger complex problems, including environmental disasters, for the inner cities as well. We need more fundamental solutions: new ways of developing our cities and land; better use of production facilities and human resources; and more investment in human resources, community-based businesses, and local manufacturing.

Environmental Racism

The race, class, and color of people affect policy makers in their environmental decision making. The communities of ethnic minority groups are often target sites for hazardous waste landfills, incinerators, sewage treatment plants, refineries, and lead smelters.[20]

According to a 1990 Greenpeace report, communities with incinerators have 89 percent more people of color than the national average; the average income in these communities is 15 percent lower than the national average; and property values are 38 percent lower. Communities with proposed sites for incinerators have 60 percent higher minority population than the national average and average property values are 35 percent lower in these communities.[21]

A Korean-American community in the Los Angeles area faced such direct discrimination. The City of Industry planned to construct a waste recycling factory in the Walnut and Diamondbar community where many Korean-Americans reside. This factory would process fifty-seven hundred tons of daily recycling waste collected from Los Angeles and Orange counties, generating traffic of twelve hundred trash trucks a day. Despite the strong opposition of the residents, the city council wanted to proceed with this plan.[22] The construction of a waste recycling factory is laudable, but why should such a factory be built half a mile away from a residential area?

Another classic example of environmental racism is the case of Altgeld Gardens in the Chicago area. The neighborhood is 70 percent African-American and 11 percent Hispanic-American. Altgeld Gardens is surrounded by 50 commercial hazardous waste landfills (active or closed), 103 abandoned toxic waste dumps, and 100 factories, including 7 chemical plants and 5 steel mills.[23]

The case of Richmond, California, also testifies to environmental racism. Over half of its population of eighty thousand is African-American and about 10 percent is Hispanic-American. Most of the African-Americans live next to the city's petrochemical hallway—a cluster of 350 facilities that handle hazardous waste.[24] On July 26, 1993, sulfur trioxide escaped from the General Chemical plant in Richmond. More than twenty thousand residents were sent to hospitals.

Since the complaint of environmental racism was first raised in 1987, African-Americans, Hispanic-Americans, Asian-Americans, and Native-Americans are even more likely to find themselves neighbors of commercial hazardous waste facilities.[25] In 1980, 25 percent of the people living in a ZIP code that comprised one or more hazardous sites were non-Euro-Americans; by 1993 that ratio rose to 31 percent. Since non-Euro-Americans make up 20 percent of the U.S. population, this means that an ethnic minority has a 47 percent greater chance than an Euro-American of living near such facilities.[26]

Economic Growth and Increasing Poverty

Since 1950 the global economy has increased fivefold; world trade has expanded even faster, raising the exports of primary commodities and manufactured goods elevenfold. We have, however, more poor people than ever before. The 1.2 billion absolute poor survive on less than the equivalent of $1 a day.[27] In terms of food consumption, 700 million people eat insufficient food to live and work at their full potential. Rising incomes and material consumption are important for improving the living conditions of the poor, but global economic growth as presently pursued enables the rich to become richer while the poor become poorer. In 1989 the richest 20 percent of the world population absorbed nearly 83 percent of global income (in 1960, they took 70 percent). In contrast, the poorest 20 percent shared just 1.4 percent in 1989 (and a meager 2.3 percent in 1960). The ratio of the income of the richest fifth to the income of the poorest thus increased from 30 to 1 in 1960 to 59 to 1 in 1989.[28]

Food production rates drop when soil conditions deteriorate. Between 1950 and 1990 grain production almost tripled (from 631 million tons to 1,780 tons or 29 million tons per year). However, between 1990 and 2030, grain production is expected to expand at the most by 12 million tons per year. Fish catches also will drop from 19 kilograms (between 1950 and 1990) to 11 kilograms per capita.[29] From 1950 to 1990 environmental damage greatly escalated: water use tripled, the industrial round-wood harvest doubled, and oil production grew almost sixfold.[30]

Global Warming

Since 1860 the mean global temperature has increased. If production of greenhouse gases (mainly CO_2) continues to rise at the present rate, in fifty years the globe will be warmer than it has been for the past ten thousand years.[31]

Warmer temperature, especially over a relatively short period such as fifty or one hundred years, would be disastrous for economic, social, and ecological systems. Such rapid climatic shifts would alter conditions faster than some species, particularly plants, could adapt (or animals migrate). Rain patterns would change, becoming wetter over all. Some areas, such as much of the Midwest, would be hotter, while parts of Africa would be cooler. Some areas would become uninhabitable because of droughts or floods following a rise in average sea levels. Over the next fifty to one hundred years the average global sea level would rise between approximately half a foot and four and a half feet. Even a modest one foot rise would flood 30 to 70 percent of remaining coastal wetlands and inundate low-land cities such as New Orleans, New York, Atlantic City, Boston, Washington, D.C., Galveston, Charleston, Savannah, and Miami.[32]

The love of God and the love of neighbor are the greatest commandments in the scriptures. These two commandments are intertwined. Our love of God must be translated into the love of our neighbor (1 Jn 4:7-21). In the same manner, love of our neighbor must be translated into love of nature. The misuse and abuse of natural resources are equivalent to theft from our neighbor and our grandchildren—and ultimately theft from God.[33] If we love our neighbor and our grandchildren as ourselves, we cannot steal the resources they need to survive.

This is the point at which the issues of social justice and ecology meet. Love of neighbor (social justice) and care for nature (ecology) should be understood as a whole. If we do not love animals and nature, we come to love our neighbor and children in the abstract. When we love nature, we make concrete our love of our neighbor. Thus, we must understand the love of God in light of the love of our neighbor, and we need to reinterpret the love of our neighbor in light of the love of nature.

We need a radical change in our thinking, a social and global repentance (*metanoia*). In this age of ecological crises, individualistic economic successes can mean collective failure. Thinking and living individualistically is not acceptable but rather a violation against God and God's creation. It is necessary for us to live collectively by planning a common future for all beings. The church can strengthen a local community through building up local economy, including local political, social, and cultural independence. The church can also be a place where people enhance global well-being. By connecting the support of local communities with the improvement of global wholeness, the church expands God's realm in the world.

MASS MEDIA

Big corporations control the media. Their primary aim is not to bring information to the public but to increase profits by raising their audience share. To boost the rating, they air sex, violence, and sensational materials. Further, since media control is largely in the hands of Caucasian males, much news information is biased against minorities, women, and third-world countries.

For example, George Bush purchased property in West Oaks, Texas in 1981. He signed a contract stipulating that the land could not "be sold, leased or rented to any person other than of the Caucasian race, except in the case of servant's quarters." The *Nation* reported this story in 1987, as well as Bush's other restrictive covenants, but no mainstream media mentioned it during his 1988 presidential campaign. On the contrary, ABC/NPR reporter Cokie Roberts narrated "George Bush's pro–civil rights record." On the other hand, during the 1984 and 1988 campaigns the same news media kept after Jesse Jackson to "pay" for his "Hymietown" joke, which he did on numerous occasions.[34]

The media frequently presents African-Americans in a negative light. Although polling statistics reported in *USA Today* reveal that only 15 percent of U.S. drug users are African-American, data from the Black Entertainment Network show that 50 percent of network news stories on drugs highlight African-Americans.[35]

Most U.S. dailies receive their news from the Associated Press (AP), United Press International (UPI), the *New York Times*, the *Los Angeles Times–Washington Post* wire services and a couple of foreign companies such as Reuters.[36] The two largest U.S. news agencies, AP and UPI, alone transmit more than eight million words a day, while the seven biggest news agencies based in developing countries together compose only a tiny portion of that amount. The United States and its closest allies regulate 90 percent of the third-world news flow.[37] Instead of cultural diversity, these news media proliferate cultural and social uniformity through feeding similar information to the world. A. Raghavan, an Indian journalist, stated: "The developing countries that have freed themselves from colonial political dependence are still saddled with information dependence."[38]

Even editors of newspapers and anchors at television stations do not have real freedom of speech. For example, Walter Cronkite, then the symbol of America's newscasters, ended his CBS news with the sentence: "And that's the way it is." The real Cronkite came out on the eve of his retirement in 1980. He acknowledged that reality was *not* the way it was: "My lips have been kind of buttoned for almost twenty years. . . . CBS News doesn't really believe in commentary."[39] Shortly following a liberal public speech that criticized an aspect of U.S. foreign policy, his television show was canceled.[40] Cronkite grumbled about the censorship by the network, but he did not explain what really happened behind the scenes.[41]

The recent wave of big media mergers has silenced some voices and forced others into a chorus. The final hurdle to Time Warner's $7.5 billion purchase of Turner Broadcasting System was removed on July 17, 1996, when it received the approval of the Federal Trade Commission,[42] creating one of the world's largest media conglomerates. On the same day, Rupert Murdock's News Corporation announced that it would pay $2.5 billion for New World Communications, making it the nation's largest station owner. The twenty-two Fox-affiliated stations of Murdock's News Corporation now reach 40 percent of U.S. homes with television.[43]

These mergers violate the new rules that were enacted by the Federal Communications Commission (FCC) in 1992 that prevent any individual or company from owning more than twelve TV stations and sixty radio stations (and up to six in the same market) or reaching more than 25 percent of the country through its stations.[44]

Furthermore, these media conglomerates manufacture a popular culture. For instance, the Walt Disney Company deeply influences the direction of our culture through its books, movies, TV shows, and toys. Its acquisition of Capital Cities/ABC extends its influence over our daily life. As Time Warner develops a new division to produce toys based on its movie and TV characters, as announced, it will also produce a popular culture for our children.

Such media mega-mergers have increased the power of media monopolies, excluding rivals, raising prices, and impeding the development of a multi-culture in the United States. As long as the large media conglomerates dominate our cultural, social, educational, and political institutions, they severely circumscribe our vision of diversity. The media present images of the arts, the family, colleges, and churches. Even religions are under the influence of the mega-conglomerates, which engender and support selected values, beliefs, and myths of religions and culture. They also have the power to spawn unfair information, if that is in their interest.

To change the present state of affairs is not a simple matter. It involves raising the consciousness of the public, the prevention of media monopoly, more sophisticated regulations by the Federal Communications Commission (FCC), the autonomy of the FCC, and perhaps even the revision of bribery laws. Change in the hearts of people plays an important role, too.

Empowerment of Citizens

In *The Quickening of America* Frances Moore Lappé and Paul Martin Du Bois describe a radio station run by low-income people in Dallas, Texas. The authors had a hard time even finding KNON in its depressed residential neighborhood. Everything about KNON seemed provisional. Paint cans were scattered around the lobby, and furniture had obviously been obtained from a salvage store. In an upstairs studio a serious live broadcast was under way. A skilled African-American interviewer was asking probing questions of two women, one a physician who was explaining in easy-to-follow detail how women should do breast self-examinations regularly to detect cancer. It was important information for the community.

Established in 1983, KNON has been owned and governed by low- and moderate-income people. It attracts 100,000 listeners. One of its aims is "to provide a voice to those usually disenfranchised from the media."[45]

KNON is one outcome of the Association of Community Organizations for Reform Now's decision in 1980 to initiate a national association of community organizations, church-based organizations, broadcast facilities, and labor unions.[46] ACORN's main aim is to use radio and television to organize and mobilize local communities. The people of ACORN call the association AM/FM (the Affiliated Media Foundation Movement). AM/FM has assembled the technical expertise to assist community groups that want to apply for an FCC license. Besides KNON, AM/FM has put two more FM radio stations (Tampa, Florida, and Little Rock, Arkansas) and a TV station (Watsonville, California) on the air. Its applications for stations in half a dozen more states are pending before the FCC.[47]

AM/FM's work is significant. It shows us that ordinary citizens can control some of the airwaves in their communities, facing media conglomerates.[48]

To change the present state of the media entails long-term political and economic reforms. The following list is not all-inclusive but provides some ideas that we can realize.

First, sponsor a tour for media people and community leaders so that they can see whatever issue you are raising. The Southwest Organizing Project (SWOP) in Albuquerque does not just wait on the media to get their news out. Louis Head of SWOP explains:

> We educate them. We spent 1985 researching environment degradation in communities of color and came up with a day-long tour for the media. It has about twelve stops. We take media people on buses into neighborhoods—to the dump, to industries, and through communities that are having big problems. People on the tours get a chance to talk with people from other organizations.[49]

After the tour participants reflected together. The experience of the tour greatly influences participants' frame of thinking and their work. Edifying media people and community leaders is a practical way of changing a local community.

Second, reaffirm the public accountability of the media. Stress the social obligation of broadcasters, reiterating the requirement of the 1934 Federal Communications Act for broadcast stations to work for "the public interest, convenience and necessity." It would be good to extend this requirement to cable system operators and program providers. Encourage each service provider to come up with its own moral standards and check periodically to improve them.[50]

Third, increase support for public broadcasting and ensure that it treats community-based programming, having full sovereignty from political influences.[51] Public schools receive government subsidies. Should not public broadcasting receive public subsidies as well, since it has greatly contributed to children and public education?[52]

Fourth, promote healthy competition for existing cable franchises among cable operators, telephone companies, and any other possible sources. At the same time, deter any kind of direct deal-making between telephone companies and cable system operators to prevent acts of monopoly.[53]

Fifth, generate citizens' programs on commercial stations to discuss important community issues. Christians could produce programs on commercial stations to edify communities. We could also use the World Wide Web to connect churches to accomplish our global missions. Christians need to get actively involved in cyberspace, actively shaping its direction.

Sixth, begin a Christian radio or/and TV station supported by mainline churches. Independent of commercialism and consumerism, it could nurture the mainline religious and educational agenda. Since the major asset of a TV or a radio station does not lie in its equipment but in its audience and credibility, the churches can manage to own and operate a media station because they have both audience and credibility in their hands.

The effort to cooperate to create a Christian network system might foster an ecumenical drive. By working together to enlarge God's community, the churches could understand each other better and be united. When the churches have a clear vision of their mission in the area of media and make a long-term commitment to it, they can spread the good tidings and reliable information. The mass media are the most important instrument for the execution of church mission. The absence of the churches in the arena of media promulgates mass media of extreme mercantilism.

Seventh, support a church credit-union so that it can build up its local community. If Christians take our stewardship seriously, we can change the world—including the media—through committing our money to proper financial institutions.

Eighth, regulate media violence, sexual materials, and exaggerated advertisements through program ratings. The Roman Catholic Church has provided a telephone service for movie-rating information. The churches also could offer TV program ratings.

A poll for *USA Weekend* magazine showed concern about violent, sexual, and vulgar programs. The average American fourteen-year-old has witnessed eleven thousand murders on TV.[54] Of the sixty-five thousand respondents, 96 percent were very or somewhat concerned about sexual content on TV, 97 percent were very or somewhat concerned about violence, and 97 percent were very or somewhat concerned about vulgar language. Most parents would prefer that TV programs be rated as movies have been.[55]

Ninth, strengthen community building through public access television. There are two thousand public access TV channels in the United States. About one-half of all households are wired for cable. Public access refers to an arrangement in which a commercial cable company agrees to offer free production facilities and air time as a condition of securing its license. Through public access, local citizens and groups can produce their own programs and televise them to all the customers in the cable system. For example, in Reading, Pennsylvania, senior citizens programmed, operated, and financed their own two-way TV system. This project became Berks Community Television (BCTV), a nonprofit community access channel on the local cable system. It televises community affairs, and people can phone in their views to public hearings, knowing their views count.[56]

Karl Barth told us that we must read the Bible in one hand and the newspaper in the other. The Bible (the text) cannot be interpreted without today's situation (the context). Knowing our world is needed to understand the Bible. This hermeneutical principle creates a problem for us. If our newspapers distort the reality of the world, we are bound to misinterpret the Bible. If we construe the world from a bias, we comprehend the message of God with a prejudice. It is crucial for us to know the reality of the world.

5

A Vision for the Church

Parousia

An inmost vision for the church is the *parousia*, the second coming of Christ. This symbol has governed Christian understanding of time (and its end) and Christian involvement in the world. Along with the *eschaton* (end or purpose), the notion of *parousia* has shaped Christians' attitude toward history. If *parousia* is misconstrued, Christian historical consciousness can be distorted. Thus, it is crucial for Christians to have a proper understanding of the *parousia* for the establishment of God's community.

The notion of Jesus' second coming has confused Christians for almost two thousand years. On the one hand, numerous Christians have waited for the physical return of Jesus. Many people have expected Jesus to come back just as he ascended. Some churches even have announced dates for Jesus' return. In the Korean and Korean-American Christian communities, the *parousia* is one of the most confusing and disturbing doctrines. It has created many social disruptions and wrong-headed directions for Christian living. Some erroneous images of the *parousia* have misled many Christians and sapped their energy and time in unrealistic and disruptive preparations. Rather than fulfill history, they have spent time negating history. On the other hand, some Christians do not take this doctrine seriously; so they ignore Jesus' *parousia*. They do not believe that there will be a second coming.

But this ancient and significant doctrine has corresponded to the direction, mission, and goal of the church. The *civitas dei*, God's city, has a close connection with the *parousia* in our daily Christian life. When we have a healthy vision of the *parousia*, we can see the right direction for our mission in the world.

THE FIRST COMING

In the Hebrew scriptures there is ambiguity about the coming of the messiah. As disenchantment grew through the period of the monarchy and the following age, a messianic hope arose.[1] The idea of the king as representative of Yahweh's lordship was transferred into the idea of a messiah. The cultic psalms encouraged this transition by proclaiming Yahweh as king.[2] The rise of the messianic hope was also fostered from the perspective of a future Davidic king.[3] Although the roots of Israel's eschatological hope go back far in its history, the experience of the exile intensified the longing for the restoration of God's kingship.[4]

Another messianic image was the Servant of Yahweh (Is 42:1-4, 49:1-6, 50:4-6, 52:13-53:12). The subject of the Servant songs in Deutero-Isaiah, however, has been controversial. It could be a historical individual (Isaiah himself or an unknown person) or a group of people (Israel), not a messianic figure.[5] Still, writers of the Christian scriptures saw an impressive foreseeing of the messiah in the songs. There is, however, no substantial validation of identification between the Davidic king and the Servant during pre-Christian times.[6]

Still another possible messianic image was the title Son of Man, found mainly in Daniel and others.[7] Whether the title refers to a messianic figure is controversial. While some scholars (e.g., M. Mowinckel) deny the messianic denotation of the title, others (e.g., H. Riesenfeld and A. Bentzen) hold that in Psalms 8:4-5 and 80: 17-18, "Messiah" and "Son of Man" are parallel.[8] A. Moore contends that of the two terms, Son of Man can take up into itself the older hope of a messiah in the strict sense.[9] A second problem with the title as a messianic image involves its corporate or individual nature. Although its individual nature is advocated, its corporate identity theory has been strongly supported.[10] The four beasts (Dn 7:3-8) are four kings, suggesting the possibility of interpreting "one like unto a Son of Man" (7:13, RSV) as the ruler of the "saints of the Most High" (7:18, RSV). If the Son of Man is accepted as the peoples' representative, he represents the suffering saints.[11]

In summary, we can interpret the messiah of the Hebrew scriptures in two ways. One is the coming of the messiah with might and majesty. The other is a humble coming. Before the coming of Jesus, many Jews waited for the glorious coming of the messiah in the form of the King of kings, the Lord of lords. The prophet Isaiah's pronouncement of a coming king was construed as pointing to the messiah's coming: "For a child has been born for us, a son given to us; authority rests upon his shoulders; and he is named Wonderful Counselor, Mighty God, Everlasting Father, Prince of Peace" (Is 9:6). All Jewish religious ideas have been built around the magnificent messiah and his kingdom, around a messiah who will reestablish a Davidic kingdom and rule with peace forever.

The other interpretation was the coming of the messiah in the form of a humble and afflicted servant. In the first century A.D. some Jews accepted Jesus. They believed that he was the Suffering Servant of Yahweh who bore our infirmities and carried our diseases. These were Jesus' disciples and the early Christians, who were convinced of Jesus' messiahship through following him and carefully studying the various texts of the Hebrew scriptures. The early Christians opted for the interpretation of a humble messianic arrival. For them, Jesus, the Messiah, had not come as the mighty God, the King of kings, the Lord of lords, but as the despised, the Suffering Servant, the crucified God, and the ruler of hearts. The image of the Suffering Servant of Yahweh (Is 52–53) fits their understanding of the messiah. However, most Jews rejected this view.

THE SECOND COMING

After Jesus' ascension a number of his followers awaited his glorious return. As with the first coming, many expected a glorious and fantastic event, doing little themselves for the transformation of society in the meantime. They prayerfully waited for the catastrophic end of the world with the coming of Christ. Unfortunately, even now many Christians wait for the glorious second coming of Jesus, and confusion about the second coming still exists in the present churches.

Let us examine this idea of the second coming in the gospel of Matthew. The Matthean writer warned against the unhealthy apocalyptic movement in the first century; the chapters concerning the end of time admonish such wrong expectations (Mt 24–25). No one, the writer stresses, knows the day and hour of the end (Mt 24:36). His focus was on preparation for the *parousia*, not the time it would come (Mt 24:43-44). This focus continues through the parables of the Wicked Servant (Mt 24:45-51) and the Wise and Foolish Bridesmaids (Mt 25:1-13). The foolish do nothing to prepare for the coming of the master or the bridegroom. They just wait while doing wicked things or nothing at all. Also, the parable of the Talents (Mt 25:14-30) encourages the diligent execution of Christian missions, disparaging the passive waiting of Christians for the apocalyptic end. The lazy servant made the excuse that he thought his work would not make any difference. The author severely criticizes such a misdirected attitude toward Christian life.

Parousia consists of two words: *par* ("beyond") and *ousia* ("being"). God is not *becoming*, but *coming* to us through Christ.[12] Christ comes to us continuously. The *parousia* denotes more than the noticeable bodily coming of Christ; it includes the unnoticeable coming of Christ.

This is the reason the Matthean writer ends the gospel with Jesus' saying, "Remember, I am with you always, to the end of the age" (Mt 28:20). Jesus is here! Jesus said that those who believe without seeing him are blessed. In this world we believe what we can see. Can we trust Christ's second coming without seeing or touching his physical body? Can we go beyond our preoccupation with the physical coming of Christ? Can we see the continual coming of Christ in the form of the least among us? The *parousia* is not a once-and-for-all event but the recurrence of Christ's coming through the disinherited and the suffering.

Most Jewish people are still waiting for the glorious first coming of the messiah, while Christians affirm that the messiah came in the form of Jesus the Nazarene. Christians profess that Jesus as the Christ has been walking with us on Earth for two millennia. However, like the Jewish people, many Christians are still waiting for the glorious second coming of Christ. They await the Wonderful Counselor and the Mighty God. This kind of *parousia* from above is the outcome of the literal interpretation of the biblical passages, which are written in metaphoric, poetic, and symbolic terms.

Let us assume that Christ comes back with glory and power. Then what do we expect to happen? Will he reign with an iron fist, condemning unbelievers? Christ would never use the traditional understanding of power (force) to reign over us; his reign will arrive with grace, compassion, and mercy. Christ's coming will not occur prematurely. The gospel of the Kingdom will be preached throughout the whole world before the arrival of the end (Mt 24:14). This means that when the gospel of grace and love permeates the frozen hearts of people in the whole world, Christ's full reign will arrive. People have awaited a *parousia* from above. But there is also the *parousia* from below, the revolution of human hearts to treat the least as Christ in history. This is the *parousia* of the downtrodden in the form of Christ. In other words, the *parousia* is from below and collective. The second coming will arrive through the coming of the oppressed.[13]

The *parousia* started with the resurrection of Christ. The risen Christ has come to his disciples a number of times. The full *parousia* will transpire when Jesus' gospel of love persuades the hardened hearts of people (Mt 24:14). The divine city slowly grows in history like a mustard seed. This is the reason God's Kingdom is in the midst of us (Lk 17:21). To establish God's city on earth, it is necessary for us to see the *parousia* of Christ in our hungry, weary, sick, homeless neighbors. They are there not simply to receive our mercy but to save us from our self-centeredness, our arrogance, and our overly busy lives.

The success of spreading the gospel hinges upon how we treat our neighbors, particularly our ethnic neighbors. If we regard them as strangers, we are still on the road to Emmaus. If we see them as inferior beings, we come to despise Christ. If we see them as the coming of

Christ, Christ resides in us. It is necessary for us to see that the city of God will arrive only through them. For Korean-Americans, Christ appears in the form of African-Americans, Hispanic-Americans, Native-Americans, and any oppressed groups. However unrealistic it may be, until we recognize this understanding of the *parousia* through our needy neighbors and exercise our faith according to that understanding, God's city will not be established among us.

If the church consists of more Christians who expect the glorious second coming of Christ in the midst of disasters and tribulations, our society will turn into a hopeless place where religious fanaticism prevails and harsh social conditions will worsen. *Parousia* is not the end of the world, but the beginning of a new world. We need more people to *usher in* the *parousia*, not just wait for it. Churches need to share the vision of the humble and collective *parousia* in our cities in order to deliver us from racism and narrow ethnocentrism. I hope that Korean-American churches realize this vision with other church groups and advance the arrival of the *parousia*. This vision of the *parousia* emphasizes that each of us is intrinsically indispensable for building the city of God—a truly inmost vision.

6

A Vision for the Self

We have discussed how the *parousia* can be a vision for the church, how such a communal vision could heal the *han* of this society. Now we will focus on the role of the self in healing our societal *han*, for one of the major sources of problems such as racism, sexism, and corporate greed is individualism, which emerges from a distorted image of the self.

In *Habits of the Heart* Robert Bellah and his colleagues contend that rugged individualism is the ethos of the United States and that it impedes people's genuine commitment to one another.[1] The authors concur with the nineteenth-century French social philosopher Alexis de Tocqueville, who warned of the possibility that Americans might isolate one another because of individualism. Freedom, which is one of the precious values in this country, does elicit individualism. Bellah and his associates worry that this individualism will eventually undermine the conditions of freedom.[2] This country has been infected by various social ills—dysfunctional families, gangs, the drug culture, profit-motivated plant relocations, and monopolistic capitalism. Fierce individualism has undergirded these national problems.

The term *individualism* has been used in many different ways. I use it in the narrow sense that the individual is prior to society and is the basic unit in society. This type of individualism is called "ontological individualism" by Bellah and his colleagues.[3] To understand individualism, it is necessary for us to examine the Western notion of the self. By dislodging an individualistic image of the self, we can lay a foundation for the construction of a society that transcends this warped image of self. The introduction of the Eastern understanding of the threefold self can shed some light on this issue. By the term *threefold self* I attempt to articulate the "tri-unity" of the self with its parents and indicate that an isolated self is an illusion.

In Eastern thinking the true self arises in its dynamic interaction with the parents. The self is threefold. On the one hand, when we lo-

72

cate its individualistic identity, we lose the motion of its dynamic interaction with the parents. On the other, when we see its interaction with the parents, we cannot locate its fixed identity. The threefold self is dynamic and living.

THE WESTERN CONCEPT OF THE SELF

In Greek culture an ideal human being was seen as the bearer of irreplaceable values.[4] In Medieval culture the notion of personhood recapitulates the Greek idea. Based on Aristotle's idea of personhood, Thomas Aquinas believed that the body (matter) constitutes individuality. Duns Scotus regarded a special individuality (*haecceitas*) as the groundwork of the soul.[5]

The Renaissance focused on the human being as the center of interest. Its ideal was the "universal man," the bearer of moral and of aesthetic values with various capacities and interests. The movement extolled human creativity and freedom.

René Descartes is a pivotal figure in Western self-understanding. His "*cogito, ergo sum*" ("I think, therefore I am") epitomizes the Western idea of the self. He started his philosophy with human consciousness (*cogito*). The *cogito* ("I think") is invested with a zeal for establishing an ultimate foundation. For Descartes, the *cogito* can arise from an extreme condition of doubt. The subject of the doubt, however, is free from its own body, which is never the foundation of the self. This free-floating "I" is problematic in terms of its own identity uprooted from its body. The foundational ambition of the Cartesian *cogito* is responsible for the great oscillation that causes the "I" of the "I think" to appear to be elevated to the heights of a first truth and then hurled down to the depths of a vast illusion.[6] Descartes's *cogito* is subjective. But the zeal for establishing a final foundation has been radicalized from Descartes to Kant, then from Kant to Fichte, and finally to Husserl.[7] Kant treated a human being not as a subject but as a bearer of moral, practical reason. The Kantian "I think" is transcendental or universal, enabling one to act according to a "categorical imperative."[8] A moral self is the final goal of nature; the self has dignity, an absolute moral value, and is a purpose in itself. Since the self is the final goal in itself, it should not be reduced to a mere means to an end. The self is rather unholy, yet it is sacred to itself in its *personhood*, because the self is the bearer of the categorical imperative, the absolute and universal moral principle of rational, self-determining self. The self with the categorical imperative must act autonomously.[9] Human freedom that can act according to the moral law within is a key to Kant's understanding of personhood. The self in German Idealism, then, is the bearer of moral, religious, and aesthetic values beyond its thinking and volitional subjectivity.

In response to the subjectivity of the self, Søren Kierkegaard underscored the I-Thou relation, which was developed further by other existentialists such as Marcel, Brunner, and Buber. For Kierkegaard, in contrast with the ethical (the world of reason), the religious moment (the realm of faith) opens up a gap of discontinuity in reason called "otherness."[10] Self-reflection can never connect the circle of its own contemplation. God is the absolute otherness. Only in the I-Thou relationship does our true self arise as we encounter the absolute otherness and unconditionally relinquish ourselves to that. To uphold this I-Thou relationship, Kierkegaard paradoxically stresses individuality.

In Freud, the Kierkegaardian "I-Thou" relation turns into the id-superego relationship at an unconscious level. The id represents our instinctive energy as the source of libido. It is formless, untamed, and illogical: "The logical laws of thought do not apply in the id. . . . Contrary impulses exist side by side, without canceling each other out or diminishing each other."[11] The id knows no values, no good or evil, no moral principles.[12] The superego is the unconscious reservoir of moral codes and standards of behavior and has three functions: conscience, self-observation, and the formation of ideals. Conscience refers to the work of the superego that limits, judges, and prohibits conscious activity. Self-observation springs from the superego to evaluate activities free from the id's drive for tension-reduction and free from the ego for its fulfillment. The formation of ideals is related to the evolution of the superego itself. The superego in its formation assumes an ancestral value-system beyond parental behaviors: "A child's super-ego is in fact constructed on the model not of its parents but of its parents' superego."[13] The superego functions as a moral counterbalance to the practical interests of the ego. One problem with Freud's superego is its repressive otherness, which finds little affinity with the id. As the shadow of our parents in terms of their values or ideas, the superego can be a threat to the existence of the id. The self or ego emerges from the tension between the id and the superego. This Freudian self describes our never relaxing and conflictive intrapersonal relationship.

Unlike Freud, George Herbert Mead presented the human self by distinguishing the "I" from the "Me." The "I" includes a private, subjective, and reflexive instance and the "Me" points to a socially resolute, objective instance. Human beings reach self-awareness by being an object to others. They internalize the attitudes of others toward them and presents themselves to others through the means of their culture. The "Me" is the outcome of generalization from the rejoinder of others, and thought is the inner dialogue between "I" and "Me." Mead recognized the relational self as a social and cultural entity.[14] The self, however, is not social at birth; the social self emerges from the process of social relations and experience.[15]

In *Oneself As Another* Paul Ricoeur tried to integrate the Western concept of the self by stating that the three great experiences of passivity—the experience of *one's own body*, of *others*, and of *conscience*—form the heart of the self in a state of dispersion.[16] The *body* mediates between the self and a world that is itself taken in accordance with its variable degrees of practicability and foreignness. *Otherness* (otherness of other people) is inherent in the self in its relation of intersubjectivity. The *conscience* is the gate of *suspicion, injunction,* and the *otherness* within.[17] Ricoeur stresses the significance of the dialectic tie of selfhood between the sameness and otherness. The *otherness* can be another person, our ancestors, God, or an empty place.

Although the Western notion of the self is not simple, its basic approach is ontological, deontological, psychological, or sociological. Frank Johnson, professor of psychiatry, outlines the history of the Western concept of self in three stages. The first period (pre-Christian times to 1850) features the philosophic, theological, literary definition of the self, underscoring the individual nature of subjective consciousness and the ontological separateness of both persons and things. The second period (1850-1945) is the stage of psychological emphasis and the development of the social self. The third period (1940 to the present) is characterized by diverse trends: psychology, sociology, and philosophy associated with existentialism and phenomenology.[18] Johnson finds several common denominators among the different disciplines. First, the self is a social construction that is symbolically and signally created between social beings. Second, the self is a phenomenological object that can be fruitfully studied through multiple disciplines. Third, the self is intimately connected to bodily experience both ontogenetically and through here-and-now awareness.[19] Although Johnson attempts to stress the Western concept of a social self, he cannot find the collective notion of the Western self at birth and is unable to repudiate the pervasive cultural understanding of the self as an individual being. The West partially acknowledges the social constitution of the self at its social relational level and at its conscious level but has primarily operated on the basis of the individualistic self. That is, the West has not convinced itself of the existence of the social self at birth, nor has it submerged the individual in the unconscious ocean of the social self.

THE EASTERN NOTION OF THE SELF

Inn and *Gahn*

The Korean term for human is *inn-gahn,* derived from the Chinese *jen-chien. Inn-gahn* consists of two words, *inn* ("person") and *gahn* ("between"), denoting that a human being exists between persons. We can be human when we, first of all, stand between persons, particularly parents. Our authentic relationship starts with our parents and extends to others. This is the reason that filial piety is the primary virtue in Confucianism, coming before loyalty to the sovereign, conjugal affection, and friends.[20] While the self can emerge from the doubting, inner moral self or the I-Thou relationship in Western thinking, the self arises from a filial interpersonal relationship in Eastern thinking. In other words, the self initially emerges from an I-Thou relationship in which the "Thou" comprises the parents in Confucius's teaching. Without our original relationship to our parents, the self cannot exist. In Eastern thinking "Thou" can never be *otherness* but must be familiar to the subject. The reality of "Thou" can be extended to others and to the divine only through establishing a right relationship with our parents. Our primary relationship with our parents must be based on truthfulness, companionship, and moral wisdom. This means that filial piety is not an isolated virtue.

> If a man is not trusted by his friends, he will not have confidence in those above him. There is only one way to be trusted by one's own friends: if a man is not affectionate toward his parents, he will not be trusted by his friends. There is only one way to be affectionate toward one's parents: if a man, looking into his own heart, is not true to himself, he will not be affectionate toward his parents. There is only one way for a man to be true to himself. If he does not know what is good, a man cannot be true to himself.[21]

A true self derives from true knowledge. True self-knowledge does not spring from the self but from human relations. True knowledge comes from one's moral sense in relationships: "Truth is not only the fulfillment of our self; it is that by which things outside of us have an existence. The fulfillment of our being is moral sense."[22]

The ground of morality is "filiality" toward parents: "The duty of children to their parents is the fountain whence all other virtues spring, and also the starting-point from which we ought to begin our education."[23] We can hardly be good, virtuous to others, if we are not good, virtuous to our parents. Concretely, Wang Yang-ming of the Neo-Confucian movement during the sixteenth century contended that detaching ourselves from our parents would be inhuman and would be tantamount to destroying our own nature.[24] It is obvious that we cannot come into being without our parents. Our very being is formed by and through our parents. Our existence always presupposes our parents' existence. It is impossible for us to know ourselves to a full extent until we relate ourselves to our parents. Thus our parental existence is not secondary but primary to our existence. Our filial piety is ontological as well as deontological to us in relationship with our parents.

Confucius further stressed our identity with our parents in a physical sense: "Our body and hair and skin are all derived from our parents, and therefore we have no right to injure any of them in the least."[25] Our body is not wholly our own but the continuation of our parents. The idea of the isolated self is a distortion of reality and a blasphemy to parents. Our true self emerges from our honorable, humble, and loving relationship with our parents. That is the infrastructure of all other interpersonal, social relationships. When this prime relationship is distorted, secondary relationships will be warped. Any individualism based on the notion of the isolated self is, therefore, an illusion. Our foundation is our threefold self, which comes to exist at birth whether we acknowledge it or not.

Ihn and Yeh

The term *ihn* (*jen*) is pivotal in Confucian thinking. It is made of two words: *inn* ("person") and *yi* ("two").[26] The term indicates that goodness (or human-heartedness) is supposed to exist between two persons. Mencius (c. 380-289 B.C.E.), a great Confucian scholar, treated *ihn* as the first among cardinal virtues. It endows meaning to all the other ethical norms that perform integrative functions in a Confucian society. It is comparable with the *Tao* in Taoism and love in Moism.[27]

Ihn is inner morality, not an external moral relationship. It is not a product of biological, social, or political forces.[28] *Ihn* is the driving force for the self-reviving, self-perfecting, and self-fulfilling process of a person. As a unifying power, *ihn* shapes and incorporates other important Confucian concepts in wholeness. Chu Hsi, the founder of Neo-Confucianism, held that *ihn* can be realized only by one's own inwardness.

While *ihn* is the virtue of the highest order in the value system of Confucianism, *yeh* (*li*), which means "propriety," is a basic concept of social relations. *Ihn* is a principle of inwardness; *yeh* is an externalization of *ihn* in a concrete social context.[29] *Ihn* needs to be embodied. *Yeh* is the process of its actualization. These two are inseparable and indispensable in their fulfillment. *Ihn* is universal, to be actualized in a particular realm of *yeh*; *yeh* is particular, to express the universal *ihn* in a concrete moral context. In this sense a human should carry out his or her moral self-cultivation in a concrete social context.[30] Tu Wei-ming, a contemporary Confucian scholar, compares the relation of *ihn* (*jen*) and *yeh* (*li*) with gospel and law in Christianity. *Yeh* underlies our living in social relations and norms. *Ihn* points to our being beyond the intersection of social forces.[31] If we take *yeh* to the extreme, we fall into legalism or formalism. If we underscore *ihn* too strongly, we succumb to normlessness or anarchism. To be gracious humans we need to keep the creative tension between *ihn* and *yeh*. These two virtues are balanced when they become inseparable from the virtue of filial piety. The virtues of *ihn* and *yeh* should be applied, first of all, to our relationship with our parents. In such a relationship these two virtues turn into filial piety (*hyo*). True selfhood is developed in the concourse of *ihn* and *yeh* with filial piety (*hyo*).

Hyo and Ihn

It is incomplete to perceive *ihn* (goodness or human-heartedness) simply in terms of social relationships. The *Analects*, one of the Confucian classics, affirm that filial piety (*hyo*) underlies human-heartedness: "And surely proper behavior towards parents (*hyo*) and elder brothers is the trunk of Goodness (*ihn*)?"[32] Filial piety—love and respect toward parents—is the primary location of the dynamic interaction between human-heartedness (*ihn*) and propriety (*yeh*). Confucius contended that no human deed is greater than filial piety.

Filial piety and human-heartedness are in unity. Filial piety without human-heartedness would be blind. Human-heartedness without filial piety would be empty of content.[33] Mencius said, "There never has been a benevolent man who neglected his parents."[34] Usually we cannot love others unless we love our parents.[35] If we do, such love is a distortion of propriety (*yeh*). According to *The Classic of Filial Piety*, "to reverence other men without first loving one's parents is to act against propriety."[36] The interiority of human-heartedness should correspond to the exteriority of propriety. Mencius said, "The richest fruit of benevolence (*ihn*) is this,—the service of one's parents."[37] That is, human-heartedness is abstract in the absence of filial piety. Filial piety is the inauguration of human-heartedness. Mencius further said, "He is affectionate to his parents, and lovingly disposed to people *generally*. He is lovingly disposed to people *generally*, and kind to creatures."[38] Considering the close relationship between human-heartedness and filial piety, we can see why the Christian doctrine of universal love has been difficult for the Asian masses to accept.[39]

Is it possible to love our enemies while we hardly love our parents? Can we love neighbors while we ignore our parents? Can we love God while we disregard our parents? How can we respect our enemy while despising our parents? To the Asian mind, such all-embracing love is hypocrisy. It is necessary to reinterpret the meaning of universal love from filial piety. Can there be universal love without particular love for parents?

Christian love must begin with filial piety. Mere emphasis on general love should be questioned and challenged. The question is not on the validity of universal love but on the *implementation* of universal love. All-embracing love that lacks concrete love is apt to fall into abstract love. Because of misplaced stress on the universal dimension of love in our time, we have lost the true meaning of love. Love cannot be love if it omits filial piety.[40]

In "Selfhood and Otherness in Confucian Thought," Tu Wei-ming points out that filiality implies obedience to the principle of the ideal parent, concurring with Mencius's teaching. With the example of the legendary Sage-King Shun, who had an unfit father, Tu implies that we may rectify and reinstate the authority of unfit parents but never challenge their authority.[41] In this present age we need not be bound by the example of Shun; with caring hearts we must defy abusive parents. Not submission but rather confrontation with respect can be the expression of true filiality for abusive cases.

A person of filial piety is very likely to extend his or her love and respect to his or her spouse, children, and others. Confucian societies suffer much less family brokenness. The cultural crisis of Christian society lies in the fact that we scarcely relate filial piety with Christian universal love. The separation between these two makes Christian love speculative and unreal. Christian love without filial piety is empty.

Asian-Americans have a background of Confucianism. According to Mullinax and Lee, the traditions of Christianity and Confucianism operate in the Korean-American Christian mind as twin gyroscopes and as dual liturgies. These researchers compare the Korean Christian church to a language and Confucianism to its grammar.[42] They conclude that "the two traditions of Christianity and Confucianism coexist within the same church and within the same believer."[43] The Confucian impact on Korea is shown in its emphasis on filial piety. Koreans have been known as "white clothes people." White is the color of mourning in Asia. One of the reasons Koreans often wear white clothes is their meticulous observation of mourning periods for some of their extended family members.[44] The white color symbolizes Korean filial piety. Korean Christians love to wear white clothes, which symbolize the resurrection. This shows the interpenetration between Confucianism and Christianity.

As Christian-Confucians, Korean-Americans have a mission to carry out in this society: to connect Christian love and filial piety. Without Christian love Eastern filial piety can be hierarchical and nepotistic, as it has been historically. In Christian love filial piety can be the mutual respect and love between parents and children. Universal love without filial piety can be nebulous, irresponsible, and idealistic. That was the reason Jesus reprimanded the Pharisees and scribes, who taught that people were free from their filial duty if they declared "korban," which meant that their giving belonged to God instead of to their parents (Mt 15:1-9). Religious duty cannot nullify ethical life. Loving God cannot cancel filial piety. On the cross Jesus consolidated his saving work and filial responsibility. By connecting Christian love and filiality we can save Christianity from its nominalism and Confucianism from its legalism and tendency to be hierarchial.

Confucian filial piety should not be confused with mere dutifulness to parents. Rather, it composes an integral approach to what it signifies to be human. Filial piety is not a burden but a natural and delightful response welling up from our very existence of authentic relationship with our parents. Its external practices are the natural outcomes of a personal self-identity in which the self is viewed not as an isolated, fundamental unit but as a part of the threefold self.[45] Its internal form is the natural expression of affection toward our parents. Therefore, Confucian filial piety denotes the most basic orientation to our authentic existence, an orientation which surmounts self-centeredness with the realization that our being is not a self-enclosed unit but something inherited, passed on from our ancestors.[46]

Individualism and Individuality

An essential premise of Confucius is "associate with others."[47] We define ourselves in relation to others, not as islands or solitary beings. It is in the mesh of reciprocal obligations or moral connections that we find and define ourselves. To be truly human, for Confucius, is to help others to flourish: "You want to turn your own merits to account; then help others to turn theirs to account."[48] Self-identity and self-cultivation arise from reciprocity.

Relationships with others, however, do not describe the self entirely. Our inner self exists to relate and communicate with others. Confucius expressed his delight in learning and in his band of friends but held that truly great persons must stand on their own even if others ignore or disparage them. In Confucius's thought a person exists in the balance between inner freedom and social environment. Inner freedom determines the circumstances of a person's life, and social environment reconciles a person's self-respect with respect for others.[49]

In Confucianism there is room for individuality but not for individualism. While individuality refers to the uniqueness of each person in connection with others, individualism refers to the tendency that espouses the independent existence of each person in freedom and autonomy. The term *individualism* that represents a Western concept of that name did not exist in traditional East Asia.[50] In describing the Confucian individual, it might be better to use the term *Confucian personalism*, which comes close to the Western forms of individualism.[51] Still, this personalism centers on the self-cultivation and self-fulfillment of the person in a social setting, not placing the individual over or against state or society.[52] The self is developed on the basis of reciprocity. A dynamic web metaphor represents the Eastern understanding of the self. The individual or self is fundamentally social, existing in relations to the family and state. In this sense the Eastern term *individual* is different from its Western counterpart.[53]

In conclusion, the West dwells on the idea of the existence of the self as a basic unit. This is partially due to two Western theoretical foundations: natural science (Isaac Newton) and social science (René Descartes). Newton held a mechanical world view that regarded the smallest thing (atom) as the foundation of the world; Descartes found an unshakable foundation of all knowledge in the doubting self (*cogito, ergo sum*). Such views are in conflict with the interconnectional view of the East, where the self is always understood in its relational context, the outcome of the dynamic interaction among at least three persons. The dictum *cogito, ergo sum* is irreverent and irrelevant to the Asian mind. To Asians, it is *parens, ergo sum*, "The parents are, therefore I am." The self exists in its convivial connection with the parents. This affable relationship can be extended to every one eventually.

Among the virtues of Confucianism, filial piety is a key to understanding the self. In the heart of filial piety lies the idea of a collegial self beyond an individual self. Western psychology has concentrated on the search for the indivisible unity of being and has assumed it to be the individual self. In the East the self is not individualistic but exists in terms of its indivisible relation with parents. Although the self is distinguishable from the parents, it also is inseparable from the parents. A self disconnected from its parents is broken; it lacks wholeness. The threefold self is the fundamental being.[54] The impact of the parents upon the formation and life of a child cannot be exaggerated. A child also permanently changes the nature of parents' existence.

The essence of the threefold self is the honor and love it holds for the others within the filial relationship. This threefold self can contribute to making an isolated self whole. It indicates a way to unite filial trust and Christian love and thus heal the family and the culture of brokenness.

Part III

METHODOLOGY

7

Sociological Theories

Since the Los Angeles eruptions in 1992 and the O. J. Simpson trial in 1995, tension and conflict between racial and ethnic groups have been intense. While it is important to reduce racial tension, it is essential to attend to its root causes. In this chapter we will examine five sociological theories on interracial relations.

THE ASSIMILATION MODEL

Traditional intergroup theories have been preoccupied with the notion of assimilation. These theories generally deal with the social behavior of European immigrants.

The fundamental assumption of this model is that ethnic, racial, and religious groups adapt to the standards, social values, lifestyles, and cultural behaviors of the dominant group. In turn, they are accepted as part of the dominant group. This model in the United States is called Anglo-conformity.[1] It promotes common usage of the English language, Anglo social values, and Anglo cultural paradigms.

According to sociologists Robert E. Park and Ernest W. Burgess, assimilation is a natural process in the life of immigrants and their children: "Assimilation is a process of interpenetration and fusion in which persons and groups acquire the memories, sentiments, and attitudes of other persons or groups, and, by sharing their experience and history, are incorporated with them in a common cultural life."[2] For Park, assimilation is the last stage of his race-relation cycle: "The race relations cycle which takes the form, to state it abstractly, of contacts, competition, accommodation and eventual assimilation, is apparently progressive and irreversible."[3] In the first stage, contacts, migration initiates exploration. This leads to economic competition and conflict between the migrating group and local people. To adjust and control competition, accommodation takes place. Then, as the last stage, the gradual process of assimilation will occur as the migrating group conforms to the dominant culture.

For sociologist Milton Gordon, assimilation is more complex. In Gordon's system there are seven types of assimilation.

1. Cultural or behavioral assimilation: An ethnic group changes its cultural patterns to those of the dominant group, including religious belief and observance (acculturation).

2. Structural assimilation: An ethnic group takes on large-scale primary group relationship with the dominant group, i.e., it enters fully into cliques, clubs, and institutions of its host society.

3. Marital assimilation: An ethnic group member intermarries with a dominant group member (amalgamation).

4. Identification assimilation: An ethnic group member develops a sense of identity based exclusively on the dominant group.

5. Attitude receptional assimilation: Ethnic group members reach a point where they experience no discrimination.

6. Behavior receptional assimilation: Ethnic group members reach a point where they experience no prejudice.

7. Civic assimilation: An ethnic group does not raise any issues involving value and power conflict with the dominant group (e.g., the issue of birth control).[4]

Gordon distinguishes cultural from structural assimilation. Whereas Park regarded structural assimilation as a natural result of acculturation, Gordon did not see structural assimilation within the life of non–Anglo Americans as inevitable; many groups remain in the stage of cultural assimilation. But once structural assimilation takes place, all the other types of assimilation will follow.[5] However, there is a price for structural assimilation: "the disappearance of the ethnic group as a separate entity and the evaporation of its distinctive values."[6]

The Anglo-conformity model seems to describe the situation of some European immigrant groups, but it cannot speak for the experience of non-European groups. There are some fundamental cultural and racial differences between Euro-American and non-Euro-American groups. Even Euro-Americans of southern-European descent have not experienced complete conformity with the Anglo-group.

The Anglo-group adamantly protects its privileges and is not willing to share its power unless it believes that other groups have been completely assimilated. This phenomenon is shown in the fact that penetration into cliques and associations of the dominant group is almost impossible for some Euro-American and non-Euro-American groups. Such groups, then, have a need for the comfort of their own communities. This need results in enclaves of ethnic groups within the society— the opposite of assimilation. Particularly for non-European immigrants, structural assimilation is almost unachievable.[7]

The difficulty of structural assimilation for Asian-Americans can be traced back to the 1882 Chinese Exclusion Act and the National Origins Quota Act, which severely limited immigration of Asians, thus institutionalizing the ideology of Anglo-conformity. This immigration policy basically remained in place until passage of the 1965 Immigration and Naturalization Act, the primary goals of which were protecting the American labor market and reuniting families.[8] In this act, hemispheric quotas superseded nationality quotas; the number of immigrants from the western hemisphere was limited to 120,000, while 170,000 visas were allocated to the rest of the world.[9] Even though this made immigration easier for Asians, a discriminatory attitude toward them was deeply entrenched in the minds of Euro-Americans.

Although it is inevitable that Asian-Americans adopt the culture of the dominant group to a certain degree, full assimilation is neither possible nor desirable. To Asian-American groups, assimilation is a form of cultural imperialism. Asian-American parents have to teach their children to be themselves and to resist the temptation to be like others. This is a laborious but very significant task necessary in order for them to find their own identity, which, in turn, makes a long-term contribution to U.S. society.

THE AMALGAMATION MODEL

Another common vision of American society is the amalgamation model known as the "melting pot"; that is, the blending of different racial groups to create a new and distinctive group. This vision can be traced back to 1782, when French-born agriculturalist J. Hector St. John Crèvecoeur depicted the United States as the place where "individuals of all nations are melted into a new race of men, whose labors and posterity will one day cause great changes in the world."[10] For him, an American is a mixture of various European antecedents who abandons all his or her previous biases and customs and embraces a completely new mode of life.

The liberal U.S. immigration policy in the first three-quarters of the nineteenth century reflected this idea. In 1893 historian Frederick Jackson Turner identified the dominant influence in American ideals as its frontier spirit rather than its European heritages: "The frontier promoted the formation of a composite nationality for the American people. . . . In the crucible of the frontier the immigrants were Americanized, liberated, and fused into a mixed race, English in neither nationality nor characteristics."[11] His vision of the melting pot of frontier America largely dealt with the diverse ethnic groups from Northern and Western Europe, leaving out Southern and Eastern Europeans, African-Americans, Asian-Americans, and Hispanic-Americans.

In 1908 the English Jewish writer Israel Zangwill produced a drama entitled *The Melting Pot*, which became quite successful. In the drama, David, a young Russian Jewish immigrant, attempts to compose a symphony that will depict America as a divinely inspired crucible in which all diverse ethnic groups with their past antagonistic histories will be melded into one group.

> America is God's Crucible, the great Melting-Pot where all races of Europe are melting and re-forming! Here you stand, good folks, think I, when I see them at Ellis Island, here you stand in your fifty groups, with your fifty languages and histories, and your fifty blood hatreds and rivalries. But you won't be long like that, brothers, for these are the fires of God. . . . A fig for your feuds and vendettas! Germans and Frenchmen, Irishmen and Englishmen, Jews and Russians—into the Crucible with you all! God is making the American.[12]

This idealistic image of the great crucible suggests a mutual adaptation of old and new groups on an equal plane. But it misdiagnoses the reality of the hierarchical structure of racial relationships in the United States and disregards the situation of non-European groups in the project. Non-European groups neither could be part of such "melting" nor did they desire such integration. However, William Newman contends that while the assimilation model preempts the dominant group's culture as the best, "the minority group doctrine of amalgamation assumes that the 'best' cultural traits of each group will be selectively contributed to the new amalgam."[13] Thus this model fails to appreciate the uniqueness of each ethnic and racial group. It is also impossible for some minority groups to melt into one, for they have distinctive looks, foods, customs, beliefs, and values. Consequently, the amalgamation theory is an impractical and myopic view that hinders the realization of the long-term potential of each group.

THE CULTURAL PLURALISM MODEL

Another theory arose to rectify the shortcomings of the melting-pot theory. Its idea is to acknowledge the diverse cultural values of each ethnic group. Horace Kallen, a Jewish immigrant philosopher, was one of the first exponents of this position. His ideas were printed in 1915 under the title "Democracy *Versus* the Melting-Pot" in the magazine *The Nation*.[14] Rejecting the assimilation and the melting-pot theories, Kallen advocated the pluralistic cultural value system that encourages ethnic groups to sustain their culture, language, ethos, and religious traditions. However, he suggested that English be the general means of communication. He envisioned the United States as "a cooperation of cultural diversities" and "a federation or commonwealth of national culture" in addition to constituting a union of geographical regions.[15] This culturally pluralistic United States, he believed, would embody democratic ideals at the level of groups as well as individuals.

Kallen's cultural pluralism features three salient points. The first stresses each person's belonging to an ethnic group in which he or she actualizes his or her potential and finds significant satisfaction. At the same time, the idea encourages the individual to get involved in social groups, political parties, educational institutions, and service associations.

The second point is that this view of cultural pluralism is entirely harmonious with the spirit of Americanism stipulated in the Declaration of Independence and the Preamble and Amendments to the Constitution. Kallen claims that in the Declaration of Independence, *equal* signifies "an affirmation of the right to be different: of the parity of every human being and every association of human beings according to their kinds, in the rights of life, liberty, and the pursuit of happiness."[16] The differences of ethnic groups imply their equality to each other.

The third major idea points to the positive value to the nation as a whole from various ethnic cultures and traditions and their interdynamics in a democratic social framework. Kallen attributes the creative dynamics of society to the diversity of ethnic heritages and holds that "cultural values arise upon the confrontation, impact, and consequent disintegration and readjustment of different orders, with the emergence therefrom of new harmonies carrying unprecedented things in their heart."[17] He uses the metaphor of an orchestra:

> The American way is the way of orchestration. As in an orchestra, the different instruments, each with its own characteristic timbre and theme, contribute distinct and recognizable parts to the composition, so in the life and culture of a nation, the different regional, ethnic, occupational, religious and other communities compound their different activities to make up the national spirit.[18]

The union of the different groups is the strength and richness of the United States.

Kallen's ideal is a democracy of diverse nationalities that finds commonality in the English language and the political system as well as diversity in ethnicity. Kallen is opposed to the ghetto model of group isolation as well as the dissolution of the uniqueness of diverse communities. This type of group existence is not easy to establish or to maintain, for various interactions through modern mass media may obstruct the balance of these two sides.

Kallen's model overlooks the fact that cultural pluralism emerges not only from a cultural democracy but also from the economic, political, and social democracy of diverse nationalities. For instance, economic monopoly has the propensity to reduce cultural diversities to a single dominant culture. Further, he misses the dimension of mutual challenge resulting from the shortcomings of each culture. Often unity cannot be obtained in smooth integration but rather from a mutual struggle to reach a higher common plane. Advocates of cultural pluralism need to delineate how it can be practically implemented.

THE TRIPLE MELTING POT THEORY

A mixture of assimilation, amalgamation, and cultural pluralism, this theory focuses on the role of religious diversity. It is not one of the major theories, but we deal with it here because of its significance for the future of Korean-American churches.

Fifty years ago Ruby Kennedy theorized that ethnic intermarriages took place among ethnic groups of the same religious group but not among the three major religious groups—Catholic, Protestant, and Jewish.[19] The triple melting pot theory contends that amalgamation or assimilation occurs *within* each of the Protestant, Catholic, and Jewish groups, but cultural pluralism operates *among* the three religious communities.[20]

Based on Kennedy's theory, Will Herberg argued further that as the sense of ethnic-immigrant origin dissipates, religious groups replace ethnic groups in providing communities of identity and belonging.[21] Herberg's thesis highlighted the third generation of immigrants. Although first-generation immigrants retain the language, customs, and traditions of their mother country, they desire to become "Americans" as quickly as possible and adopt the dominant way of life in the United States. However, they keep their allegiance to their home countries and attend their own ethnic churches on Sundays because of the language barrier.

The second generation, those born in this country or brought here very young, undergo an ambiguous existence of marginality between the two cultures and societies. They try to stay away from their ethnic culture and to uphold the cultural values of the United States. They often speak English only, emphasizing their Americanness over their ethnic origin.

The third generation is characterized by a return to its roots for self-identity. Herberg observes that this return of the third generation is not directly to its lost ethnic heritage, but rather to its authentic heritage through the religion of its parents and grandparents. Other values of the original culture were changed in the process of Americanization, but not the family religion. Religious association thus becomes the primary axis of self-identification and cultural location.[22]

In the 1950s Herberg's analysis spoke to his social situation. But after the liberalization of immigration policy in 1965, many Asian immigrants have poured onto the American scene, changing the traditional contour of American religions. Whether Herberg's theory on the return of the third generation to its parents' and grandparents' religions will be upheld is questionable. (His theory focuses on Judaism, Roman Catholicism, and Protestantism.) In 1978, 28 percent of Japanese-Americans were Christians, while only about 1 percent of Japanese in Japan were Christians.[23] These data show that Japanese-Americans, many of whom belonged to the third generation, converted to Christianity instead of returning to Buddhism. It seems Herberg's theory does not apply to Asian-Americans.

A NEW ETHNIC IDENTITY: A SYNTHESIS

Nathan Glazer and Daniel Patrick Moynihan published *Beyond the Melting Pot* in 1963. In this work they attempted to complement the theory of cultural pluralism with the idea of the melting pot. Their theory holds that an Irish person becomes an Irish-American and an Italian becomes an Italian-American in this country; that is, American ethnic groups are different from the folks in the home country. Comparing some big ethnic groups (African-Americans, Italians, Puerto Ricans, Jews, and the Irish) in New York City, they conclude that each ethnic, racial, and religious group blends into American society at different speeds, forming the new identities while keeping its own ethnic distinctiveness in spite of its assimilation into the society. They underscore two basic points in this transition. First, ethnic minority groups become a part of the bigger whole; they do not become an isolated entity in the process of assimilation. Second, the American ethnic groups become politically organized in order to procure their share of political power. These groups signify political power blocs. Glazer and Moynihan contend that ethnic distinction diminishes on the road to Americanization except for the significance of its political presence. While they deemphasize various cultural, social, historical, and economic dimensions of different ethnic groups, they focus on their unity as political interest groups.

Glazer and Moynihan expected race and religion, instead of ethnic diversity, to be the most significant dividing factors between groups in the 1970s. However, up to the present, ethnic dividing lines have *not* diminished in ethnic American life. The Los Angeles eruptions in 1992 provide counter evidence to their theory, since ethnic tension and conflict created the conditions for such violence. They were also wrong in their expectation of a decrease in the economic discrepancy between the Euro-American and African-American communities. Such a decrease was the trend of the post-World War II era, but the 1990s witnessed a wider gap between these two groups. Not only political factors but also economic factors play an important role in intergroup relations.

The above theories of assimilation, amalgamation, and cultural pluralism have at least three shortcomings. The first is their Euro-centric perspective; while they have given some attention to non-European groups, they have inadequately treated Asian-American issues. The second is their concentration on the cultural aspect, overlooking the economic, social, and political dimensions. While involved with culture and assimilation, they have been less concerned with the structural problems of economic injustice and political subordination. Related to this second problem, the third shortcoming is that these theories espouse the status quo of the social order. They all basically assume that if cultural problems are addressed, social order will return. They stress the "ubiquity of social order [rather] than of social change."[24] These theories are all consensus theories of social life, aspiring to peaceful coexistence.

8

Current Korean-American Models

Church and Culture

There are several sociological models for racial and ethnic relations. The church, however, has not developed such models, which are necessary if the church is to pursue the community of God on earth. Theological models would not necessarily contradict sociological models but might go beyond them.

Here we come face to face with the relationship between church and culture. H. Richard Niebuhr's classic *Christ and Culture* presents five different models of this relationship.[1] These basic models need to be modified for today's situations, for his analysis of culture was general, overlooking cross-cultural situations and ignoring economic, social, and political problems. Finally, he composed his models from the perspective of the dominant group, not considering the ethnic churches. Korean-Americans need a theological model that is inclusive and is concerned about ethnic American churches in general and Korean-American churches in particular.

Ethnic churches have a three-part role in dealing with cultural and Christian encounters; they have their own ethnic culture, the dominant American culture, and other American-ethnic cultures to consider. Their task is neither merely to confirm these cultures nor to reject them, but to keep a creative tension between them. The ethnic churches need to choose which parts of these cultures they support or change. This selective process is an ongoing task. The issue that ethnic churches face is not "Christ and culture," but the relationships among their own church, their own culture, other American-ethnic cultures, and the dominant American culture. By examining the Korean-American community, we can see how its churches guide its people as they come to terms with new and strange culture.

THE WITHDRAWAL MODEL

Encountering a language barrier, different foods, different social values, and racism in a new and strange land, most Korean-Americans tend to flock together, withdrawing into their Korean enclaves. They realize that the United States is a place where they are not welcome, where they are discriminated against and rejected. It is very difficult to break through social prejudice and discrimination. To survive the hostile environment, they "ghettoize" their community. They are not emotionally and socially ready to adjust to the dominant culture.

Good examples of these communities are Koreatown in Los Angeles along Olympic Boulevard and Korea Town in Orange County along Garden Grove Boulevard. A feature of these Korean immigrant enclaves is that they are business-oriented. Korean-Americans live in suburbs, scattered here and there, but they flock together to do business. Their business signs are written in Korean only, clearly showing that they intend to do business with fellow Korean-Americans. They read Korean newspapers published in Los Angeles or in Chicago and watch Korean TV produced in Los Angeles. They eat Korean foods, speak Korean most of the time, and find friendship almost exclusively among fellow Korean immigrants. For business purposes or other social occasions, they use a functional English that enables them to communicate with the outside world at a minimal level.

The church plays a very significant role in immigrant life. Compared with Chinese and Japanese immigrants, Korean immigrants are very much churchgoers. (While 32 percent of Chinese immigrant respondents and 28 percent of Japanese immigrant respondents to a Chicago survey were churchgoers, 71 percent of Korean immigrants were churchgoers.[2]) As centers of immigrants' activities, Korean-American churches exercise great influence on the life of Korean-American communities. Korean-American churches provide the security and identity that immigrants cannot find in the society. The churches are the bastions from which they receive their *raison d'être*. Thus, the Korean-American churches play a great role in establishing and sustaining the ghettoization of Korean immigrants and their children.

Furthermore, these churches tend to transplant Korean church systems to this country and repeat their traditional emphasis on church growth and faithful commitment to church activities. In a metropolis such as Los Angeles, Korean-American churches expand by absorbing other church members through various evangelical meetings or extending their influence through overseas missions, neglecting social missions in their own backyard—the inner cities.

The churches serve Korean immigrants as important social-service centers. Pastors provide rides for the needy, find jobs for them, and interpret for the newly arrived. By hosting various traditional celebrations, Korean-American churches function as "community squares," and their leaders are community leaders. The Korean-American churches of this model greatly ease the sorrows and pains of their community. They have been the healing places for Korean-American immigrants.

Korean-Americans, however, need to move beyond their security zone. The purpose of their being in this country is not only to have their own community but to interact with other groups for mutual enrichment. Exclusive communal life was partially responsible for the Los Angeles eruptions. The withdrawal model misses interaction with other groups in a democratic social framework. Thus, the withdrawal model stresses cultural diversity without conferring true unity on the society.

THE ASSIMILATION MODEL

Unlike those who form enclaves, some Korean-Americans dissociate themselves from other Korean-Americans. They believe that the sooner they are assimilated by the dominant culture, the better their lives will be. They attempt to put their Korean identity behind them by distancing themselves from Korean traditions, customs, and language. They tend to avoid contacting other Korean-Americans. They encourage their children to adopt the dominant social values, attitudes, and traditions as soon as possible. While they believe that Korean culture is basically secondary to the dominant culture, they may want their children to maintain certain Korean family values and practice certain Korean customs and traditions at home—particularly the virtues of filial piety and propriety. Many Korean-Americans who came to the United States when they were young and many second generation Korean-Americans belong to this category.

Korean-American Christians of this type usually attend non-Korean churches, in which they try to find their own support communities. Some associate Christianity with the dominant American culture. When they accepted Christianity, they embraced Western culture as a whole. Thus their church life can be construed as part of their assimilation process. They attend Anglo-American churches or more integrated churches. Unlike other social groups—cliques, sororities, fraternities, and prestigious clubs—mainstream churches welcome them and assimilate them within their systems.

Cultural assimilation inevitably takes place when a new ethnic group arrives on the shore. It is not, however, an exclusively one-sided process but rather an interaction between two groups (although one may be much more influenced by the other).[3] Strictly speaking, there never can be unilateral assimilation, however powerfully the major group dominates assimilation processes.

Korean-Americans of this model can expect to find that it is extremely difficult to be structurally assimilated in the United States. Their assimilation process usually ends with acculturation.

THE PARADOXICAL MODEL

Some Korean-Americans strive to preserve their Korean ethnic identity, on the one hand, and adopt the dominant culture, on the other. They disagree with the melting-pot theory. The United States is not a melting pot, states Michael Novak, an American of Slavic descent. The dominant white Anglo-Saxon Protestant (WASP) group empathizes less with lower-middle-class white descendants of southern Europeans and Slavs than with nearly any other groups in the country. Novak calls these groups the "unmeltable ethnics."[4] The WASP culture has dominated since the settlement of the United States, leaving little room for a fresh fusion with new immigrant groups. And, unlike the southern Europeans or Slavs, who, according to Novak, are accepted individually although rejected as groups by the WASP culture, Asian-Americans experience both individual and group rejection.

In response to the dominant culture, Korean-Americans of the paradoxical model attempt to maintain their own culture. Nevertheless, they believe that assimilation by the dominant culture is inevitable. Their ideal is to sustain the Korean culture while learning from the mainstream culture. Thus they live in the polarity and conflict between the two cultures. They belong to both cultures, yet identify with neither fully. Both Korean family values and American individual freedom attract them, for example.

These Korean-American Christians keep the ambiguous balance between their Korean Christian identity and worldly citizenship. Their Christian identity has a conflictual relationship with the worldly realm. Their loyalty is to the reign of God, yet they acknowledge the reality of the society. They accept the polarity and tension in their Christian identity and their society. They learn how to live precariously in this country. As immigrants, they are not fully accepted in this country, yet they know that they must be involved in this society as U.S. residents or citizens. They experience life in this country as marginal.

Many Korean-American Christians of this model find their true identity in scripture as citizens of the Kingdom of God. As heavenly citizens, they live the life of sojourners in this world. Living in the United States as immigrants helps them realize their temporal existence in the world. Thus, their marginal existence is not mourned but accepted, even appreciated. *Ambiguity* and *paradox* describe their experience in the life of immigrant marginality.

Theologian Sang Hyun Lee's pilgrim theology can represent this group.[5] Introducing pilgrimage as a theological paradigm, Lee stresses that Korean immigrants' marginality is a sign of a "sacred calling." As God called Abraham into the land of Canaan through the wilderness, so calls God us into this new country through the experience of marginality—our wilderness.[6] Using Everett Stonequist's terminology, Lee writes that a marginal person is "on the boundary" or "in between" two cultures without belonging to either.[7] In Lee's theology the marginality experience is not all negative; it is positive in terms of providing creative opportunities for pilgrimage. He finds the ultimate paradigm for marginality in Jesus. The crucified One represents the pioneer and perfecter of the Asian-American's pilgrim faith on earth. This calling to be pilgrims of marginality is sacred in the sense of its divine providence for new creation.

The pilgrimage does not allow us to settle permanently at any location but exhorts us to move forward to a better country or to a heavenly one. This does not mean, however, to escape or withdraw from this world, but rather to participate in building houses, planting gardens, and rearing sons and daughters in this land (cf. Jer 29:1-7).[8] His emphasis is on our sojourning through this world as we work for God's Kingdom.

Lee's position is a classical case of the paradoxical model. Korean-American Christians of this type live in the United States but find their true home neither in this country nor in Korea. They are meant to wander through this wilderness, yearning for the better home in God's city. The tension and paradox of their identity will follow them all the days of their life.

People of this model are pietistic and serene. Their faith is in always looking for the ultimate, not the relative. By detaching themselves from their earthly desires, they paradoxically take part in the life of society more fully. Detachment here does not denote a withdrawal from the world but unselfish genuine participation in the world of God. They take their responsibility seriously, believing God calls them into this journey.

A difficult area for these people is understanding the relation between this world and the next. Their attitude is dualistic. They project God "out there," not underscoring that life is a journey to God and that God is *here*. This country too is the Creator's world. We must settle in this country to establish God's society.

A more positive evaluation of this life is necessary in this model. Furthermore, this model has little concern with social transformation. Its focus is on the people who are called, not the society that needs change. By valuing the experience of marginality, people of this model may show insufficient interest in reforming the structures that create such marginality. This model fails to confront the racism, sexism, and government structures that create and sustain marginality and boundary existence.

Moreover, this model may view Asian-American Christians as the newly chosen. It might imply that non-immigrants are not called by God. If God calls Korean-American Christians to God's mission as God called Abraham, what about other Christians in this country? There can be a danger of attributing some subtle manifestation of divine destiny to Korean-American Christians.

The above three models—withdrawal, assimilation, and paradoxical—are basically survival models. They provide little guidance or motivation for changing the *han*-causing elements of the society and healing the *han* of the Korean-American community. With these models Korean-Americans cannot be full participants in the society or work toward its reorganization. At this time of high racial and ethnic tension, it is necessary for the Korean-Americans to develop a new model that brings forth racial harmony by changing the sin and *han* of our communities.

Embodying the Community of God

A Transcendent, Transmutational Model

Compared with all the sociological efforts to guide this country to a racially and ethnically congenial society, the church has developed few viable models for its ethnically diverse community and society. If we take the earthly city of God seriously ("Thy kingdom come and thy will be done on earth as in heaven"), we need to work toward a concrete plan for realizing God's community.

H. Richard Niebuhr provides five theological models for cultural change: Christ against culture, the Christ of culture, Christ above culture, Christ and culture in paradox, and Christ as the transformer of culture. He indicates that he favors the last model. He suggests that Christians reflecting the authority of Christ transform the culture, which means the "total process of human activity" or "civilization" including "language, habits, ideas, beliefs, customs, social organization, inherited artifacts, technical processes, and values."[1] Although his definition of culture is broad, the concept is limited to his perception of the cultural and social realities of the 1950s.

We need to broaden Niebuhr's model and provide a new perspective that embraces the racial, sexual, economic, cultural, and political dimensions of life. The transcendent, transmutation model aims at embodying the community of God in the midst of our racially and economically divided society.

TRANSMUTATION

The term *transformation* can be a dangerous one, if it implies imposing one's own idea upon others. The *Tao Teh King* recommends that we do not interfere with others' lives: "Behave indifferently—without trying to impose your own ideas upon the lives of others."[2] Oppressors use coercive power to change others and deprive them of various human rights, a deformation of existence. Authentic transformation is instead a *natural transmutation* that comes from within. We cannot compel change in others; at most we can be an instrument for their spontaneous change by preparing them to realize all their promise. People transform themselves by divine beckoning. Our goal is not to work for transformation in others but to toil for fuller divine flow in them.

I use the term *transmutation* to express a change in nature, substance, content, and appearance. Although *transmutation* and *transformation* both refer to change, the word *transmutation* stresses its internal, biological, and natural aspect while the term *transformation* underscores its external and structural aspect. We need both terms. To avoid the notion of compelled change, I tend to employ the word *transmutation*. Transmutation does not indicate, however, a passive and weak work of change; it is an active and assertive confrontation, although in a cordial spirit. The way of transmutation is the way of Tao, changing an object not by force but by gentle strength.

Consider a huge rock in flowing water. Water carves and rounds the rock tenderly and slowly but surely. Like water, the way of transmutation changes a being by soft strength without coercion. Such transmutation never means passivity toward the power of evil. We confront oppressors with the strength of truth, however, not with compelling force. Our strength includes genuine consideration for the persons we challenge because we understand that true change takes place in voluntary reformation, not in forced modification.

INWARD AND OUTWARD ASPECTS OF TRANSMUTATION

For our society to change, each person, community, and culture needs to undergo inward and outward transmutation. The inward aspect presumes personal self-criticism, self-rectification, self-permutation, and self-healing. Inward transmutation is a self-reflective process, reforming the consciousness and structure of the oppressor.

Outward transmutation presupposes the inhumane, oppressive traditions and structures of the society and recognizes the need for social reformation through proper challenging, confronting, and questioning. It requires careful, critical examination of unjust social policies, agencies and systems.

For example, racism must be dismantled. Its nature has two aspects: discrimination and prejudice. Racial prejudice is an idea or attitude about a racial group, whereas racial discrimination is the expression of racial prejudice in harmful treatment. To eliminate racism, we need to change the practices of racial discrimination through protests, education, and legislation (outward transmutation) and to challenge people's racial prejudice through persuasion, edification, and inspiration (inward transmutation).

For authentic reformation, inward and outward transmutations should occur together. Outward transmutation without inward transmutation is empty; inward transmutation without outward transmutation is hypocritical. The genuine merger of the two transpires when people see a community vision and begin to actualize it.

THE FOURFOLD TASK OF KOREAN-AMERICAN CHRISTIANS

Niebuhr's transformation model treats culture as the only object that Christians should unilaterally transform. We cannot, however, unequivocally separate Christians from culture. Even Jesus was not fully free from the effects of his culture, for the civilization of the first century influenced his life and thinking. And even if Christ were not so influenced, his followers certainly are. Thus Christians should not only transform but also be transformed by God and culture. For Korean-American Christians the job is more complex than Niebuhr's idea of Christ and culture conjures. We face two cultures: the Korean-American culture, and the United States culture (which itself takes several forms). In addition, we see Christ through two dimensions: Christian truth, and the Korean-American church. Thus Korean-American Christians face at least a fourfold task: self-transmutation, the transmutation of the Korean-American church, the transmutation of Korean-American culture, and the transmutation of U.S. culture.

First, Korean-American Christians need to change North American society, which suffers from sexism, racism, economic injustice, intolerance, media monopoly, violence, a drug culture, and bad politicking. These are the causes of *han* in the world. Using effective Christian resources and positive Korean traditions, we must confront these problems and unravel the *han* of the society. As we transmute these culprits of social *han*, we are involved in the cultural, economic, social, and political reformations of the society.

Second, Korean-American Christians need to change our own community, which is patriarchal, exploitative, and racist. Traditional patriarchy allows domestic violence and lowers the status of women in the community. Economically, a number of Korean-American business people depend on the labor of fellow Korean immigrants or other immigrant workers, who work long hours for low wages. Fair employment should be practiced in Korean-American business. Finally, in racial relations the unequal treatment of other racial and ethnic groups has been a serious problem within the community.

Third, Korean-American Christians must change our churches, which are still patriarchal, hierarchical, and exclusively ethnocentric.

Women are not treated fairly in many Korean-American churches. Most Protestant churches are reluctant to ordain women and hesitate to accept women as their senior pastors. Concerning hierarchy, most Korean-American churches have the vertical structure of church spiritual order: ministers, lay elders, encouragers, deacons, and members. Regarding exclusive ethnocentrism, many Korean-American churches neglect or overlook non-Korean members affiliated through interracial marriages. Korean-American Christians must transmute the ethic and ethos of our churches.

Fourth, Korean-American Christians must be transformed by the renewal of the heart in the Spirit of God (Rom 12:2). Incessant self-critical reflection is an important step to the transmutation of the world. We need to be transmuted by our community and society, too. To change our community we need to be affected by its creative influence.

TRANSCENDENCE

As Christians we cannot work for the mere integration or assimilation of various ethnic groups, because these cultures nurse such distortions as racism and sexism. Consolidation of these cultures (the melting-pot theory) will miss the opportunity to rectify cultural as well as social shortcomings and distortions. Also, the incorporation of these cultures into the dominant culture (the assimilation theory) will bypass the chance to confront the major shortcomings of the dominant culture. While the melting-pot and assimilation theories might result in a homogeneous society, they will not meet the expectations of the community of God. Nor can the model of diversity in unity (cultural pluralism) change the structures that cause *han* and engender the needed elements for the healing of a group's *han*. If an individual group wants to maintain an unfair aspect of its culture in the name of diversity, the society cannot do much about it in the cultural pluralism model.

The equilibrium of diversity and unity is desirable for ethnic relations but cannot be the goal of the transmutation model. In the dominant culture and ethnic cultures lie deep-seated *han* and destructive sin. Without transmuting the *han* and sin of the groups, the unity and diversity of our various cultures and traditions will be superficial, empty, and repressive. Genuine unity and diversity of our social groups occur as we work together to alter social *han* and sin. For example, without changing the culture of individualism, unity of different groups is untenable. Without eliminating the culture of racism and sexism, the unity of society is nominal. To change such conditions as individualism, racism, and sexism, sociological theories are helpless.

Diversity and unity in Christ denote *transcendence*, for Christ points us to the fulfillment of our natural cultural gifts. This transcendent dimension becomes a gentle force for the transmutation of culture and the direction of that transmutation. Christ does not reject what we are but directs us to what we can be. In this sense Christ is the symbol of our transcendence. He calls us to change *han*-causing structures.

THEOLOGICAL CROSS-CULTURALISM

However important it is to spread cross-culturism in this society, we should not be complacent with its mere promulgation. We need to contribute to shaping American cross-culturism in a creative way. This is the distinction between sociological cross-culturism and theological cross-culturism. Sociological cross-culturism intends to create environments in which multiple cultures interact for their mutual benefit. Theological cross-culturism expects to foster shared transmutation (group repentance), moving all peoples toward the community of Christ.[3] Even an oppressed group needs collective penitence. Marx's great mistake was to miss this point, elevating the proletariat to an ideal, repentance-free group. However, if we overemphasize the penitence of the sin of an oppressed group, we increase the subjugation of the group. (This has happened in several Latin-American countries.)

It is necessary for a wronged group to be healed of its own *han* and freed from obsession with its own sin. Its priority should be on healing its *han* through commitment to the eradication of the sources of *han*. A collective pardon occurs when the wronged group sees an inmost vision of the avenue to healing its *han*. For an oppressive group, a turnabout can happen as it engages in rectifying its unjust acts. True multiculturism comes from a group that knows how to repent of its wrongdoing. Theological cross-culturism does not lead multiple cultures to either cultural pluralism or a Christian monoculture but rather promulgates diverse Christian cultures that encourage every individual culture to maximize its own potential in Christ. There is no single Christian culture; there are diverse Christian cultures because the authentic Christ is received and expressed only through a group's own culture.

THE CROSS: SYMBOL OF TRANSMUTATION

In the transmutation model each ethnic group needs to open its clannish boundary of community without losing its uniqueness—its important cultural and traditional values. The Korean-American community needs to break the external shell of its enclave in order to take root in the wider society yet preserve its own life. Even though Korean immigrants should lose their reclusive Korean identity, they should keep their Koreanness in this country. This process of reformation will elicit a new Korean-American identity.

Let me illustrate the transmutation model with an example. To make food tasty, we season it with salt. But unless the grains of salt lose their outer form to permeate the food and become part of it, they cannot change its taste. Like the grains of salt, Korean-Americans have to part with our outer form (the exclusive Korean identity, which is elite, ethnocentric, and intolerant of other groups) in order to permeate the society, but we should never lose our inner essence (a Koreanness that is open and tolerant toward other groups). If we maintain our exclusive form, we fall into our own ghetto. If we lose our form without keeping our own essence, we become assimilated into the dominant culture. Korean-Americans need to keep our Koreanness to share with others. Sharing our own being is a way of transmuting the society. Of course, transmutation is more than sharing; sometimes it confronts the systemic evil of society through the strength of truthfulness and justice.

Korean-American Christians can spur Korean-Americans to change society. In this sense, Korean-American Christians are the "catalysts for the catalysts." Korean-Americans should keep our own "flavor" in order to transmute others, and we should prepare to be transformed by other groups, finding our own Korean-American identity in the process. This reciprocal transmutation is the excitement of living in the United States.

The symbol of transmutation is the cross. On the one hand, as we live in this multicultured country, we wonder about our Korean-American identity. The situation forces us to delve into the meaning of our Korean-American identity and deepen it with new understanding. This effort is the vertical dimension of Korean-American identity.

On the other hand, we extend our hands in fellowship to other groups to enlarge our historical, economic, and social mission. This means working with other groups toward a community of Christ. Widening our social boundary may appear to attenuate the Korean identity, but it is actually a way to find and form our authentic identity. This execution of our historical mission is our horizontal dimension. Our being (person) always converges with our doing (work). Being and doing create our identity. Becoming true Korean-Americans means participating in creating an authentic society beyond our Korean-American boundary. Our Korean-American identity is not a substance to possess but a happening at the crossroads of the vertical and horizontal dimensions of transmuting life.

The cross of Jesus Christ speaks to this symbol of transmutation. To find a new identity, we must lose our old one. The cross represents the death in our old self. Jesus said, "Very truly, I tell you, unless a grain of wheat falls into the earth and dies, it remains just a single grain; but if it dies, it bears much fruit" (Jn 12:24). To preserve the Korean-American identity, we must forsake it, and when we forsake it, we find our authentic identity. For Korean-Americans, forsaking our outmoded identity means negating our old identity formed by various oppressors (*han*). We must die to our old negative identity in order to live with a new image of ourselves. When we die to our group identity as second-class citizens, we will find our genuine identity and bear much fruit. The cross is the symbol of our new self, our redeemed identity.

RADICAL OPENNESS

The transmutation model goes beyond mutual integration and acceptance of ethnic groups. It presses toward shared challenge, transmutation, and remedy. The goal of this model is neither to achieve harmony nor to attain peace in inter-ethnic relations, but to open out to life, to the creative tension between groups. Its openness points to self-reflective thinking and a creative attitude. Its basic assumption precludes any naive absolutism. It defies any ultimate unity or diversity within society and points to the organic transmutation of our ethnic relations based on iconoclastic yet compassionate criticism. The destiny of transmutation is to reach a Christic community, which is not a perfect society but a society of openness, where people genuinely accept each other, freely admit their own feebleness, and candidly point to each other's shortcomings in the spirit of support.

In this sense the transmutation model affirms Karl Popper's "open society," opposing the historicism that espouses the development of history by certain historical principles.[4] While dialectical determinism underlies Hegelian historicism, historical dialectic operates Marxist historical utopianism. Neither of them, however, can measure up to the notion of the transmutation model. Hegelian historicism assumes the arrival of the divine Kingdom through the smooth process of the divine spirit without repentance. Marxian historicism presumes the establishment of utopia on earth through proletarian revolutions. Without constant transforming self-examination, any utopia will turn into a tyrannical society. Openness in the transmutation model is not a condition but a direction toward which we are moving. Our future is not determined but open and unfolding.

AUTHENTIC VISIONS

In addition to proper questioning, confrontation, and care, genuine transmutation takes place when people begin to see an alternative vision. Without a vision, people become apathetic. A vision is the matrix of transmutation as well as its destiny. A vision is important, but a communal vision is vital for bona fide transmutation.

In intergroup dynamics a common vision helps bring about the unity and harmony of groups. Without it, cooperation and collaboration among groups are impossible. Furthermore, a communal vision will bring forth interdependence, mutual appreciation, and affection between groups even in the midst of tension and conflict. Transmutation coincides with an authentic vision. While utopian visions might bring despotism and totalitarianism, authentic visions generate reciprocal strength between groups.

Within the sociological models, the assimilation model circumscribes the scope of change within the boundary of the dominant group. Its vision is uniformity. The amalgamation model drives the goal of ethnic interactions to the idea of the preparation of cultures. Its vision is unity. Cultural pluralism accepts the diversity of various cultures. Its vision is unity in diversity and diversity in unity (although unity is actually lacking).

In the Korean-American models, the withdrawal model adopts seclusion for the survival of the group. Its vision is diversity without unity. The assimilation model espouses adaptation to the dominant culture to succeed in the society. Its vision is homogeneity. The paradoxical model expresses the ambiguous identity of marginal people. Its vision is to prepare for the ultimate home through detachment from the present life.

The transmutation model underpins both unity and diversity *in transformity*. It advocates the unity of diverse groups through transmuting social *han* and social sin, while undergirding the diversity of these groups by transmuting the *han* and sin of each group and deepening each culture. For Korean-Americans, it can be a practical direction to challenge social sins and *han*, change our *han* and sins, and heighten Korean-Americanness. Our common and communal visions, along with respect for diversity, will bring forth the unity of diverse groups, and the implementation of the visions according to racial groups will affirm the diversity of the groups. In other words, moving toward a vision is a moment of unity, and working separately toward a vision is a moment of diversity. The strategy of this model is to move toward a communal vision through which we affirm our diversity and unity. Moving toward the vision means transmuting the present culture, economy, and power structure. Diversity or unity (or both) is not the goal of this model; its goal is the creation of a Christic community. Transmutation is a major tool of this model. A Christic community in this country is not a melting-pot society, a Euro-American cultural society, or a cultural-diversity society but a community that enhances all cultures. Mutual enhancement involves mutual enrichment, which aims at horizontal progress and the mutual challenge that works for vertical improvement. To reach its goals, the transmutation model espouses self-critical reflection, mutual cultivation, intrinsic appreciation, gentle confrontation, indispensable cooperation, collective critical thinking, and shared respect. The process is natural, spontaneous, and creative.

10

Koreanness

Toward a Christic Community

The goal of the transmutation model discussed in the previous chapter is to change the *han* and sin of society so it becomes a Christic community. Such a Christic community would enhance the culture of each racial and ethnic group. But what spiritual and cultural ethos will Korean-Americans contribute to establishing the Christic community? This chapter will focus on answering this question.

There are two types of Korean ethos: existential and essential. The existential ethos is *han*, the ineffable agony of the *minjung*; the essential ethos is *hahn, jung,* and *mut*.[1] The existential ethos is transitory—*han* can be overcome someday—but the essential ethos is permanent. By promoting the essential ethos of Koreanness, we can contribute to the whole society. That is, we propose to transmute the *han* of society into *hahn, jung,* and *mut*. Since we have discussed *han*, the existentialist ethos of Koreanness, in Chapter 1, we focus now on the essential aspect of the Korean ethos.

HAHN (PARADOXICAL INCLUSIVENESS)

Hahn is a complex concept to define. Koreanologist Nam Sun Choi was the first modern scholar to study the idea of *hahn* in the early twentieth century. Other Koreanologists, such as Ho Sang Ahn and Min-Hong Choi, furthered the study of *hahn* philosophy in its historical and philosophical aspects respectively. Tongshik Ryu has readdressed the significance of *hahn* as a major mode of the Korean mind.[2] Recently, Sang Yil Kim published several books on *hahn*, affirming it as the essence of the Korean mind.[3]

First, *hahn* denotes divine supremacy, referring to heaven or the sky. Koreans—whether Confucianists, Taoists, shamanists, or Christians—

call the Supreme Being *Hahn-u-nim*.[4] The name consists of *hahn* and *nim* (an honorific). *Hahn-u-nim* is the personal God for Koreans. *Nim* makes the word *hahn* personal. *Hahn* characterizes the attribute of the divine, pointing to greatness, sublimity, immensity, brightness, honor, ultimacy, infinity, majesty, and magnificence. *Hahn* is a comforting yet ultimate notion to Koreans. It is the utmost, highest, and the most sublime word in Korean.[5]

Second, *hahn* signifies *Oneness*. It indicates a circle that has no beginning and no end. In the *Chunbugyong* the cosmos "begins with One (*hahn-a*) yet that One has no beginning . . . ends with One yet that One has no end."[6] A circle symbolizes wholeness or totality. The *hahn* mind sees both sides of a coin, both forest and trees, and both ocean and its water at the same time. The beginning and the ending of an event coincide within *hahn*. Its philosophy eschews the segregation of reality and the polarization of truth.[7] According to Min-Hong Choi, life and death were not viewed as opposing realities in the *hahn* mind of ancient Koreans. By analyzing ancient tomb murals from the fifth and sixth centuries, he verified that the *hahn* mind is non-dualistic.[8] It corresponds with Tao (One or Great) in Taoism.[9] Tao both cares and does not care for all things. It cares to "originate and suckle, rear and develop, protect and provide for, and guide and perfect all things."[10] At the same time, Tao also has no anxiety for the welfare of all things, including human beings, for everything will come naturally to an end (death).[11] Tao encompasses life and death as natural processes. Concurring with the notion of Tao, *hahn* undergirds the continuity of reality.

Third, *hahn* symbolizes *paradoxical inclusiveness*, pointing to an indeterminate boundary. It embraces one and many, and whole and part, simultaneously.[12] In *hahn*, the part unrolls the whole and the whole envelops the part. *Hahn* can mean the whole and the part without self-contradiction; in the same notion of *hahn*, the two terms coexist naturally.[13] The beauty of *hahn* is that ontological antitheses (whole and part) are united in paradoxical harmony (oneness). The *hahn* mind embraces yin and yang, "either . . . or" and "both . . . and" without self-contradiction. Thus, the boundary between one and many, whole and part, becomes ambiguous and uncertain. The uncertainty and ambiguity of life create room for openness. There is no sharp boundary of reality in the Korean mind.[14] The radical openness of *hahn* emphasizes tolerance, acceptance, and creativity in spite of difference and lack of accord. *Tolerance* is passive inclusion, *acceptance* is active embracing, and *creativity* is the dynamic interaction between yin and yang.

In Korean history the *hahn* mind has blossomed through contact with imported religious and philosophical thoughts. Silla Buddhist monk Wonhyo (617-698) grasped and realized the mind of *hahn* fully.

To actualize the *hahn* mind, he used Buddhism as a medium. "Return-ing to the root of the *One* [*hahn*] heart" was the kernel of his idea. The Buddha mind was the *hahn* heart—the one mind.[15] Seen from the per-spective of the *hahn* mind, all things return to the *One*. The enlight-ened Buddha and the masses, life and death, the sacred and the secu-lar are not two, but one. Wonhyo's life was free from any dualism. With one mind he delivered discourses before royal families at the palace and taught prostitutes in the street. His was the incarnation of the *hahn* mind.

Hahn was not only expressed through the mind of Wonhyo, but also through the mind of Yulgok (1536-1584), a prominent Korean Confu-cian scholar. Yulgok used Neo-Confucianism as a medium for express-ing the *hahn* mind.

Whereas Chu-Hsi (1130-1200), founder of Neo-Confucianism, as-serted that principle (*li*) and material force (*ki*) are absolutely two dif-ferent things and that they are mixed together or confused, Yulgok held that principle and material force are neither two things nor one.[16] He argued that because they are not one, they become two; at the same time, because they are not two, they become one. Thus, on the basis of the *hahn* mind, Yulgok declared that *li* and *ki* cannot be separated into two different things.[17] The *hahn* mind does not separate things, but embraces them. It is the heart of inclusiveness, oneness, tolerance, and sublimity.

Another important incarnation of the *hahn* mind was through the development of the *Donghak* movement in the nineteenth century.[18] As the great modern *minjung* movement, *Donghak* has greatly con-tributed to the formation of modern Korea. It evolved into the greatest revolution by oppressed farmers in Korean history in 1892, changed its name to *Chundogyo* (Heavenly Way Religion) in 1905, led the March 1st Movement of 1919 under the Japanese occupation, and provided the spiritual ethos for the *minjung* movement of the 1970s.

The basic teachings of *Chundogyo* can be summarized in the idea of *In-nae-chon* (the divinity of humanity) and *Si-chon-ju* (the human tend-ing of the divine). *In-nae-chon* stresses the inseparable relationship between the divine and the human and the immanence of the divine in the thought and action of the human.[19] The core of its idea is that the human is the divine. *Si-chon-ju* denotes that the human should trust and serve the divine, underlining the transcendental dimension of God. God is the original and total life and the source of the human, and the human bears the divine.[20] This idea does not espouse pantheism, but monotheism. The result of the divine immanence within us is genuine reverence, peace, and joy in our hearts and lives.

Treating the human as the divine (*sain-yochon*) was *Chundogyo's* major teaching. *Chundogyo* particularly emphasized respect for wives, daughters-in-law, and children during a time of strict patriarchy. Furthermore, it taught people to respect not only human beings but also things, including animals and nature (*kyoungmul*). This teaching was far ahead of its time. Its ethical concern was to close the gap between the "small I," the individual, and the "Great I," the Totality.[21] The goal of *Chundogyo* was to have perfect union of the human and the divine.

Koreans have pursued the life of *hahn*. They call themselves *hahn* people. The people of *hahn* are characterized by honor, paradoxical inclusiveness, and unreserved acceptance.

JUNG (AFFECTIONATE ATTACHMENT)

To understand the Korean heart, we need to look into *jung*, the consolidation of emotion (*jung-suh*), affection (*ae-jung*), passion (*yul-jung*), sentiment (*jung-cho*), human-heartedness (*ihn-jung*), sympathy (*dong-jung*), and heart (*shim-jung*). Koreans use this term on many different occasions. Although *jung* is a heavily loaded concept, we can unravel it in three ways.

First, *jung* is the feeling of endearment. In Korean pottery, we can find such *jung*fulness. According to Soon-Woo Choi, a former head of the Arts Department in the Korean National Museum, Korean art works, particularly pottery, depict the heart of the national ethos. The indirect, graceful, and humorous beauty of Korean pottery can be summarized in the word *jung-dah-um* (endearment). While Chinese pottery contains solemn, authoritative, and dynamic beauty, and Japanese pottery holds tidy, synthetic, detailed, and decorous beauty, Korean pottery emits cozy, courteous, amiable, and gentle beauty—the beauty of endearment.[22] Taking after the shapes of the mountains, rivers, creeks, and fields of Korea, the ethos of Korea is *jung*ful. Nature and people in Korea are amiable and adhesive.

In Korea most people overcome loneliness through sharing their *jung*. People are fond of people. In contrast with limited natural resources and capital resources, the endearment of *jung* among people is bountiful. The nature of Koreans is gregarious and friendly.

Second, *jung* is the warmth of human-heartedness. Korea is a nation of *jung*. *Jung* as a major mind-set can easily transcend the rational mind in many affairs. The *jung* mind overwhelms the business mind. The following story is an example:

> I got on a bus running from Tae-Jun to Bo-Eun and saw cosmoses blooming on the roadside. The bus passed golden-ripe rice fields and was climbing up a hill. In the middle, the bus stopped and about twenty school children got on. I asked the person next to me, "Aren't they paying bus fares?" "No. Whenever it rains or the children are late for school, the driver gives them free rides," re-

plied the old man. The bus stopped in front of the school and the children, getting off the bus, bowed and said, "Thanks a million, *Ah-guh-see* [uncle]." "You are welcome. Take good care of yourselves," responded the driver. Warm *jung* was exchanged. My heart was filled with warmth, too.[23]

The warmth she is describing is *jung*. A culture of independence and self-sufficiency can rarely yield the culture of *jung*. Only a culture of interdependence can engender the heart of *jung*.

Korean culture is a *soong-yoong* (toasted-rice tea) culture. Its smell and taste are like *nooroongi* (slightly-toasted rice). We feel *jung*ful. *Soong-yoong* symbolizes gracefulness and generosity. The *soong-yoong* culture can be seen in food-sharing. People love to share their food with their neighbors and strangers. When Koreans invite friends to their homes, they serve plenty of food. After dinner, the hosts distribute any remnants to their guests as an expression of *jung*.

Jung also can be seen in gratuitous gift-giving. Unlike Western gift-giving, Korean gift-giving is often an expression of *jung*. On New Year's Day grandparents give money to their grandchildren, who pay homage to them through *seh-bae* (the bow of prostration). Students give gifts to their teachers on special occasions. The head of a company gives personal gifts to employees on particular occasions. By exchanging gifts Koreans communicate their mutual care and *jung*.

Third, *jung* is compassionate attachment. Koreans are people of suffering. When they see other people of suffering, their hearts are filled with *jung*. There is a saying in Korean: A widow knows another widow's hardship. People of sorrow or suffering are connected through mutual *jung*. The strength of the *jung* of affection enables them to transcend many of the tragedies of their life—shameful subjugation to the tyrannical Japanese rule, the division of the nation, the Korean War, the separation of families, the oppression of military dictatorships, and the economic exploitation of big corporations. *Jung* arises as compassionate attachment when people share their deep *han*. This *jung* helps people stick together through thick and thin.

Fourth, *jung* is an intense longing for somebody or something. People yearn to see their lovers, family members, and friends. Many Koreans have suffered separation from their *jung*-relationships for a long time. Such longing produces the *han* of the *minjung*. *Jung* is both the material cause of *han* and the power to transcend *han*. The *jung*-filled *minjung* usually suffer from *han*. When they fulfill their dreams by seeing their *jung*-related people, their *han* can ebb.

The mind of *hahn* is expressed in *jung*. When *hahn* comes to an interpersonal level, it turns into the mode of *jung*. While *hahn* is more or less vertical, *jung* is horizontal, connecting people in affection and fondness. When we cannot exchange our *jung*, it turns into *han*. Many Koreans left their *jung*-related families, friends, and hometowns because of the Korean War, the division of the country, and urbanization. Any kind of separation in Korea can create deep anxiety, breaking their *jung* and generating the *han* of people. So-wol Kim's poetry epitomizes Korean *jung*. His poems are based on *jung* and *han*. "Azalea" represents the *jung* of the Korean literary world.

Azalea

When you leave me behind, feeling
    burdensome to see me,
I will silently let you go.

I will pluck an armful of azaleas from Yacksan
    Hills, Youngbyun, and spread it over your
    path.

Every step on your way,
laid azaleas
Gently and softly traverse on the flowers.

When you leave me behind, feeling
    burdensome to see me,
I will never shed tears before you, though I
    might die.[24]

"Azalea" symbolizes *jung*. When the beloved leaves, the lover's *jung* toward the beloved turns into *han*. The poem sublimates the *han* of departure with the heart of self-resignation in *jung*. It is difficult to separate *jung* from *han* in this poem.

Koreans are the people of *jung*. When the heart of *jung* is broken by separation, oppression, or repression, *jung* becomes *jung-han*. The world of Koreans has been filled with both *jung* and *han*. Korean songs and literature, popular or classical, express the heart of *jung*, that the *minjung* cannot shake off. *Jung* with *han* delineates the ethos of Koreanness.

MUT (GRACEFUL GUSTO)

Mut is the other important Korean ethos. Sung Bum Yun and Tongshik Ryu particularly underscore this expression of Korean thought.[25] Its rough translation is "beauty of natural harmony," "splendor of asymmetry," or "grace of gentleness." The incarnation of *hahn* in *jung* produces the elegance of *mut*. If *hahn* remains a concept, no grace of *jung* and its *mut* can come out. When we embody the idea of *hahn* in the life of *jung*, *mut* flows from it. *Mut* is the world of art.

There are three ways of defining it. First, *mut* comes out of zestfulness balanced with rhythmic movements. It is not only the rhythmic equilibrium of symmetric factors but also that of asymmetric elements. *Mut*, the beauty of asymmetry, can be seen in the Buddhist towers and designs of *Bool-gook-sah*, the oldest temple in Korea.[26] Both the compatible beauty of a race and also the harmonious beauty of diverse races can produce *mut*. Second, *mut* is the beauty of action. It is the dynamic grace of realizing the vision of *hahn*, that is the gusto of praxis. As we move toward the vision of *hahn*, *mut* can be seen in the process. Third, *mut* also implies the beauty of inner creativity. "Do it in your *mut*" means "Do it in your own way." *Mut* coincides with our freedom. It is the creative struggle of life. *Mut* is the gusto of artistic life and the creativity of organic beauty. Artificiality cannot produce *mut*, but creativity can.

Koryo (918-1392) *chungja* (blue porcelain) reveals the elegance of *mut* in addition to *jung-dah-um*. Its first feature is the beauty of its curves. Compared with Japanese art, which is characterized by the beauty of an orderly and straight line, Korean art features the beauty of a curved line. Koryo *chungja* unveils the curved and spiral beauty of *mut*. Its second feature is its sophisticated damascening method. A blue porcelain vase shows its pattern indirectly. The beauty of the pattern lies in its soft, alluring design. Its third feature is its dark blue color symbolizing the sky, the *hahn-ul* (heaven). The color of *hahn* is blue, and blueness hints at the transparency of the *hahn* mind. Koryo *chungja* is the expression of the *hahn* and *jung* mind in a vase.[27]

Another example of Korean *mut* is the invention of *Hahngul* (the language of *hahn*). This was the greatest invention of the Yi dynasty (1392-1910). Before the invention of *Hahngul*, Koreans used the clumsy *Idu*, the linguistic system that phonetically used Chinese characters for Korean grammatical endings and inflection. It was very unnatural for Koreans to use this odd *Idu* for daily communication. During the reign of Sejong the Great (1397-1450), a royal commission of linguists and philologists invented (after years of study) a Korean alphabet by observing the images of heaven, earth, and humans, and by employing the cosmic principle of yin and yang. They also explored the shape of lips, tongue, teeth, and throat to learn how we naturally pronounce various sounds (twenty-four letters). In short, Korean was a language of *mut* out of the harmonious balance of heaven, earth, and humans.[28] Korean was the epitome of *mut* expressing the *hahn* mind.

The *Hwarangs* of the Silla dynasty were persons of *mut* (*mut-changi*). In the beginning of the seventh century, the three kingdoms—Koguryo, Packche, and Silla—fought against one another. China to the north threatened these three kingdoms. Thus the prime task of the time was to unify the three kingdoms and prevent an invasion by China. Silla accomplished this historical task of unification owing to its *Hwarangs*.[29]

The *Hwarangs* were disciplined in three areas. First, they learned the teachings of the three religions—Buddhism, Confucianism, and Taoism. They sought the virtues of these religions and led people to edification. They held that virtue, not power, would unify the three kingdoms. Second, they were trained in singing and dancing—specific training in *mut*. To be in the divine spirit was a pleasant matter for them. *Mut* is an outcome of the union between the divine (*hahn*) and the human (*jung*). Third, they visited beautiful mountains and rivers for play (*noli*). Mountains and rivers are the place where the divine spirit is present. Play takes place in nature, outside ordinary working places. It is a transcendental dimension beyond ordinary life. *Hwarangs* developed a transcendental world view through play.[30]

Their life was full of *jung* and *mut* based on *hahn*. They were taught that their strength did not depend on military force, but on the harmonious art of humanness (*jung*) and justice, singing and dancing, and playing in nature. The *Hwarangs* lived the quintessential life of the integration of *hahn, jung*, and *mut*.

Mut is the gentle and harmonious beauty that has created the artistic and cultural history of Korea. It has inspired the pens of writers, touched the hands of artists, moved the hearts of poets, and empowered youths to realize their gifts.[31] *Mut* is the ultimate expression of justice, affection, and peace.

In conclusion, Koreanness can be epitomized as *hahn, jung*, and *mut*. *Hahn* is the mind of the divine, the cosmic Oneness. *Jung* is the concrete incarnation of *hahn*. When the transcendental dimension of *hahn* enters human life, *jung* arises. When the congruity between the transcendental *hahn* and the immanent *jung* is achieved, *mut* emerges from it. *Mut* is the stylish beauty of balance. When we pursue a *hahn* vision, the warmth of *jung* takes place and the elegance of *mut* flows out from them. *Mut* originates in the ecstasy of union with the divine and the human. When *hahn* and *jung* are united, the harmony of harmonies, a cosmic art of peace, emanates from it as *mut*.

KOREANNESS AND CHRISTIANITY

The goal of Korean Christians is to embody the vision of *hahn*, the heart of *jung*, and the integration of *mut*. In the beginning, God did not create us to be Christians, but to be true human beings, as God created Adam and Eve to be true human beings. They were not meant to be Christians but to be authentic human beings in the image of God. God's purpose for Koreans is to make them true Koreans in the image of God. Christianity is not meant to supplant the purpose of God's creation but to restore the original goal of the creation. Christianity is a medium to bring forth their Koreanness. To become genuinely Korean is thus inseparable from their Christian calling. Seeing Nathanael coming toward him, Jesus said, "Here is truly an Israelite in whom there is no deceit" (Jn 1:47). Before they became Christians, they were Korean. They were born Korean, not Christian. Without becoming Korean they cannot be Christian. Their call to be Christians is not the call to be religious people, but the call to become authentically Korean, people who fulfill the dreams of *hahn, jung,* and *mut.* The mind of *hahn* is the divine mind for Koreans. Korean Christians have adopted *hahn,* not God or Yahweh, as the name of the divine (*Hahn-u-nim*). For Korean Christians, to fulfill the will of *Hahn-u-nim* is the ultimate mission. Here they can distinguish the vision of Koreans pursuing the mind of *hahn* from the mind of God expressed in Christ, but they cannot separate them. *Hahn-u-nim* had been working hard in Korea to realize God's own mind (*hahn*) long before the arrival of Christian missionaries. In this sense the redemption of Christianity never precedes or replaces the creation-purpose of their Koreanness.

CONTRIBUTIONS OF *HAHN, JUNG,* AND *MUT* TO SOCIETY

What about Korean-Americans in relation to Koreanness? What can the notions of *hahn, jung,* and *mut* contribute to this country? I believe that we can actualize the vision of *hahn,* the heart of *jung,* and the art of *mut* through Christianity in the United States. If we carry out the mind of *hahn,* the heart of *jung,* and the elegance of *mut,* we can contribute to alleviating the *han* in the interracial relations in our society. First, the *hahn* mind points to paradoxical inclusiveness. We can nurture this attitude toward other groups. The *hahn* mind guides us to tolerance toward other groups in spite of their differences.

Second, the *hahn* mind highlights acceptance of the ambiguity of life. Surpassing uniformity or polarization, this mind epitomizes the openness of life. The *hahn* mind accepts the ambivalent reality of one in many and many in one (the whole in the part, and the part in the whole). Linear thinking finds no room in *hahn,* but a multiplex mode of thinking attains its support. For instance, the *hahn* mind sees in the issue of racism more than a matter of racial differences involving the economic, psychological, social, and political benefits of the dominant group. As its diagnosis of racism is multifarious, so is its remedy.

Third, the *hahn* mind is one of reverence. We do well if we treat every person as our precious friend. The *hahn* mind, however, exhorts us further, to attend every person as the divine. Every person is the house of *hahn* (the divine). Furthermore, the *hahn* mind, which reveres all things, illuminates our ecological point of view. Its reverence for all beings is ontological, not teleological. In other words, we do not revere others because we can use them, but because they are in *hahn*. The *hahn* mind sees racial differences as great assets of society. At first, the *hahn* mind passively acknowledges and tolerates racial differences. At the next level, the *hahn* mind actively accepts and embraces them. At the mature level the *hahn* mind builds them up.

In connection with *hahn*, *jung* can engender a social atmosphere of endearment. In spite of racial and ethnic differences, we can promote the culture of *jung* through the traditions of cherishing each other. *Jung* can thaw the icy conditions between racial groups and help people relax with and care for one another. Second, the culture of *jung* can contribute human-heartedness to the business-oriented society. In their business relationships Korean-American shopkeepers need to show other racial groups warm-heartedness. Although there is no duty to help clients beyond business relations, we need to care about their well-being as a whole. *Jung* can challenge the profit-glorifying ethos of corporate culture by showing that accumulating wealth is not the goal of life but a means of sharing our *jung*. Third, *jung* can spread attached affection beyond racial and ethnic boundaries. We give *jung* not only to fellow Korean-Americans but also to all types of people, particularly to the downtrodden. *Jung* brings people true repose and enjoyment of fellow human beings beyond ethnic and racial lines.

As the union of *hahn* and *jung*, *mut* seeks the natural beauty of harmony in racial relations among ethnic groups. Its beauty arises when the dissimilarity and variation of groups are recognized and accepted. Its beauty diminishes when homogeneity is imposed upon ethnic groups. The beauty of *mut* flows from the harmony of natural divergence, not from artificial uniformity. When people appreciate the difference of ethnic groups, the genuine beauty of asymmetric *mut* emanates.

Second, *mut* appears when the strength of virtues overwhelms the power of force. A society of *mut* cannot be attained through any kind of force, including police force, but only through the strength of goodness. Law can bring forth social order but never the art of life in *mut*. Only religious ethos, not even ethical injunctions, can bear the fruit of *mut* in our society.

Third, *mut* promotes the life of play through intercultural singing and dancing. When ethnic and racial groups play together, they grow to understand one another and to appreciate their differences. Play creates mutual affinity and provides space to be different. Ethnic and racial groups can play together and enjoy the gusto of multicultural life, creating the beauty of asymmetry, *mut*.

In this country, Korean-Americans can share the ethos of *hahn*, *jung*, and *mut* with other groups. This sharing can be challenging and transforming. Other groups can enhance the Korean-American ethos by appropriating some of it—and Korean-Americans can do the same with the ethos of other groups. In a society that is racially, ethnically, economically, and culturally torn apart, *hahn, jung,* and *mut* can contribute to the reforming of warped intergroup relations and the healing of this divided society. In the midst of striving for the life of *hahn, jung,* and *mut,* the *han* of alienation, marginality, and fear will turn into the indispensable medium of experiencing and receiving the gift of bountifully gratifying life.

11

The Extended Family

We have discussed sharing the ethos of *hahn, jung,* and *mut* with other racial and ethnic groups. The family is a specific place we can apply the ethos to transmuting the social structure. The nuclear family is dissolving. In 1975 the number of divorces passed the one million mark for the first time. Although the divorce rate declined from 5.8 percent in 1979 to 4.7 by 1988, about 60 percent of first marriages in 1991 are destined to end in divorce.[1] In the same year, half of the nation's children (32.3 million) lived in a situation other than the traditional nuclear family; they reside with a single parent, a stepparent, a grandparent, another relative, or a non-relative. About 4.7 million children lived with a grandparent.[2]

Schools are besieged by problems originating in students' homes, and society is bogged down with crime and punishments. Senator Daniel Moynihan worries that this society might become more stringent and legalistic in an attempt to discipline young adults who are not adequately trained at home because of the breakdown of family.[3]

This country needs to improve its family and community life. It would be difficult, at this junction, to go back to the traditional nuclear family system. Nor is it possible to resolve the present problem of the disintegration of the family by restrengthening the traditional extended family system. Unless we diagnose the causes of the disintegration of the American family and treat them, the process will continue.

French social philosopher Alexis de Tocqueville warned in the 1830s that American individualism might separate citizens from one another and eventually undermine the conditions of freedom.[4] Robert Bellah and his colleagues worry that the family is no longer an integral part of a larger moral ecology, in which the individual is interwoven in community, church, and nation; it has become the core of a private sphere, whose aim is to escape from the public world. At most, the altruism of Americans is limited to the family circle.[5] Americans need to extend the boundary of the family.

A deeper problem in America is that many individuals not only escape from the public world to the family, but they also withdraw from the family into themselves. Strong individualism undercuts the family system. While we should respect and advocate the rights of individuals, we need to confront ontological individualism. It is also necessary for us to work on some viable famly systems for the present and next generations.

THE KOREAN-AMERICAN FAMILY

A contribution Korean-Americans (along with other Asian-Americans and ethnic group members) can make to this society is to redefine the family by introducing a form of the extended family. In Asia, the family is the core part in the economic, social, moral, and political aspects of life. The members of a family stand by one another. Old and needy family members depend on younger family members. To a certain extent, the family fills the roles of health, unemployment, life, and retirement insurance. At home, children receive moral education. They learn about family loyalty, affection, and honor. Within the extended family organization, three or four generations live together under one roof: great-grandparents, grandparents, parents, and children. Grandparents have a great influence on the education and edification of their grandchildren; grandparents' wisdom, personal care, and gentle relational skills guide and instruct them. The extended family is where the mind of *hahn* (the mode of inclusiveness), the heart of *jung* (the relationship of endearment), and the life of *mut* (the beauty of asymmetric harmony) are lived out.

In the United States, many Korean-Americans have adopted the nuclear family system.[6] Nevertheless, according to sociologists Kwang C. Kim and Won M. Hurh, the great majority of the 622 respondents to their interviews in the Chicago area cleave to the cultural values of family and filial piety.[7] Generally, Asian immigrant families deal with two sets of family conditions: one set of conditions strengthens their kinship ties, and another stresses the nuclear family system. Korean immigrant families integrate both sets of conditions: they adopt the nuclear family system, while keeping their extended kinship network.[8] A high percentage of the respondents "strongly agree" or "agree" with the following statements: "Respect is due to elderly parents, no matter how good or bad they have been as parents" (92.4%); and "For a successful marriage, the couple's smooth relationship with their kin is as important as the personal happiness of the husband and wife" (92.2%). Over one-fourth of the respondents have parents in the Chicago area, and 8.5 percent live with members of their own nuclear family and the elderly parents.[9] Over one-third of the respondents live in a form of

extended family. A Korean immigrant family consists of the independent nuclear family as well as close kinship relations. Based on third
and fourth generation Japanese-Americans, Kim and Huhr expect Korean-Americans to preserve the extended family.[10] The Korean form of
extended family implies the coexistence of the nuclear family and its
relatives, along with the traditional virtue of filial piety.[11]

THE MODIFIED EXTENDED FAMIL
AND THE EXTENDED CONJUGAL FAMILY

The nuclear family with close kinship ties can be found in the lifestyle
of this country. Several sociologists find the coexistence of nuclear family and kinship networks in the United States. Sociologist Eugene Litwak
calls the family-kinship system the *modified extended family*, an association of nuclear families in a state of partial dependence for emotional support, mutual aid, visiting, and interchange of other services.[12]

Litwak holds that the modified extended family system adjusts better to the industrial-bureaucratic society than the isolated nuclear family or the traditional extended family does. It has four major traits. The
first is voluntarism. Kinship is in a sense voluntary; that is, kinship ties
are used optionally on a sporadic basis or activated in time of need.
This replaces the basic kinship tie of the family.[13] The second is equality. On an egalitarian basis, the modified extended family incorporates
a series of nuclear families with a strong emphasis on the family bonds
as an end value.[14] The third is that a modified extended family is harmonious with occupational mobility in the mature industrial economy,
while the traditional extended family is antithetical to occupational
mobility.[15] The fourth is that modified extended family relations can be
sustained despite differential geographical mobility because of tech-
nological improvements in communications systems.[16] The modified
extended family is a mutually supportive system.

It is crucial for today's society to establish a sense of community
through the family. For some people, friends fulfill various functions of
the extended family. For others, a religious or ethnic community fills
the roles once reserved for the extended family. For example, uprooted
from their hometowns and families, Jewish-Americans gather regularly
to socialize and partake in discussion in Connecticut cities and towns.
This is called the *havurah* movement (Hebrew for "fellowship").[17] This
type of meeting serves as a surrogate extended family.

Most ethnic groups in this society have had strong traditions of extended family systems. They can help revitalize the society by modify-
ing their own traditional family systems in accordance with the need
of the time. Let me illustrate this point with the traditional family system of Korean-Americans.

The *extended conjugal family* of the Korean immigrants has three characteristics. First, its system is basically vertical. Children pay respect to their parents regardless of their worthiness. Second, the extended conjugal family is based on close social ties among geographically accessible kin. Third, it is an obligatory relationship, not a voluntary one. Children have their strong commitment to the cultural value of filial piety. Such an obligatory relationship comprises parental and sibling relationships. Their kinship ties are inseparable.[18]

Korean immigrants have undergirded the extended conjugal family system with a strong sense of commitment to the value of filial piety. Traditionally, filial piety was focused on the father, but in the United States Korean immigrants show filial duty to both father and mother. Incorporating the virtue of filial duty could bring forth a renewal of family unity in the United States.

By sustaining the extended conjugal family system, with some modifications, Korean-Americans can make a difference in the renewal of the family in society as a whole. The revitalization of the extended family will bring forth a wholesome society. The modified extended family can be a good communal model in the culture of American rugged individualism, and so is the extended conjugal family. Although the extended conjugal family is hierarchical and needs to be more democratic, its spirit of honoring parents and its accountability for siblings need to be stressed in this society. While the extended conjugal family must learn the horizontal autonomy of human relationships from the modified extended family, the modified extended family must learn the spirit of a strong filial tie from the extended conjugal family. These two can complement each other.

Faced with the lack of family and community connections, this society needs to adopt a form of the extended family. Whether we choose a form of the modified extended family or the extended conjugal family, we should refine it through complementarity.

The present demise of the American nuclear family is partially due to an extremely individualistic spirit and industrialization, which foster *laissez faire* capitalism. Even the present trend of postmodern deconstructionism is an outcome of an individualistic market economy. Postmodern philosopher Jacques Derrida's category of the self-referential text corresponds to the autonomy of the market under late capitalism.[19] Although it may be the best way to propagate the wealth of the rich, free capitalism smashes cultural diversity, subverting healthy local communities and fostering an individualistic spirit and competitiveness.

A way to ease familial and social problems can be to stress the life of commitment in a form of the extended family. Such a family system will uplift the mutual commitment of true care among family members, teaching children about honoring the grandparents and parents as well as being accountable for their siblings. It is hopeful for us to see a shift away from an ethos of excessive individualism to an ethos of family responsibility and commitment in the present society. One of the major forces generating this "new familism" is the changing lifestyle of large numbers of the so-called baby boomers.[20]

The practice of the extended family can eliminate ageism, too. Grandparents no longer pass time but live a true life together with their family members. If we reorganize our family structure well, grandparents and grandchildren play and enjoy each other's company. During such time grandparents transmit their ethnic or cultural customs, traditions, and values to their grandchildren. In an extended conjugal family, parents model for their children how to honor parents, and children have the opportunity to show their love and respect toward their parents and grandparents.

Recently, "adopt-a-grandparent" programs have been started at the thirteen American House residences in southeast Michigan. The program matches school children with elderly people in retirement homes.[21] The "adopt-a-grandparent" program also operates in other places, such as the Tower School in Marblehead, Massachusetts. Through the programs, children become acquainted with "grandparents"; "grandparents" have opportunities to play with young children. This kind of contact is essential for an intergenerational connection. A study conducted by the American Association of Retired Persons on the images of aging found that most children who know old people but have never played with them regard the elderly as sick and crabby. The association calls for more intergenerational projects.[22]

To bridge the gap between grandparents and grandchildren, a program called "Grandtravel" arranges tours for grandparents and their grandchildren.[23] Catholic Social Services in Wayne County, Michigan, organized the Foster Grandparent program, which places in-home foster grandparents with pregnant or parenting teens twenty hours a week.[24] When grandparents and children meet, they naturally play with each other. These programs spread hope in a disconnected society, where dumping grandparents is practiced to avoid financial and filial responsibility.

A recent trend shows more single parents living with their parents. A Census Bureau survey shows that the number of single parents living in households headed by others increased from about 859,000 in 1980 to 2.1 million in 1991.[25] It will be good if we can live with our elderly parents or live near them for mutual support. If that is not feasible, we need to have close contact with them.

FAMILY DECLINE

The extended family system might also prevent families from breaking down in the first place. One reason married couples in this country divorce is the lack of a familial support system in times of crisis. When a couple is deciding about divorce in a nuclear family, no one besides themselves can give advice on the matter. Such crucial decision-making is based on one or two people's judgment. In an extended family system, such a decision is the decision of the whole family. The former is an independent decision; the latter is an interdependent decision.

American family life has undergone drastic transformation since the late 1950s: a steep increase in divorce, two-career families, and single parenting. Some of the driving forces behind the transformation were shifts in values. During the 1960s and 1970s, the United States enjoyed unprecedented economic affluence. Median family income tripled between the 1950s and 1970s. This affluence heightened educational and travel opportunities and deepened personal aspirations for happiness and achievement. New psychological and philosophical trends that underpinned self-actualization and growth coincide with the economic prosperity.

Another great influence on the family was the sexual revolution. In the 1960s the Supreme Court struck down a series of state laws that forbade the prescription or distribution of contraceptives, and in 1973 the same court decriminalized abortion. In the late 1970s a number of public schools instituted birth-control clinics. These actions indicated that the government was out of the business of regulating the private sexual conduct of its citizens.[26]

Another significant component of change in the family has been "working mothers." In 1940, around the time of World War II, less than 12 percent of Euro-American married women participated in the work force. The rate was almost 60 percent in the early 1980s; over half of all mothers of preschoolers were working mothers.[27] By the late 1980s, over two-thirds of all three-to-five-year-old children were going to a day-care center, compared with one-fifth in 1970.[28] Fewer children had full-time mothers or fathers. Children who were born between 1965 and 1975 are called "baby-busters" or "Generation X," aloof, emotionally withdrawn, and individualistic.[29] They need the sense of belonging. The rise of street gangs is a response to such a need.

Economic affluence, a new psychological philosophy, the sexual revolution, and the flow of married women into the work force joined together to spawn a growing desire for personal achievement, an immersion in the self—the spirit of individualism. A number of social critics—Peter and Brigitte Berger, Christopher Lasch, Robert Bellah, and Daniel Yankelovich—believe that today's ideals of love and marital relationships, based on therapeutic ideals of openness, emotional honesty, and communication of intimate feelings, have proved incapable of withstanding anything stronger than undemanding, short-term, narcissistic sexual relationships.[30]

TWO VIEWS

Regarding the issue of the crumbling of the family in the United States, people argue whether the government should be involved in the improvement of family life. Conservatives have driven a religio-political pro-life movement since the 1970s, convinced that soaring divorce rates, single parenthood, and working mothers produce a break-down of family values. They have attempted to block ratification of the proposed Equal Rights Amendment to the Constitution, control tele-vision eroticism and violence, reject gay rights, limit teenagers' access to contraceptives, and hamper abortion. Their philosophy is that the state has a positive accountability to specify and enforce family stan-dards and values.[31] On Capitol Hill, Republicans trace America's woes to the breakdown of the family, and they offer tax breaks to families that remain intact. This is item four of the GOP's Contract with America, the Family Reinforcement Act.[32]

In contrast, liberals have attempted not to use government social policies to control family matters, but rather to employ them to help individual families. Some of their proposals include federal subsidies for child-care centers for low-income families, family-planning pro-grams, health and safety requirements in child-care centers, and un-paid leave for birth or adoption.[33]

One thing is clear: the government can help to improve external fam-ily conditions such as family health and children's programs, but it can-not stipulate the internal cohesion of the family in areas such as family morality (the virtue of filial piety, the prohibition of divorce). Thus the government cannot be the solution for the problem of the family.

The nuclear family system did not evolve without reason. The preindustrial American family of the seventeenth and early eighteenth centuries was an extended family. But the characteristics of the ex-tended family such as solidarity, paternalistic leadership, and invisible individuality became irrelevant in the industrial society. A major rea-son for the initial existence of the extended family was protection from hostile outsiders, such as other extended families. Urbanized, native-born Americans no longer needed the clan membership that had ex-isted on the frontier. Exposed to a different sort of frontier, newly ar-rived immigrants, however, have had an acute need for the extended family.[34]

In addition to working mothers, two-career families, single parenting, and widespread divorce, the American family now faces eco-logical and economic crises. To deal with these crises, society needs a refurbished lifestyle—an extended household for ecological and eco-nomical living. Not just to protect ourselves from danger, but for the sake of engendering genuine humanity and community, we need to move toward a form of the extended family. Doing so will renovate and enrich the quality of American life; connect grandparents and grand-children; and interweave the ecology, economy, and ethic of society.

THE EXTENDED FAMILY AND CHRISTIAN FAITH

The renewal of external and internal family conditions and structures is the task of the church. The church can reach where the government cannot. The church needs to emphasize external improvement of family life and internal family responsibility.

In the Hebrew scriptures, family members had to keep together to protect their lives and their livestock.[35] Sin and salvation were not individual matters but involved the family, tribes, and Israel. To maintain an extended family or a clan, it was necessary to emphasize the virtue of filial piety. Parents were procreators, and God the Creator. Without honoring the procreators, it was not possible to honor the Creator.

In the Christian scriptures, God is the heavenly parent. Without honoring the visible parent, it is nonsensical to worship the invisible God. In this sense familial accountability is directly related to faith. Faith in what is unseen is evidenced in filial duty. Without filial piety, it is impossible to please God. Filial piety and faith underpin each other. Filial piety, however, precedes faith. We understand God only through our faith in our parents. It is very difficult or impossible to have faith in God while disbelieving or dishonoring our parents.[36]

This country, though predominantly Christian, has trouble understanding the meaning of Christian faith. With the practice of filial duty ebbing, people lose their grip on Christian faith or distort its meaning. Christian faith is not a pathological, baby-like clinging, a phobia of punishment, or an obsession with God. It is a mature, trustful relationship with God.

Filial piety is not mere unilateral trust in our parents. It is a growing relationship of trust, respect, and love for our parents. The relationship is always reciprocal. In Confucianism, filial piety is an inward respect or reverence for one's parents. However, the relationship is mutual: kindness in parents and filial piety in children.[37] When *hahn* and *jung* are applied to our relationship with parents, *mut* arises from within. That *mut* is called filial piety.

Sallie McFague delineates various models of our relationship with God.[38] She expresses our deepest personal relation with God in the metaphors of mother, lover, and friend. These three metaphors are explained in *agape*, *eros*, and *philia*. For McFague, these metaphors of our relation with God point to the "destabilizing," "inclusive" and "nonhierarchical" vision of fellowship.[39] In spite of the nonhierarchical nature of relationship, she underscores the significance of the transcendence and immanence of God. The God of *agape* transcends our present state of love. This transcendent dimension of God's love is extravagantly loftier than ours and invokes our filial piety toward God.

We grow into the maturity of being God's friend, yet this friendship with God does not supersede our faith in God. In the same manner, our relationship with our parents should grow into friendship when we reach our parental plane. This friendship, however, never reduces our filial piety in any manner. The more mature we grow in our friendship with our parents, the more we will cherish our parents with filial piety. The relationship with our parents maintains always the transcendent and horizontal dimensions of friendship. Likewise, we develop a friendship with God through filial piety—the content of faith.

In conclusion, filial piety is indispensable in understanding Christian faith and relating to God.[40] This nation needs to take up the subject of filial piety, through which we might reconstruct our familial and social systems and revitalize the church. The task of Korean-American churches and other Asian-American churches is to keep practicing a form of the extended-family lifestyle, thrive on it, connect it with Christian faith, and heal the wounds of broken families and communities through *hahn*, *jung*, and *mut*.

Part IV

AN EMERGING THEOLOGY

12

Theology of Seeing

Biblical Insights for Racial Healing

"In the beginning when God created the heavens and the earth, the earth was a formless void and darkness covered the face of the deep" (Gn 1:1-2). Creation was closely related to God's vision. Before creation, there was divine vision seeing the formless void and darkness. After seeing the void and darkness, God started creation. *Seeing* precedes creating. After the third day of creation, God "saw that it was good" (Gn 1:10). God's creation was incomplete on the third day, but God saw beauty in it. However imperfect, creation looked good to God because God was going to perfect it. Therefore, to see good in any incomplete creation is to participate in the divine work of creation. Seeing the divine in the imperfect creation is necessary in order to move toward completion of creation.

In a society permeated with racial and ethnic conflict, seeing the good in other groups will remedy the tainted images of our ethnic and racial relations. It is important to achieve ethnic and racial harmony in our society, but a more urgent matter is to see good in each other in spite of our shortcomings.

Many people are pessimistic about the ability of the United States to achieve a harmonious racial and ethnic society. Cornel West articulates the rampant nihilism in the African-American community: economic decline, racial conflict, the absence of self-love and love of others, the breakdown of the family and neighborhood, lack of supportive networks, and the social rootlessness and cultural barrenness of urban dwellers. West believes that the decay of spiritual communities is causing the crises of our society.[1] *Seeing* is a practical answer to a confused and pessimistic society, and a necessary factor in the construction of future society.

Our God is the God of revelation. God reveals reality, and we perceive God's revelation. Most theologies have concentrated on the revelation of God—the word of God—but a theology of *seeing* stresses how we *see* God's revelation. Our *seeing* is as crucial as God's revelation. Without our *seeing*, God's revelation is not revelation to us. Our understanding of faith, affection, and hope derives from our perception of God's revelation. Inseparable from God's revelation, *seeing* is the key to bringing salvation and liberation to creation. How we *see* the following three biblical events has implications for ethnic relations.

PENTECOST

The spreading of the good news (gospel) is cross-cultural in nature. When a group of people begins to see others' life, culture, and tradition as valuable, the story of Jesus Christ can be transmitted. In Acts, the Pentecost event created a cross-cultural community of caring.

The descent of the Holy Spirit empowered the disciples to launch the Christian movement. When the Holy Spirit grasped them, they could *see* "tongues, as of fire," and they "began to speak in other languages" (Acts 2:3-4). This event is pivotal in the formation of the church. We have most often interpreted this event from the perspective of the propagation of the universal gospel. That is, the speaking in tongues was construed as a means to transmit the gospel. We need, however, to see that the event itself was the very content of the gospel, not its mere form. The occurrence denoted the understanding and accepting of other cultures. It was a breaking away from the narrow interpretation of Judaism, transcending its ethnocentrism and seeing its new mission toward the world in the form of neo-Judaism.

There are diverse interpretations of the miracle of Pentecost. Some believe that the disciples spoke different foreign languages, while other scholars deny an actual language-miracle, assuming that the report was Luke's redaction. Our aim is to comprehend the theology behind Luke's report, not to examine the nature of the language-miracle itself.

Luke tells us that on the day of Pentecost the Holy Spirit started the new movement of the church by inspiring the 120 disciples to proclaim the message of Jesus Christ in the languages of other peoples. Luke had made the universal nature of the gospel explicit at the outset of the book (1:8). Acts 2:1-4 runs parallel to the descriptions of the rabbinic notion of the Sinai event (Ex 19).

First, Pentecost was the fiftieth day after the Passover, also called the "Feast of Weeks." Historically, it commemorated Moses receiving the Law on Mount Sinai. For Christians, Pentecost recalls the disciples receiving the Holy Spirit, marking the birth of a new Christian community. For Jews, Pentecost has become the day of receiving the Torah; for Christians, Pentecost is the day of receiving the new Torah (gospel).

Second, the Jewish themes of the theophany at Mount Sinai correspond to the Christian phenomenon of the theophany of the Holy Spirit on the day of Pentecost. The Jewish theophany is described thus: "Now Mount Sinai was wrapped in smoke, because the LORD had descended upon it in fire; the smoke went up like the smoke of a kiln, while the whole mountain shook violently" (Ex 19:18). The Christian theophany is recounted this way: "And suddenly from heaven there came a sound like the rush of a violent wind, and it filled the entire house where they were sitting. Divided tongues, as of fire, appeared among them, and a tongue rested on each of them" (Acts 2:2-3). The fire is the primordial fire issued from God. God speaks through the fire. Alfons Weiser holds that the stress on the interconnection of fire, voice, and language is particularly striking.[2]

Third, in the rabbinic tradition (midrash) of a language-miracle at Sinai, the voice of God divided itself into seventy world languages and communicated the Torah to all nations, but only Israel accepted it.[3] Luke, presumably familiar with this rabbinic tradition, differs from it. He holds that God's new Law (gospel) through *glossolalia* (speaking in tongues) was proclaimed to various groups of people who eventually accepted the new Law through Peter's speech (Acts 2:14-41). At Pentecost, God spoke through the fire, and Jesus' disciples *saw* the fire of God's speaking.

Furthermore, Luke's story is contrasted with the story of the tower of Babel (Gn 11:1-9). According to Etienne Trocmé, Luke took the narrative of verses 1-6 and 12-13 from a source that reported how divine grace had finally removed the confusion of languages that came from the tower of Babel.[4] On the surface the story of the tower of Babel addresses the origin of multiple languages; it says they resulted from the sin of pride. The narrative of Pentecost explains the origin of new languages that derive from the power of the Holy Spirit. Luke conveys that this *glossolalia* event transforms the story of the confusion of language into a story of the ecstasy of language. *Glossolalia* is generally unintelligible ecstatic speech.[5] Luke recasts incomprehensible *glossolalia* as comprehensible language in the Pentecost episode. Thus the confusion of languages is converted into the unmistakable sign of languages that proclaim the wonderful works of God. *That* is the miracle of Pentecost. The story of the tower of Babel recounts the division of language as a divine punishment; Pentecost redefines the division of language as a divine gift for the lucid communication of the divine message.

In Pentecost we see the positive value of multiple human languages, for God inspired the disciples to speak diverse languages to spread God's story. Speaking many languages at the beginning of Christianity means a lot to ethnic people, because it symbolizes the significance of ethnic diversity in Christian mission. It highlights not only the universal nature of the gospel, but also shows respect for the variety in ethnic languages and cultures. It was unnecessary for the disciples to proclaim the gospel in various languages; most people in Jerusalem could understand their common language (Aramaic). In this account of the Pentecost, Luke focuses on the importance of Gentile (*ethnei*) cultures as he emphasizes the boundlessness of the gospel.

Luke is the only known Gentile (*ethnei*) author in the Christian scriptures. He wrote the gospel from the perspective of a Gentile addressing the Gentiles and the marginalized. For instance, his genealogy of Jesus is different from Matthew's. While Matthew started from Abraham in order to affirm the Jewish origin of the gospel, Luke traced Jesus lineage to Adam in order to declare the universality of the gospel. Luke highlighted the faith of the Roman centurion (Lk 7:1-10), the compassion of the Samaritan, the widow at Nain (Lk 7:11-17), and the sinful woman (Lk 7:36-50). The report that the disciples spoke different languages at Pentecost highlights Luke's ethnic theology.

To begin proclaiming the gospel of Jesus Christ, we must *see* the flame of the Spirit as the disciples did. The gospel is good news when people hear it in their own languages. Speaking in others' tongues is the first part of sharing the good news.

In the Holy Spirit, the diversity of tongues does not result in confusion but turns into the blessing of sharing the good news. When the Holy Spirit grasps us, we begin to perceive the confusion of Babel as the gift of God to proclaim the healing work of God. The power of the Spirit turns the confusion of multi-ethnic and multiracial America into the blessings of God by affirming our differences. Speaking in others' languages at Pentecost did not result in destructive confusion; its dynamic energy created the new community of Christ.

The birth of the church under the guidance of the Holy Spirit provides a new paradigm for the dynamics of inter-ethnic relations in the United States. When we *see* the primordial fire, Pentecost takes place. When the fire touches us from head to heart, we speak other languages—embracing diverse cultures and appreciating them. The primordial fire that created the world re-creates us to appreciate and enjoy each other's presence. The Spirit of God melts the confusion among peoples, languages, and cultures into a celebration of our differences.

THE ROAD TO EMMAUS

In the Lukan resurrection story (Lk 24:13-35), two disciples were going to a village named Emmaus on the third day after Jesus' crucifixion. A stranger approached them, joined in their conversation on the suffering and risen Messiah, and explained the crucifixion and resurrection of Christ. Near Emmaus, they invited him to share their dinner, and as he took the bread, broke it, and gave it to them, their eyes were opened, and they recognized the stranger as the resurrected Jesus.

The meal is an extraordinary one, as the guest turns into the host. Luke's words echo the grace before meals pronounced by the head of the Jewish household: "He took bread, blessed, and broke it, and gave it to them" (Lk 24:30).[6]

Some scholars wonder whether the sharing of the bread in this incident represents the Eucharist. According to C. F. Evans, although it is widely accepted that the setting presupposed is the Christian Eucharist, dependent on the Last Supper, in reality it is no more than the traditional wording for saying grace. There is no indication of anything as distinctive as of the Last Supper.[7] Joachim Jeremias argues that the *koinonia* of Acts 2:42 refers to the *agape* or fellowship meal, while the "breaking of the bread" of Luke 24:35 connotes the subsequent Eucharist. He supposes that the risen Christ grants the Emmaus disciples fellowship at his table and that during the holy meal their eyes were opened and they recognized him.[8] Arthur Just, Jr., contends that the Emmaus meal is the *transitional meal* between the historical meals of Jesus, including the Last Supper, where he was physically present and visible, and endless eucharistic meals where he is present but invisible.[9] To Eduard Schweizer, since Jesus gave the two disciples the reality of his presence in table fellowship, it is no longer possible to make a sharp distinction between an everyday meal eaten in the fellowship of faith and the Lord's Supper in the larger circle of the community.[10]

Indeed, the church has distinguished too sharply the Lord's Supper from our everyday meal. We need to highlight the Emmaus meal, which pulls the historical meals of Jesus and the Eucharist together. The Emmaus meal indicates that our fellowship meal with a stranger is a meal where Jesus is present. Both the fellowship meal and the Eucharist are significant in terms of Jesus' presence, although the intensity of his presence will be experienced differently depending on the susceptibility of partakers.

Another crucial issue is how the two disciples recognized the risen Christ. Some explain that the Lord's words and deeds brought about the recognition. Jeremias speculates that his special way of tearing the loaf or a special form of words in blessing might have made it possible.[11] J. E. Alsup postulates that the two disciples came to recognize him through supernatural power.[12] A. R. C. Leaney suggests that the reception of the blessed bread restored their weary mental and spiritual faculties and they recognized him.[13] Luke used the familiar phrase "breaking of the bread" to emphasize that Christ is recognized at the meal: "Then they [the two disciples] told what had happened on the road, and how he had been made known to them in the breaking of the bread" (Lk 24:34).

Recognition of strangers as our companions does not happen until we invite them to share our meal. Our heart might be inspired and changed when listening to their stories, but only when breaking bread together do we see them as our companions—and as the risen Christ.

In breaking the bread with a stranger they came to recognize the stranger as Jesus Christ. Sharing our bread with strangers will open our eyes to *see* strangers—as Christ. This complements the scene of the last judgment (Mt 25:31-46), where Jesus appears in the form of the needy. If the two disciples had not invited him to the meal, Jesus would not have had the chance to bless it and open their eyes.[14]

The term *epignôskô* (recognition) is different from *ginôskô* (knowledge). Luke wrote an orderly account so that Theophilus might *know* (*epignôs*) the truth (1:4). *Knowledge* is also used in 24:18: "Are you the only stranger in Jerusalem who does not know [*égnôs*] the things that have taken place there in these days?" For Luke, the disciples *knew* the passion facts, but did not *see* (recognize) them. The opening of their eyes indicates that the event was a revelation for them. In Luke's theology, seeing or recognizing differs from knowing. Luke stressed recognition over knowledge, probably in opposition to the Gnostic emphasis on knowledge. For Luke, *recognition* is an alternative term for faith (*pisteúô*).[15] We cannot simply know Jesus; we need to recognize or see him. The action of sharing our resources with the needy makes this seeing possible.

Chi-ha Kim, a *minjung* poet, explains how we are interconnected through rice (the basic staple for Asians).

> Rice is heaven
> As you can't go to heaven by yourself
> Rice is to be shared
> Rice is heaven
> As you see the stars in heaven together
> Rice is to be shared by everybody
> When the rice goes into a mouth
> Heaven is worshiped in the mind
> Rice is heaven
> Ah, ah, rice is
> To be shared by everybody.[16]

Rice and God are inseparable. Sharing rice is sharing God. Until we share rice, we do not see God in the hungry world. Abstract theology is "pie in the sky." Eucharistic theology connects God with rice. This Emmaus episode points to the inseparability of bread (resources) and Christ. Without the theme of bread, Luke's Christology is incomplete; he firmly links the Emmaus event and the Last Supper.

It is a strange paradox that the stranger becomes our host. By inviting a stranger to our meal, we can be blessed. By providing us with the opportunity to serve, the stranger blesses us. A stranger is not there to receive our pity and compassion but to save us from our sins—the sins of self-centeredness. In this sense, a stranger can be our messiah, delivering us from our blindness.

In *The Ongoing Feast* Arthur Just, Jr., explains why Jesus disappeared when the disciples recognized him. Jesus Christ no longer reclines at table as he once did; he relates with his disciples in a new way. The presence of Jesus at the Emmaus meal prepares his disciples for his invisible presence at the Eucharist.[17]

Luke could intend to point to something further: Jesus disappeared in order to appear through a stranger again. The stranger who is recognized as Jesus is no longer a stranger. Jesus is a permanent stranger to us. Only we recognize him in a stranger. This was the reason Jesus disappeared when they recognized him. His absence opened their eyes further to his permanent presence in the stranger. Here absence is true presence and true presence is absence.[18]

But who are strangers among us? Strangers are not "us," but "them." Native-Americans have lived here longer than any other group, yet they have become permanent strangers in their own land. Along with other ethnic groups, Asian-Americans also experience such permanent-stranger status. Most Korean-Americans and second generation Korean-Americans are often asked, "Where are you from?" "When are you going back to Korea?" We are strangers in our own country.

In our society, many people suffer from egoism, meaninglessness, depression, and despair. Others are disillusioned. They have tried for years to change the structure of racism, but discern little or no change in people's attitudes. Reared in an affluent society, many young people struggle in their search for some meaning in their lives.

Aliens who have undergone various kinds of human suffering can bring valuable insight to this society. The marginalized—undocumented workers, immigrants, and discriminated-against ethnic peoples—can serve to open the eyes of people so they can see the reality of the human struggle. These strangers might be the messiah for our affluent society. Perhaps God perhaps renews and redeems this self-complacent society through these strangers.

THE LAWYER'S QUESTION

A promising young lawyer came to Jesus to test his mettle (see Lk 10:15-37). The lawyer asked how he should inherit eternal life. Jesus had him answer his own question. The lawyer responded correctly: love God and love our neighbor as ourself. The lawyer then asked the definition of *neighbor*. At this juncture Jesus told him a story, turning knowledge into praxis, making religion into life, and extending the definition of *neighbor* beyond racial boundaries.

The Samaritans were schismatics, holding to the Pentateuch as scripture, and were often the object of greater hatred than Gentiles. They were excluded from the covenant fellowship, but they carried out the requirements of the covenant.[19] They claimed descent from the patriarchs, but this claim was rejected by the Jews, who attributed to them a heathen origin.[20]

A Samaritan, one of the marginalized, became the center of Jesus' story. Jesus tells us that when the priest "saw him [the victim of the robbery], he passed by on the other side" (Lk 10:32). So did the Levite. They avoided seeing him by passing by on the other side of the road. But the Samaritan did not change his course; he *saw* the victim and was moved with pity (v. 34). Looking at a victim of violence takes the courage to care.

However painful it may be, we must see suffering people around us. Only by seeing the reality of suffering people can we eliminate suffering. We often, however, cross the road to avoid seeing victims. By moving our churches to the suburbs or making them islands in the inner cities, for example, we insulate ourselves from seeing burdensome people and the problems in the inner cities.

The Samaritan had the courage to see the wounded, for he was wounded too. A traumatic event—a physical or mental wound—usually results in *han*. With *han* inside, the Samaritan could face the wounded and take care of him. The wounded can heal the wounds of others.[21] Jesus picked the Samaritan character to be the healer of the society. His selection of the Samaritan was no accident. He knew that the wounds of a society could be healed through the wounded.

The wounded can be healed through the community of the healthy, but deep healing takes place in the community of grief, wounds, and brokenness. In other words, the healing of *han* occurs in the community of *han*. Only the deeply wounded can see and understand the inmost wound of a sufferer. In this sense, the marginalized can be the healers of the wounded of our society. Wounded ethnic groups can create communities of healing. Compared with groups having little experience of racial and sexual discrimination, a racially and sexually wounded group can see clearly the pain caused to others by racism and sexism; it can become the agent of cure for the injured, for it can *see* their wounds.

The Samaritan *saw* the victim, and this led him to take action. When we *see* others' affliction, we begin to get involved with it, to participate in their suffering. The Samaritan was not a priest, or a Levite, or a Jew, or a religious official. He was an outcast who *saw* the injured. This man was the focus of Jesus' religious teaching. *Seeing* the wounded is religion.

The Korean-American community is a *han*-ridden community; it can be, therefore, an agent of healing this *han*-filled society. The marginalized Samaritan cared for the victim. His marginality was not a disadvantage but a creative edge. Our *han* of victimization is painful, but it has potential for seeing the wounded society and healing it. We not only moan for our own victimization, but we also should take the role of the creative Samaritan in this racially broken society.

Beyond the biblical story, we realize "Samaritans" need not to be attentive to healing victims only; they also need to pay attention to robbers. They must see who the robbers are, why they rob strangers, and how such robbery can be prevented in a systemic way. With the present social condition, more evildoers will rise and "rob" people. More racial eruptions are expected in the future. It is important for "Samaritans" to change the social system that produces robbers.

Christianity is the religion of revelation. *Seeing* is the key to understanding God's revelation. When we *see* divine revelation through the downtrodden, the healing of our broken society takes place and the hope of humanity arises.[22]

13

Seeing Others Well

Dissolving the *Han* of Group Conflict

THE STORY OF THE KING AND THE MONK

Sung Kye Yi was the first king of the Yi dynasty (1392-1910) in Korea. Monk Moohahk was an advisor for the king.

> One day Sung Kye Yi teasingly put down Moohahk, "To me, you look like a pig."
> The monk gently replied, "To me, you look like Buddha."
> "Why are you saying that?" asked the king.
> "If you have a pig inside, you will see pigs in others, and if you have Buddha inside, you will see Buddha in others," modestly explained the monk.[1]

What we see outside corresponds with what we see inside. An untrained person may see a fine painting but appreciate only part of its beauty and value. A well-trained painter sees much more. Two people can have different opinions about a view. One may greatly appreciate its beauty, while the other may be indifferent. How we *see* is pivotal in our self-understanding as well as our understanding of the world. What we see is what we are.

How we see can be applied to intra-personal and interpersonal relationships. People with no self-respect do not know how to respect others. People who don't know how to care for themselves cannot care for others. People who have little self-love cannot love others. This is the reason Jesus asks us to love others as ourselves. If we do not love ourselves, we cannot love others.

This dynamic also affects group interaction. If a group has little self-respect, it cannot respect other groups. If a group suffers self-hatred, it cannot appreciate other groups. What we see inside circumscribes what

138

we see outside. A major reason for social and racial conflict and strife is the broken collective image of ethnic groups. Healthy intergroup dynamics start with sound group self-images. How can we have wholesome group self-images? How can we resolve the *han* of ethnic America? Learning to *see* will help us dissolve *han* by attaining a healthy self-image.

SEEING OTHERS

In this society, where ethnic groups live in conflict and tension, we need to find unity and at the same time affirm our ethnic identities. The first step toward unity is to see each other more often. Avoiding other groups is the prototypical sin that creates all kinds of prejudice and problems and prevents efforts at resolution.

Not all ways of looking at others are good, however. Whereas the term *seeing*, especially when it carries the meaning of recognition and understanding, contains a warm intention and can yield constructive transformation, the word *staring* has nuances of ill will and may engender harmful consequences. *Seeing* is a visual dialogue and understanding, arousing sympathy. *Staring* is a visual monologue, an unpleasant or suspicious leering.

African-Americans sometimes complain that Korean-American shopkeepers watch their moves while they are shopping but do not look them in the face when they check out at the counter. The tension is partially due to cultural differences and the antagonistic nature of the relationship between store owners and shoppers. But it can also be attributed in part to the suspicious *staring* on the part of the shopkeepers. To alleviate inter-ethnic tension, we need to convert staring into seeing.

A CULTURE OF SEEING

Korean culture is a culture of seeing. Korean people know and experience many things through seeing. *Bon-dah* means seeing: *mot-bon-dah* (seeing taste), *namseh-motah-bon-dah* (seeing smell), *dle-uh-bon-dah* (seeing hearing), *yehbae-bon-dah* (seeing worship), *gah-bon-dah* (seeing going), *hae-bon-dah* (seeing doing), and *jang-bon-dah* (seeing shopping).[2] Besides these, there are many more expressions that affirm that Koreans' basic pattern of perception is seeing. All other forms of perception are secondary.

Further, Korean culture is a culture of seeing *well*. The expression *Jahl-Bwah-Joo-Seh-Yo* (See me well or graciously) is used on various occasions, particularly when people need favors. "Seeing others well" is crucial for good human interaction. Good relations between storekeepers and customers require that they see each other well. When employers hire people, they must see their employees well.

The Korean folk song *Milyang Ari-rang* clearly expresses the theme of "seeing well":

> See me well please, see me well please, see me
>   well please
> See me well please as if you saw a flower in
>   cold January
>
> Shy, shy to greet my lover at his arrival,
> smile, smile at him holding the apron rim
>   between the lips
>
> Ari-rang, seu-ri seu-ri-rang, ara-ri-ga natneh
> Send me across over Ari, Ari-rang Hill please.[3]

This is the love song of a woman who is joyful at her lover's coming yet hides her real feeling behind her blushing smile. She wants to look good to her lover. By being seen well, she will glow in elation. It is her longing to be seen at her best.

In many Korean songs, we find lovers or family members yearning to see each other. Since many wars have divided families and lovers, their aspiration to see each other is ardent. Love does not happen without seeing. Seeing kindles and rekindles love. Without seeing, understanding and love are empty.

The lovers in these songs represent Koreans, who like to be seen well by others. When others see and understand us well, we operate better. Others' generous seeing of us brings out the best in us.

In turn, we must see others well. When we see and understand others well, they too act better. Seeing is the first step for understanding. Between groups, seeing precedes any dialogue, understanding, and caring for each other.

It is necessary to see other ethnic groups well for any improvement in racial relations in our society. *Staring* at other groups with disparaging eyes chills those observed and closes down their being. Only *seeing* others can elicit true understanding of the seen. By being seen well, the downtrodden can have the courage to be what they ought to be and what they can be.

Jesus came into the world to see sinners well. In his eyes, they were precious sons and daughters of God. His presence in the midst of sinners was good news for all the downtrodden. It was natural that the community of God grew around Jesus, who saw them as God's family.

SEEING IN EASTERN RELIGIOUS TRADITIONS

Seeing is stressed in major Eastern religious traditions. In Buddhism, authentic seeing is the first path of the Eightfold Noble Path.

As I have said before, the seeing plays the most important role in Buddhist epistemology, for seeing is at the basis of knowing. Knowing is impossible without seeing; all knowledge has its origin in seeing. Knowing and seeing are thus found generally united in the Buddha's teaching. Buddhist philosophy therefore ultimately points to seeing reality as it is. Seeing is experiencing enlightenment. The *Dharma* (Truth, Reality, Norm) is predicated as *ehipassika*, the *Dharma* is something "you come and see." It is for this reason that *sammaditthi* is placed at the beginning of the Eightfold Noble Path.[4]

Enlightenment means "seeing Truth." The foundation of all knowledge is seeing. In relation to seeing, it is important to know the *prajna* (wisdom), which sees into all the implications of Emptiness. Emptiness is not nothingness or relativity, but "suchness," "so-ness," or "state of being so."[5] Buddha united seeing with knowing; without seeing, knowing is superficial and life becomes incomprehensible. This is the reason that right seeing comes before right knowing in the Eightfold Noble Path. "Seeing is experiencing, seeing things in their state of suchness (*tathata*) or is-ness. Buddha's whole philosophy comes from this 'seeing,' this experiencing."[6]

For Buddhists, enlightenment is the goal of life. Enlightenment means opening the *prajna*-eye that sees into the realm of Ultimate Reality and landing on the other shore of the ocean of suffering where everything takes its suchness, its purity.

In Taoism a temple is called *kuan*, which means "to view or see." *Kuan* is the house of seeing or viewing. *Kuan* is different from merely looking; it is to see Tao. Enlightened by Tao, we can see deeper reality: "Can you become enlightened and penetrate everywhere without knowledge?"[7] Ultimate wisdom will arrive through the *seeing* of insight. According to the *Tao Teh King*, "Without even looking out of his window, one can grasp the nature of everything. Without going beyond his own nature, one can achieve ultimate wisdom. Therefore the intelligent man knows all he needs to know without going away."[8] Merely looking is not *seeing* in Taoism; *seeing* is the finest way of grasping utmost knowledge and wisdom.

In Korean Buddhism, Wonhyo (617-686) emphasized *kuan* (seeing or visualization) in his discussion of the practices of *Maitreya* (the future Buddha) belief. He is considered a key figure in the organization of an indigenous Buddhism in Korea. *Seeing* as a technical term in Buddhism involves the technique of Buddhist meditation. Through visualization, Wonhyo intended to achieve perfect enlightenment, the summum bonum of Mahayana Buddhism. The procedure of visualization is twofold. It is to visualize "one's own conditions and one's direct recompense of the setting of one's next rebirth and of the body one will then have."[9] In other words, the first is to see oneself in the majestic adornments of a heaven as the setting for rebirth, and the second is to see oneself in the superiority of rebirth there as a bodhisattva. A bodhisattva is one who has attained enlightenment yet delays entering Nirvana in order to help others reach enlightenment.

Although *seeing* was generally referred to as *samadhi*, an advanced technique of concentrated mental absorption, Wonhyo's *seeing* was not the advanced *samadhi* that directly produces wisdom (*prajna*) and requires attaining a substantial degree of serenity. For him, such a prerequisite of the advanced technique would put the practice out of the reach of lay Buddhists and even many monks.[10] His seeing (*kuan*), is distinguished from the other forms of practice (*hang*).[11] Visualization, however, is inseparable from practice. Although diverse forms of practice, including visualization, can be combined for the goal of enlightenment, it is the visualization technique that ensures the most desirable effect. The goals of visualization practice are (1) to relieve the negative *karma* (work) amassed as the result of past sins, (2) to avoid undesirable rebirths in the future, (3) to be reborn in *Tusita* Heaven as a bodhisattva,[12] and (4) to attain the degree of nonrelapse on the bodhisattva path.[13] Wonhyo's *seeing* is the way to resolve our *han* of life and to attain the highest level of path to enlightenment. The purpose of his visualization is not for benefit to self but for the bodhisattva vision of saving others.

SEEING AND TRANSMUTING

Seeing as transmuting is best shown in the new physics. According to Young's two-slit experiments, matter has a dual nature: waves and particles.[14] When light shines through a slit in a card, it acts like particles on a screen; when shining through two slits, it behaves like waves. Matter can be waves or particles; the reality depends on how we observe. That is, how we see influences what we see.

Seeing involves a more holistic grasp of reality than knowing. Knowing is concerned with mental and conscious activity, while seeing is engaged in holistic (including unconscious) activity. True seeing transcends visual perception and reaches a nonsensory mode of *sight*. This seeing is not sight but *in*sight. It can behold with the eyes closed. Insight penetrates the appearance of an object by exposing the artificial bifurcation of subject and object and restores their original unity. It is direct interpenetration between subject and object, deterring the use of any medium of sensory communication. The power of *insight* makes this interpenetration possible.

Seeing recasts what we see. In turn, what we see transmutes the seeing. The new physics states that the observer affects what is observed at a quantum level; that is, the presence of the observer causes matter to act in ways it does not otherwise act. This does not mean that the observer creates reality, but that an observer's way of measuring reality makes a difference. Since we cannot precisely measure reality, how we measure shifts the reality we measure. Probabilities rather than definite states constitute the world. This is confirmed by the Heisenberg Uncertainty Principle. When observing a subatomic particle, we may choose to measure either its position or its momentum. Every particle is constantly moving. Thus, we are unable to measure its position and momentum simultaneously. We can either have precise information about the particle's position, overlooking its momentum; or we can obtain knowledge about the particle's momentum, neglecting its position; or we can have an incomplete and imprecise knowledge about both quantities.[15] The limitation has little to do with the imperfection of our measuring techniques, but is based on a principle limitation inherent in atomic reality.

The idea of such an observer-created reality troubled Einstein: "I cannot imagine that a mouse could drastically change the universe by merely looking at it."[16] But in 1964 John Bell proved that the notion of reality as consisting of separate parts, joined by local connections, is inconsistent with the statistical predictions of quantum theory.[17] In other words, the universe is an inseparable whole. In the interconnected universe, how we see affects what we see—and we are affected by what sees us.

A Greek myth tells us about the frightful Gorgon—three sisters named Stheno, Euryale, and Medusa. The Gorgon was commonly represented as a three-headed monster with snakes for hair and eyes that turned any person looking into them into stone. Medusa was beheaded by Perseus. Pallas, the goddess of wisdom, set the face into her shield to petrify—literally—any enemies who gazed at her. The myth signifies the power of the face at which we gaze. It has a transforming power in our lives.

In atomic physics a scientist cannot play the role of a detached observer but becomes engaged in the subject he or she observes. Seeing this engagement of the observer as the most important feature of quantum theory, John Wheeler suggests changing the word *observer* to *participator*.[18] The universe is a participatory one. In a strict sense, an observer does not exist, but a participator does. A participator cannot escape transmuting and being transmuted by the what he or she sees.

SEEING AND UNDERSTANDING

To resolve *han*, understanding is very important. *Understanding* means "standing under." When we stand under others' *han*, we can see their agony. Understanding comprises rational, intuitive and incarnational dimensions.[19] Rational understanding is intellectual comprehension, with which we analyze others' situations. This aspect of understanding is important for us to discern others' *han*. Intuitive understanding goes beyond our conscious level. It delves into the emotional and instinctive dimension of others' positions, touching the world of the unconsciousness. This aspect of understanding grasps others' conditions more holistically. Others' *han* sinks into our heart. Their *han* becomes flesh to us. This understanding is the understanding of praxis followed by necessary action. In case of oppression, understanding denotes up-standing.

When we are forced to kneel at others' feet, we should not keep on *standing under* them. We should *stand up* to measure up to them. The downtrodden must not be forced to understand (stand under) the oppressors. The oppressors must understand them. The downtrodden must stand tall to be equal with their oppressors. Seeing is the medium that provides the courage and wisdom to do this.

14

Balm for Healing

How to heal *han* is an urgent matter in the church. *Han* accumulates in images, not in words. Outward healing can occur through religious reformation, cultural and social transformation, political revolution, and economic equity. Inward healing, however, transpires only in our seeing the reality of *han* and in envisioning a better world. Genuine and total healing takes place when inward healing converges with outward healing.

Seeing is different from hearing or reading. If someone describes a beautiful scene, we have to listen or read word by word. If we see a color picture, however, we can instantly perceive the scene. While we can analyze and interpret a problem through words, imaging enables us to grasp it in a larger context. Ultimately, we change reality through shifting our images, not through altering words. Thus, a hermeneutics of imagery is suggested here for resolving *han*.

Seeing is complex. There are at least four ways of seeing the reality of *han* in order to overcome the *han* of the Korean-American community and our society as a whole. I will call them the *visual, intellectual, spiritual,* and *soul* dimensions of *seeing*. These types of seeing heal the *han* of people, not through a hermeneutics of text, but through a hermeneutics of imaging.[1]

Teilhard de Chardin was interested in *seeing*. He desired to unify his theological and cosmic visions. He saw these two converging in his vision of God and pined for others to see what he saw: "I want to teach people how to see God everywhere, to see Him in all that is most hidden, most solid and most ultimate in the world. These pages put forward no more than a practical attitude, or, more exactly, perhaps, a way of teaching how to see. . . . Seeing. We might say the whole of life lies in that verb."[2]

Hugh of Saint-Victor (1096?-1141), a Christian theologian of the twelfth century, also valued seeing. He speaks of the soul's three ways of seeing—thinking (*cogitatio*), meditating (*meditatio*), and contemplating (*contemplatio*).[3] These roughly correspond to the visual, intellectual, and spiritual seeings in our hermeneutics of imagery. For Hugh, thinking happens "when the image of some real thing, entering through the senses or rising up out of the memory, is suddenly presented to it"; "meditation is the concentrated and judicious reconsideration of thought that tries to unravel something complicated or scrutinizes something obscure to get at the truth of it"; and "contemplation is the piercing and spontaneous intuition of the soul which embraces every aspect of the objects of understanding."[4] Thus meditation investigates one matter, while contemplation embraces the complete understanding of many things. To a certain degree, "contemplation possesses that for which meditation seeks."[5] Hugh further describes two types of contemplation: contemplation on created things, and contemplation on the Creator. In Hugh's interpretation, Solomon begins at the stage of meditation in the Book of Proverbs, rises to the first type of contemplation in Ecclesiastes, and then betakes himself to the higher level of contemplation in the Song of Songs.[6]

Imaging differs from meditation or contemplation, for it focuses on imagery for healing the wound of *han*. Like prayer, imaging is practiced with a calm mind. Through imaging in four different ways—visual, intellectual, spiritual, and soul-seeing—we surpass our *han*-laden self and reach our deepest self, in which the divine resides. Each of these four ways of seeing or imaging has a number of dimensions that reveal its meaning for us.

VISUAL SEEING: A HERMENEUTICS OF QUESTIONING

Visual seeing is what we perceive. This is different from obtuse seeing, which is mere viewing without understanding.[7] Visual seeing discerns the reality of a landscape. With visual seeing—a perceptive eye—people do not judge others by their appearance only; they see beyond color, race, and gender. Visual seeing is empirical. It is similar to Hugh's thinking, but while Hugh's thinking is the work of the spirit, visual seeing is the work of the senses and reason. It helps us recognize the reality of our surroundings by attending to them with a questioning eye.[8]

Visual seeing uses perception to discern reality. It beholds the *han* of the world through the hermeneutics of questioning, which examines the present order of the society.

Awakening

First, a hermeneutics of questioning helps us visualize our *han*-ridden life. Undergoing the painful experience of our own *han*, we come to perceive the reality of the pervasiveness of *han*. When God nudges us through various occasions, we begin to discern our own *han* in a clearer image.

Clodovis Boff shares a story:

> One day, in the arid region of northeastern Brazil, one of the most famine-stricken parts of the world, I met a bishop going into his house: he was shaking. "Bishop, what's the matter?" I asked. He replied that he had just seen a terrible sight: in front of the cathedral was a woman with three small children and a baby clinging to her neck. He saw that they were fainting from hunger. The baby seemed to be dead. He said: "Give the baby some milk, woman!" "I can't, my lord," she answered. The bishop went on insisting that she should, and she that she could not. Finally, because of his insistence, she opened her blouse. Her breast was bleeding; the baby sucked violently at it. . . . The mother who had given it life was feeding it, like the pelican, with her own blood, her own life. The bishop knelt down in front of the woman, placed his hand on the baby's head, and there and then vowed that as long as such hunger existed, he would feed at least one hungry child each day.[9]

Questioning

Second, the experience of awakening to *han* raises questions in us. We question why we have not awakened to *han* before, what we have contributed to the *han*, and what we can do to resolve it. The direction of these questions is internal.

Its direction is also external. The hermeneutics of questioning guides us to investigate the root causes of *han*, to go beyond the symptoms of *han* to expose its deep-seated structural causes. It discloses connections, often obscure, among personal, communal, social, national, and global dimensions of *han*. The process of questioning never ends.

Righteous Anger

Third, the hermeneutics of questioning makes us angry. The anger we express is healthy and constructive for building a new society. If we do not rage against injustice, our hearts are dead to justice. It is Christian to be angry at inequity, injustice, and inhumanity (Mt 21:12-17). On the other hand, we are not to be swept away by anger, but rather to avoid its destructive effect on us (Eph 4:26). This is the biblical meaning of meekness (*praotes*), the medium between excessive anger and excessive passivity. For people of *han*, it is quite easy to be angry all the time. Such anger can distort our personality and character.[10] However, the absence of indignation in the face of injustice fosters *han*-causing situations.

Bewailing

Fourth, the hermeneutics of questioning helps us express deep sorrow for our *han*. Shivering over the wound of *han*, anger moves us to tears or deep grief. Lamenting or grieving is the cleansing or purifying of *han*, a necessary process moving toward its healing. This society avoïds crying; it has reserved its tears. It needs to learn how to mourn for its violence, its loneliness, and its brokenness. The absence of tears only escalates deeper *han*. In a culture of tearlessness, the hermeneutics of questioning opens the eyes of society so that people of *han* can burst into tears.

There are some kinds of *han* that do not result from unjust people or structures: tragic accidents, natural disasters, unintentional injuring. People with *han* of this type cannot direct their anger toward specific persons or structures, although they sometimes become angry with God. For them, lamenting can help them *transcend* their undirectable *han*. Usually their wailing is deep.

Deconstructing

Fifth, the hermeneutics of questioning defies the present state of affairs. It deconstructs the ideology, authority, expertise, and power of the world. Deconstructing means *detheologizing* the gods of the ego, power, control, individualized religion, and hierarchy (patricide).[11] It remythologizes the world of oppression by dismantling the stories of the oppressors and retelling the stories from the perspective of the *han*-ridden. Since the present system of the world has created our *han*, we revolt against this world of absurdity.

INTELLECTUAL SEEING: A HERMENEUTICS OF CONSTRUCTION

Before the eye of questioning, the reality of *han* and its causes are exposed and deconstructed. It is not enough, however, to deconstruct the reality of *han*. We need to reconstruct a new community order for its healing. This goes beyond the eye of questioning and requires intellectual seeing. Intellectual seeing is reflective, considerate, and inclusive seeing. Although it begins with visual seeing, intellectual seeing can deepen our perception. No one can see at first glance all that there is. The more we are trained to see, the more we understand.[12]

Intellectual seeing opens the eye of *hahn* (oneness, inclusivity, and sublimity). *Hahn* is the divine mind—merciful, tolerant, sublime, and whole. Persons of *hahn*—like Christ—unlock the vision that is grounded in divine grace and divine mercy. Beyond the fragmented vision of the visible world, persons of *hahn* seek the wholeness of reality, including the world of the noumenon.[13]

Intellectual seeing begins with the imagery hermeneutics of construction, which has four dimensions, which may vary according to particular contexts.

Letting Go

The first dimension is opening the *han*fulness of the afflicted. People of *han* can easily retreat into ourselves, shunning a society that is indifferent or hostile. We often blame ourselves and injure our own minds and hearts, attributing our suffering to our own inabilities or the vagaries of fate. This vicious circle of self-blame must be stopped. People of *han* must learn how to care for ourselves, so we can stop damaging ourselves and turn around to heal our deep wounds. One way to care is to let go of our *han*, open our wounded hearts, and treat ourselves with care and understanding.

To let go is to transcend our self-image of victimhood. It is to free us from the self-imprisonment of bitterness.

We also need to let go of our notion of perfect control over life. Letting go is the courage to admit our vulnerability. When we share our vulnerability with the suffering, we are closely connected with them. Letting go of our *han* means sharing our weakness with others.

Furthermore, letting go means to quit individualizing *han*. We tend to blame *han* for our own shortcomings. We need to see that our *han* is correlated with the communal and social structure of *han*. Letting go is to stop assuming private responsibility for our *han*.

Moreover, letting go is to forgive oppressors. Forgiving them does not mean forgetting the past but rather foreseeing their fresh future. We do not forget their responsibility for their wrong, but we pray for and expect their new, accountable life. Forgiveness does not come from our own effort but as God's gift. When we let go of our control over forgiveness, true forgiveness can take place in God's forgiving spirit.

At a genuine human level the afflicted learn to care for our oppressors and for the society, too. We see the pitiful blindness of the oppressors. When we deal with them, we do it with a caring spirit, not with malice. The mind of *hahn* instead of hatred challenges them to change their unjust behavior.

Envisaging

The second dimension begins to see alternatives to the present state. The hermeneutics of construction opens the doors of insight so we can see different paths. An alternative may be to suggest an indispensable goal or inmost vision that reforms interpersonal relationships and social structures. Providing such an alternative vision may be difficult or painful; it can be too heavy and cumbersome for the afflicted. It is not a necessary step for their healing but is a gracious move on the part of the afflicted, for many times the wrongdoers do not perceive reality and have no map to exit from where they are.

Confronting

The third dimension challenges offenders and social systems to change. Facing offenders means helping them see their oppression and reverse it. Such an act allows them to repent their sin and offer recompense for what they have done. Facing systems means to reject and restructure the status quo. When we confront others, we need to do it in the spirit of *hahn*; otherwise, confronting can be interpreted as sheer rejection. And although we do reject the world, world view, and acts of wrongdoers, we must always acknowledge the possibility of their regeneration. The world of divine grace allows for their redemption. In the absence of a pardoning mind, we cannot seek to confront our oppressors; without forgiveness, we can only seek to avoid or destroy them.

Confrontation is a way of pursuing a further relationship between oppressor and oppressed. Creative dialogue is possible only when the offender and the victim are related as I-Thou, not I-It. If the offender is treated as "It," confrontation turns into a destructive conflict. The *han* of the victim must be communicated to the offender through creative dialogue. However difficult it may be, a dialogue between the oppressed and the oppressor must be pursued for the healing of our society. Without confrontation, no true healing can take place.

Transmuting

A fourth dimension in the hermeneutics of construction is to become involved in the change of the oppressors and the oppressive structures of the world. This is an effort to remove the root causes of *han* at the interpersonal and structural levels. Transmutation does not take place at the symptoms level but at the social/global levels. With justice and fairness, we seek to carry out structural reformation. Such reformation does not force our way upon others but offers an alternative that both groups can pursue. True change does not take place in coercion but through the power of inspiration. While participating in the change of *han*-causing groups and structures, people of *han* can experience the burning of their own *han* as energy for constructing a rejuvenated community. Intellectual seeing does not seek to change only the external structures of the society but also the deep structures of the soul by changing the inner image of the oppressors.

People with this vision begin to recognize themselves as symbols of God in the world of *han*. Symbols are different from signs. Signs point to themselves, but symbols point beyond themselves, participating in the reality to which they point.[14]

In the intellectual vision, we can no longer live the life of signs that point to ourselves. We point beyond ourselves to the cross of Jesus, which is the ultimate symbol of God's presence in the *han* of the world. We participate in God's *han* through our *han*, and the transformation of *han* is not our own work, but the work of God in which we participate. If we think that we transform the world, we become signs; but if we acknowledge that God does the transforming, we become divine symbols. Seeing this *han*-ridden world we are not crushed or despairing, because we know we are symbols pointing to God's transformation, not to our own work. Thus we can have true repose in the midst of endless work.

SPIRITUAL SEEING: A HERMENEUTICS OF AFFECTION

The eye of construction opens spiritual sight in the process of transmutation. But intellectual seeing is not sufficient to heal the world of *han*. Deeper image-shifting is necessary for the healing of the world, a seeing that emerges from the heart of affection in the world of *jung*.

Jung involves endearment, emotional attachment, humanity, and predilection. Whether we like it or not, we become *jung*-entangled with the people in our lives. In a world of limited opportunities, we cannot contact everybody but only those around us. Thus, the people we contact every day are extremely significant for the meaning of our life. With them, we come to share our *jung*. Even our oppressors become part of our destiny. *Jung* expresses the thought of the *hahn* mind through endearment and affectionate attachment.

As God's light shines upon us, we begin to see our true self and the world. By the divine light, we transcend our self-denigration and move toward unconditional divine acceptance. This spiritual seeing changes the "I" into the pervasiveness of Christ. As the spiritual vision breaks, we say that "it is no longer I who live, but it is Christ who lives in me" (Gal 2:20). Spiritual seeing uses the imagery hermeneutics of affection, which has three dimensions: listening, affirming, and appreciating.

Listening

The first dimension is listening. We listen to many external voices, which usually results in cacophony. It is, however, rare for us to listen to our own voice from within. The spiritual eye shows us who really we are—our divine origin. Through hearing our inmost voice, we can listen to the divine voice. The deep voice coming out of the inner spirit attests to our yearning for friendship with God. This divine-human dignity comes from the vision of affection.

Listening entails learning to trust our inner voice and thought. The more we make friends with our inner voice, the more comfortably we relate to others. Listening to our inner thought enhances our ability to listen to others. Spiritual seeing is the capacity to listen to the voice of *han* crying from within and from others at a deeper level: "*Eli, Eli, lema sabachthani?*" Spiritual seeing is the "eye" by which we listen to our own and others' inner voices.

The imagery hermeneutics of affection not only hears but also sees the depth and width of the inner voice of *han* within and without. Seeing the interconnectedness of *han* in its root, we develop compassion with other *han*-filled people. When *han* is shared, it slowly opens the eyes of *jung*.

Affirming

The second dimension is affirming our good self-image. Rather than escape from our own self, we accept whatever we have, including our *han*. We do not reject whatever we are, whatever we feel, whatever we have. As God unconditionally accepts us, we accept ourselves. By embracing our being, feeling, suffering, and pain, we transcend our *han* and affirm who we are and who we can become.

We should guard against distorting our self-image due to our *han*. Nor can we yield to the temptation to internalize our oppressors' false projections. We are apt to play by the rules of the oppressors' game, but in spite of inhumane treatment, it is critical for us not to lose our sacred self-image. Sustaining a healthy self-image is a key to the resolution of *han*.

Meantime, we need to avoid projecting demonic images onto our oppressors. Real forgiveness includes not engraving bad images of the wrongdoer on our heart (idolatry). We have to move away from negative images of wrongdoers that exclude the possibility of their repentance. This does not imply that we naively believe in their good nature, but that we believe in their capacity to be good. Unless they change their self-image, they do not change their nature.

Appreciating

The third dimension of the hermeneutics of affection is to recognize our own value. At this stage, we genuinely appreciate our own existence. Too often we, the oppressed, do not appreciate ourselves because of our damaged self-image. As long as we do not appreciate ourselves, we neither have the ability to heal ourselves nor do we know how to appreciate others. Genuine self-appreciation can even lead us to appreciate the intrinsic value of our oppressors. They too are part of God's creation.

In Hinduism and Buddhism the "third eye" is equivalent to the eye of *jung*. Both are illuminated and enlightened eyes. The third eye has been acknowledged for a long time in Asia. D. T. Suzuki articulates the goal of Zen (meditation) as the opening of the third eye:

> Generally, we are blind to this fact that we are in possession of all the necessary faculties that will make us happy and loving toward one another. All the struggles that we see around us come from this ignorance. Zen, therefore, wants us to open a "third eye," as Buddhists call it, to the hitherto undreamed-of region shut away from us through our own ignorance. When the cloud of ignorance disappears, the infinity of heavens is manifested where we see for the first time into the nature of our own being.[15]

Zen Buddhism is the art of introspective seeing. The third eye is the eye of enlightenment, which "liberates us from all the yokes under which we finite beings are usually suffering in this world."[16] It releases us from our futile desires and anxiety.

In Tantric Buddhism (Tibetan Buddhism), which is influenced by Hinduism, *Ajña-chakra* is known as the third eye. *Chakra* or *cakra* (wheel or circle) is the center of refined energy (*prana*) in the human energy body. There are seven *chakras*. *Ajña-chakra* is the sixth *chakra*; its physical correspondence is between the eyebrows. The third eye is the lotus that has two petals radiating from its middle. This lotus is regarded as the seat of consciousness. People who concentrate on this *chakra* destroy all karma from previous lives and liberate themselves in this lifetime.[17]

While the third eye can open through the practice of meditation, the *jung* eye comes through reflection, prayer, or meditation. Looking beyond appearances, both the Buddhist third eye and the *jung* eye work to remove the stumbling blocks of life: karma for the third eye and *han* for the *jung* eye.[18] However, the Buddhist third eye meditates for liberation *from* the self and life, whereas the *jung* eye aims at liberation *into* an authentic self in the divinely abundant life of affection.

Through spiritual seeing we can see our own or others' *han* in a fuller sense. The vision of *jung* takes in all the dimensions of *han*. Beyond what we see in the *han* of the world, this vision discerns the archetypes of *han*, including its rational (conscious) and transrational (unconscious) aspects. The eye of *jung* releases the *han*ful mind from its self-prison to envisage the greatness and limitlessness of divine forgiveness, mercy, and affirmation. *Jung* nudges *han* to transcend its suffering by inviting it to partake in a divine vision for a bounteously affectionate life.

In addition, the eye of *jung* pierces the interconnectedness of the *han* of various ethnic groups. Through the process of reflective affec-

tion, we come to realize our *han* and the *han* of others more holistically. The eye of *jung* grasps that Korean-Americans' *han* and African-
Americans' blues intersect on inner-city streets, and that the *han* of
Korean-American women and the *han* of Hispanic-American women
converge in their patriarchal homes. Using meditation and prayer to
decipher the presence of *han* in our society, the spiritual eye leads us
to see our own power, which enables us to unravel the unconscious
levels of the causes of *han* that collectively oppress ethnic communities. Through the eye of *jung*, we realize that the islands of ethnic *han*
are interconnected by the subcontinent of collective unconscious *han*.
Jung creates the compassion of the *han*-ridden.

Furthermore, the eye of *jung* envisages an indispensable vision for
han-ridden people. Above and beyond the bondage of *han*, the *han*-
ridden see the indispensability of one another for creating a new community. In commiseration, they work together to break through the
density of *han* in their society and free the energy of greatness, tolerance, pardon, affection, endearment, and mercy. With the eye of *jung*,
people not only understand their differences but also appreciate them.

In a multicultural setting, persons of *jung* not only care for others
but also begin to see beauty within them. In a *jung* society a diversity
of people is not a problem but rather a strength; the more diverse voices
we have, the healthier our societal decision will be.

SOUL-SEEING: A HERMENEUTICS OF CELEBRATION

Soul-seeing coincides with a *mut* eye. *Hahn* is the mind of the divine, the cosmic Oneness. Freely traversing through all categorical levels, *hahn* is transdimensional but mainly runs in consciousness. *Jung*
has conscious and unconscious dimensions, but operates primarily
unconsciously. *Mut* (zest, gusto, and the harmonious beauty of asymmetry) is the ecstatic beauty of the harmony between *hahn* and *jung*.
When we live out a *hahn* vision with the heart of *jung*, the elegance of
mut flows out. *Mut* originates in the ecstasy of union with the divine.
In a Korean expression, *shin-nam* means the divine descending to us.
Mut arises with *shin-nam*. When *hahn* as the divine mind is united
with *jung* (endearment), *mut* takes place, transmuting our *han*. The
mut eye is not merely a kind of abstract seeing but the materialization
of a *hahn* vision through the life of *jung*.[19] Embracing the visual, intellectual, and spiritual eyes, the *mut* eye fathoms our own as well as others' condition in the deepest sense.

The terms *spirit* and *soul* are interchangeable, although their origins differ.[20] There are several ways of understanding the terms *spirit*
and *soul*, most frequently because they are defined by the theological,
philosophical, or cultural context. I use *spirit*, however, to describe the

center of our unconsciousness. To express the center of our super-consciousness, I employ the term *soul*. Meister Eckhart distinguishes *deus* (God) from *deitas* (Godhead), which is the dark, unfathomable, ineffable, and unutterable side of the divine. The spirit corresponds to *deus*, whereas the soul corresponds to *deitas*.

Superconsciousness refers to cosmic consciousness. When the self is united with the divine Soul, superconsciousness transpires.[21] It is the state of beauty and integrity of head (intelligence), heart (intuition), and hand (action). In this state our action with attentive conscious-ness surrenders to the universal Spirit.[22] When superconsciousness becomes active in us, we lose sight of our individualistic ego: "Then the superconsciousness or transcendental consciousness arises wherein the ego idea vanishes like mist before the sun."[23] By losing our ego we find our true identity—true self.[24] According to philosopher Ken Wilber, our mind evolves from subconsciousness (prerational) to self-consciousness (rational) to superconsciousness (transrational). He ar-gues that Sigmund Freud and Carl Jung were mistaken in thinking that we move from consciousness to unconsciousness.[25] From a view of developmental psychology, his hypothesis may be correct, but for prac-tical purposes I hold that consciousness and unconsciousness run side by side and that unconsciousness is much deeper and larger than con-sciousness. I use *spiritual* for transrational at an unconscious level, and *soul* for trans-spiritual at a superconscious level.[26]

The deepest seeing is *soul-seeing*, which is submerged under the di-vine Soul. It can be called an imagery hermeneutics of celebration. This hermeneutics involves three aspects: receptivity, praxis, and celebration.

Receptivity

The first dimension of the hermeneutics of celebration is the state of being grasped by an inmost vision. At this stage we cannot grasp the vision, but the vision grasps us. In other words, we come to experience the vision of the divine. In this state we do not need to struggle to re-solve *han*, for God's strength gracefully dissolves it. The grace is the grace of grasping what we cannot grasp. In this state we do not have to attain water from a well through a bucket, a water wheel, or a trough; it comes through a heavy shower from above.[27] We just open our hands and receive healing, peace, and joy of life. This does not mean we do nothing. We change the *han*-ridden world by letting God's gift flow through us. Such work arises from and produces serenity, meaning, and elation.

Praxis

The second dimension is the state of living out the inmost vision. When we have hold of an inmost image within, we naturally strive to live it out one way or another. In this sense praxis is not our own effort but God's gift.

An Asian term, *kyoung* (reverence, seriousness), describes this understanding of praxis. *Kyoung* is awe before God; it embodies God in daily life. To receive the grace-*fulness* of God, we must keep our soul and heart empty.[28] *Kyoung* empties all things, reveres all things, and fills life with sincerity and integrity in humbleness.

In soul-seeing, image is inseparable from praxis, for virtue is constructive inmost imaging. An inmost image guides us to act in the *han*-ridden world. All the moves in accordance with our inmost visions directed toward liberation can be "praxis" in this stage. Through the parable of the Cave in his *Republic*, Socrates exhorted that after finding the reality of the world, the philosopher should go back into the Cave to tell others about it. In the Cave, people are chained to see the shadows of the real world only. For Socrates and Plato, praxis is inseparable from knowledge (*episteimei*), since virtue (*aretei*) is knowledge. Aristotle chose not to return to the Cave. In his philosophy, *theoria* is always superior to praxis. Plato chose to return to the Cave. That is praxis.[29]

Celebration

The third and final dimension is to bless and rejoice in what we are and what we can be. The hermeneutics of celebration opens the eye of the soul, freeing us from all kinds of restrictions, boundaries, and oppression, including that of our own *han*-ridden ego. It is the artistic world of *mut*, where we all acclaim the beauty of the integration between the life of *hahn* and *jung* beyond the existence of *han*. In this state the *han*-ridden learn to celebrate the joy of life in spite of its *han*fulness. Joy is an unmistakable sign of divine presence (Teilhard de Chardin). Joy in a joyous occasion is not full joy; joy in sorrow is full joy. Beauty in the midst of beauty is not full beauty; beauty in ugliness is full beauty. In *mut*, we can say yes to the *han*-ridden life at this stage. In actuality, *han* becomes the energy to move us toward the vision of *hahn* and the heart of *jung* in the creative celebration of *mut*.

The *mut* eye can be called a "fourth eye," for it incorporates an inmost vision. When spiritual seeing reaches union between image and life and between inspiration and practice, a new eye develops; that is, emerging from the unconsciousness of seeing, the third eye tries to grasp reality further, but when the third eye is unable to grasp reality any longer, it is grasped by the divine soul.[30] That is the moment when the fourth eye opens.[31]

Soul-seeing is our soul's window; it opens to the divine sky. Unlike Hugh of Saint-Victor's contemplation, soul-seeing is not piercing and spontaneous intuition; rather, it is the intuition of being pierced. More accurately speaking, it is the state of *intasy*, not *ecstasy*.[32] We are pervaded by the Spirit rather than invading it. Through contemplation and prayerful life, we are carried to the cosmic ocean of super-consciousness.

The world of *mut* is the world of images, not of symbols. As we noted, for Tillich symbols point beyond themselves and participate in the reality to which they point. For him, however, the statement that God is being-itself is not a symbolic statement, for it does not point beyond itself.[33] In his thought, there is the gap between a symbol and its reality. In the *mut* world nothing stands between an image and its reality. While symbols are ways to reality, images are the immediacy of reality, pointing to actuality. A picture of a mountain is reality, whereas the mountain itself is actuality. The picture here is an image.[34] There is nothing that is more real to actuality than an image (super-reality). Even paradigms (Thomas Kuhn) and metaphors (Sallie McFague) end up with images. We cannot perceive any actuality in abstraction, but only in images. Images are more spontaneous and immediate than symbols in their relationship with reality. In this sense, Christ is not the symbol of God, but the image of God. By opening the *mut* eye, we embody the image of God. Soul-seeing lets us be images of God in our relationships with others and with the world. We present the immediate portrait of God in the world, as Jesus did. Jesus as God abides in us. Thus, the divine image in us transmutes the *han* of the world.

The *mut* eye opens our humble, reverent, and prayerful actions for the healing of our own and others' collective unconscious *han* in divine peace. Through the *mut* eye we promulgate inmost visions that can allow us to transcend the deep valley of our collective unconscious *han*. *Han* cannot be resolved by a simple psychotherapy but only by a deeply felt image by which we can truly become alive. As our image is changed, our *han* will disintegrate. *Han* is frozen matter. It can be negatively unraveled and exploded, or it can be positively unraveled and used as fuel to establish the community of God. This *mut* vision is not a conceptional vision but the art of a copious life in the integration of the vision of *hahn* and the heart of *jung*. It is not our production but God's gratuity.

Until we embrace others with soul vision, we cannot fully celebrate others' presence with us. With soul-seeing, we accept, understand, and cherish them wholeheartedly, experiencing joint enhancement. In soul-seeing we come to hope against despair; we express the community of God, where God's grace wipes away the tears of the *han*-ridden through our collective imaging. Soul-seeing melds our *han* with that of others and guides us to cooperate. Thus our *han*-resolving work transpires as divine grace overflowing from the divine Life and filling the deep ravine of *han*.

At the soul level, our seeing naturally becomes our act for the celebration of life, and we can genuinely include others' *han* in our realm
of care. The dichotomy between person and work, being and doing,
seeing and acting disappears in the *mut* eye. Mary and Martha are
working together at this level, celebrating the blessings of life, including *han*.

The concern of the fourth eye is not only to remove the root causes
of *han* but also to transmute the culture that produces other causes of
han. The method of transmutation for the fourth eye is to transvisualize
the archepattern of culture, in which the structure of *han* is a symp-
tom.[35] To change the culture of our society, it is necessary to change the
vision of religion, which is the flower of its culture. The transvaluation
of religion derives from the transvisualization of our seeing. Our
superconsciousness will undo the unconsciousness of the culture of
the spirit, which will, in turn, rectify the mind of consciousness. When
our intellectual seeing becomes sounder, our visual seeing will turn
out to be more whole.

It is necessary for the United States to change its cultural ethos of
individualism. In the name of religious freedom, rugged individualism
has mushroomed in this culture. Based on the notion of an isolated
self, such individualism has brought forth racism, ethnocentrism, sexism, consumerism, and corporate America. Even religion itself has been
shaped by individualism. Subsequently we have an individualized form
of Christianity that interprets sin, faith, justification, and sanctification from an isolated perspective. This is a distortion of the true Christianity that flourished in the early church. The scriptures, Eucharist,
sanctification, salvation, and the ecclesia, which are outcomes of the
early community of faith, cannot be understood in the setting of the
isolated individual self. By reshaping our images, we can make long-
term changes in the religion and culture of this society.

With the fourth eye, we see an inmost vision of the preciousness of
people celebrating their intrinsic indispensability. We care for others
apart from their usefulness or functionality. Our soul eye accepts and
rejoices in their being, doing, and feeling. In the Spirit of God, soul-
seeing unites the ethos of *hahn, jung*, and *mut*—the incarnate community of divine tolerance, acceptance, creativity, endearment, affectionate attachment, affirmation, appreciation, asymmetric beauty, the
creative celebration of life, the peace between justice and affection.

•

We have discussed the four layers of seeing for the healing of *han*.
Each layer has several dimensions. Since we have four eyes to see, we
need to maximize our vision. As I noted earlier, these four layers of
seeing do not have a linear upward movement, but take place simulta-

neously to heal our *han*. We can traverse these visions of the four eyes horizontally to strengthen any weak dimensions. The dimensions of each layer are not strict steps that we must follow but guidelines that might help our journey to wholeness.

One thing we need to keep in mind is that we must stop controlling every aspect of healing our *han*. When we release our control over our life, we come to accept the divine healing that wells up from our imperfection. To accept our weakness is to attain our strength in the divine spirit.

In our quest for healing *han*, our goal is not the healing of *han* itself but union with God. As we are united with God, we cease playing God and let God work in us. In this sense, *han* can lead us to the divine mind (*hahn*), the unshakable compassion of the divine spirit (*jung*), and the graceful serenity of the divine soul (*mut*) in our community and society.

Our journey to union with God through the healing of *han* is similar to the birth of a pearl. When some irritant enters a shellfish and dwells between the shell and the outer layer of flesh, the shellfish encloses the irritant in a sac and secretes layer after layer of smooth nacre (mother of pearl) around it. It deposits these layers of mother of pearl to cope with the pain caused by the irritant. After long years of struggle, a beautiful pearl finally forms. It is interesting to note that pearls can have many different colors—black, brown, red, yellow, or white. And if by chance the pearl grows against the shell wall instead of being completely enveloped by nacre, a blister pearl, a creation of little value, develops.

Han can grow into either the beauty of the soul or its blister. Beyond healing, *han* can be a gateway to the unending affirmation, appreciation and joy of divine life in our society. Because of *han*, this society can mature more beautifully, more richly, and more graciously, accepting the differences of each group, embracing the pain of one another, celebrating the particularity of each racial group, and weaving our hopes together. Through our struggle we can develop our own hues of beauty.

Notes

Introduction

1. Ferdinand Toennies, *Community and Society*, trans. Charles P. Loomis (New York: Harper & Row, 1965).

2. Hereafter, unless I specify otherwise, the term *Korean-Americans* refers to Korean immigrants and their descendants.

3. See Andrew Sung Park, *The Wounded Heart of God* (Nashville: Abingdon Press, 1993).

1   *Han*-Talk

1. Young-Hak Hyun, "Minjung the Suffering Servant and Hope," unpublished paper presented at Union Theological Seminary in New York, 13 April 1982. The term *minjung*, in spite of the extreme difficulty of its definition, can be explained as "people who have been politically oppressed, economically exploited, socially alienated, or culturally despised for a long time."

2. Carl Jung, *Letters*, ed. G. Adler (Princeton: Princeton University Press, 1973), p. 408.

3. Ibid., p. 433.

4. Carl Jung, "Individual Dream Symbolism in Relation to Alchemy," in *Collected Works*, vol. 12, ed. R. M. Fordham and G. Adler (London: Routledge, 1934), p. 41.

5. See Andrew Sung Park, "Theology of *Han*," *Quarterly Review* (Spring 1989), pp. 51-52.

6. Cf. David Kwang-sun Suh, "A Biographical Sketch of an Asian Theological Consultation," in *Minjung Theology*, ed. Commission on Theological Concerns of the Christian Conference of Asia (Singapore: The Christian Conference of Asia, 1981; revised edition: Maryknoll, NY: Orbis Books; London: Zed Press; Singapore: The Christian Conference of Asia, 1983), pp. 27-28.

7. For a further description of these examples, see Andrew Sung Park, *The Wounded Heart of God* (Nashville: Abingdon Press, 1993), chap. 2.

8. *Matthew's Chinese-English Dictionary* (Cambridge: Harvard University Press, 1963), p. 310.

9. Soon-Tae Moon, "What Is Han?," in *Han ui Yi Yah Ki* (*The Story of Han*), ed. David Kwang-sun Suh (Seoul: Borhee, 1988), p. 148. The taste of chewing a dry gall bladder is very bitter.

10. Andrew N. Nelson, *The Modern Reader's Japanese-English Character Dictionary* (Tokyo: Charles E. Tuttle, 1962), p. 400.

11. Kosuke Koyama, "'Building the House by Righteousness': The Ecumenical Horizons of Minjung Theology," in *An Emerging Theology in World Perspective*, ed. Jung Young Lee (Mystic: Twenty-Third Publications, 1988), p. 142.

12. John A. Hutchinson, *Paths of Faith* (New York: McGraw-Hill, 1969), p. 291.

13. See Luat Trong Tran, "Understanding Minjung Theology from the Perspective of the *Han* of Vietnamese *Dan-Chung*, 1989," unpublished paper, School of Theology at Claremont, California, pp. 6-7.

14. Ko Eun, "*Han ui Kuek-Bok ul We-Ha-Yuh*," ("For Overcoming *Han*"), in Kwang-sun Suh, *Han ui Yi Yah Ki* (*The Story of Han*), ed. David Kwang-sun Suh, pp. 33-34.

15. Ibid.

16. Woo-Keun Han, *The History of Korea* (Seoul: The Eul-Yoo Publishing Co., 1970), p. 447.

17. Tyler Dennett, "Roosevelt and the Russo-Japanese War," Ph.D. diss., John Hopkins University, 1924, p. 68.

18. Kyung Bae Min, *The Church History of Korea* (Seoul: The Christian Literature Society, 1972), pp. 174-75.

19. Patrick M. S. Blackett, *Fear, War, and the Bomb* (New York: Whitley House, 1948), pp. 127-42. The second nuclear bomb, dropped on August 9, forced Japan's surrender on August 14, 1945.

20. Bruce Cumings, "The Division of Korea," in *Two Koreas—One Future?*, ed. John Sullivan and Roberta Foss (Lanham, MD: University Press of America, 1987), p. 7.

21. *Foreign Relations of the U.S.*, 1945, vol. 6, Dean Rusk, memo for the record, July 12, 1950, cited in Cumings, "The Division of Korea," p. 7.

22. Dean Rusk, in Cumings, "The Division of Korea," p. 7.

23. Dean Acheson, in ibid., p. 6.

24. *The Korea Times*, 17 January 1992, p. B5.

25. Jin Sook Lee, "The Case of Korean 'Comfort Women,'" *Korea Report* (Spring 1992), p. 18.

26. Ibid., p. 19.

27. *The Korea Times*, 16 January 1992, p. B5.

28. Quoted in Jin Sook Lee, "The Case of Korean 'Comfort Women,'" p. 19.

29. Ibid.

30. *The Korea Times*, 15 January 1992, p. B4.

31. *The Korea Times*, 17 January 1992, p. B20.

32. Jin Sook Lee, "The Case of Korean 'Comfort Women,'" p. 19.

33. "The Korean Christian Church in Japan: Appendix I, Introduction to the Problems in the Korean Community in Japan," A Proposal for Human Rights and Community Development Project (Osaka, Japan: 1981, mimeographed), p. 1.

34. *Time*, 14 November 1983, p. 46.

35. Michael Moore, "Scapegoats Again," *The Progressive* 52 (February 1988), pp. 25-26.

36. Ibid., p. 27.

37. Chung Ha Kim, "The Plea of the Rejected Woman," *The Chosun Daily*, 27 June 1994, p. 3.

38. Ibid.

39. *Korea Times: Monthly English Edition*, 7 September 1994, p. 8.

40. Ibid.

41. Warren W. Lee, *A Dream for South Central: The Autobiography of an Afro-Americanized Korean Christian Minister* (self-published, 1993), p. 13.

42. Ibid., p. 19.

43. Nancy Hill-Holzman and Mathis Chaznov, "Police Credited for Heading Off Spread of Riots," *Los Angeles Times*, 7 May 1992, cited by Sumi K. Cho, "Korean Americans vs. African Americans: Conflict and Construction," in *Reading Rodney King Reading Urban Uprising*, ed. Robert Gooding-Williams (New York: Routledge, 1993), p. 201.

44. Ibid. The LAPD was not only racist but also sexist under police chief Daryl Gates. Many policewomen were raped and harassed by fellow policemen. Some of them bravely accused their assailants and reported the assaults to Chief Gates, but they were fired instead of being vindicated. These policewomen did not know where to go with their problem. Many policewomen work in fear within the police department (ABC-TV "20/20," 4 March 1994).

45. The U.S.–Japan Committee for Racial Justice, *Unmasking Racism at the Intersection of U.S. and Japan Racism: A Handbook for Analysis and Action* (self-published, 1994), p. 16.

46. Mike Davis, "Burning All Illusions in LA," in *Inside the L.A. Riots* (New York: The Institute for Alternative Journalism, 1992), p. 99.

47. Sumi K. Cho, "Korean Americans vs. African Americans: Conflict and Construction," p. 204.

48. Twenty-five Korean-American shopkeepers had been killed by robbers between 1990 and1992 (Eui-Young Yu, "We Saw Our Dreams Burn for No Reason," *San Francisco Examiner*, 24 May 1992, editorial page, cited by Sumi K. Cho, "Korean Americans vs. African Americans: Conflict and Construction," p. 199).

49. Ivan Light and Edna Bonacich, *Immigrant Entrepreneurs* (Berkeley: University of California Press, 1988), pp. 6-7.

50. Michael Parenti, *Inventing Reality: The Politics of the Mass Media* (New York: St. Martin's, 1986), p. 27. For further information on the eight corporations, see "Mass Media" in Chapter 4 below. I have taken the liberty of updating this information supplied by Michael Parenti.

51. The war against Iraq in 1991 can exemplify the media bias by corporations. NBC is owned by General Electric, which manufactured or supplied parts for most major weapons for the war, including the Patriot and Tomahawk cruise missiles, and the AWACS plane. When correspondents and paid consultants on NBC television praised the performance of U.S. weapons, especially that of the Patriot missiles, they were extolling the very hands that feed them (*Convergence* [Summer 1991], pp. 8-10).

52. This and all subsequent biblical quotations are from the NRSV, unless otherwise specified.

2 The *Han* of the Korean-American Community

1. Herbert Hill, "The Racial Practices of Organized Labor—The Age of Gompers and After," in *Employment, Race, and Poverty*, ed. Arthur M. Ross

and Herbert Hill (New York: Harcourt, Brace and World, 1967), pp. 365-402.

2. Richard T. Schaefer, *Racial and Ethnic Groups* (HarperCollins Publishers, 1990), p. 119.

3. Ibid.

4. Ibid., p. 396.

5. Leonard Bloom and Ruth Riemer, *Removal and Return: The Socioeconomic Effects of the War on Japanese Americans* (Berkeley: University of California Press, 1949), chap. 5.

6. *Korea Times*, 23 April 1994, p. A.

7. See Sung-Ryu Shin, *Hawaii Imin Yahksah* (A Brief History of Hawaii Immigration) (Seoul: Korea University Press, 1988), pp. 15-16.

8. Vincent N. Parrillo, *Strangers to These Shores*, 3d ed. (New York: Macmillan, 1990), p. 294.

9. *Social distance* means the degree of closeness or remoteness one desires in interaction with racial group members.

10. Sources are from Emory S. Bogardus, "Comparing Racial Distance in Ethiopia, South Africa, and the United States," *Sociology and Social Research* 52 (January 1968), p. 152; and Carolyn Owen, Howard Eisner, and Thomas McFaul, "A Half-Century of Social Distance Research: National Replication of the Bogardus Studies," *Sociology and Social Research* 66 (October 1981), pp. 89.

11. Won Moo Hurh conducted the predominantly Euro-American sample in 1976, and Richard T. Schaefer did the African-American sample in 1987. Won Moo Hurh, "The 1.5 Generation: A Cornerstone of the Korean-American Ethnic Community," in *Korean Immigrants in the United States*, comp. Kwang C. Kim (Chicago: Dept. of Sociology and Anthropology, Western Illinois University, 1992), p. 21.

12. Partial report of NAPALC reported in *Korea Times*, 23 April 1994, p. A.

13. Timothy Bates and William Bradford, *Financing Black Economic Development* (New York: Academic Press, 1979), p. 12.

14. Mike McNamee, "Color-Blind Credit: How the Banks Can Do Better," *Business Week*, 29 June 1992, p. 99.

15. Zamgba Browne, "Justice Dept. Rules in Favor of Black Bank Loan Applicants," *Amsterdam News*, 10 June 1995, p. 8:1.

16. Bates and Bradford, *Financing Black Economic Development*, p. 13.

17. Its first national study of housing market discrimination was initiated in 1977. Because of loopholes in its survey methodology, the study did not come up with any decisive conclusion. See Billy J. Tidwell, ed., *The State of Black America 1993* (New York: National Urban League, 1993), p. 114.

18. Ibid.

19. McNamee, "Color-Blind Credit," p. 99.

20. U.S. Commission on Civil Rights, *Statement on Metropolitan School Desegregation*, February 1977, pp. 21-34.

21. U.S. Commission on Civil Rights, *The State of Civil Rights, 1979* (1980), pp. 8-9.

22. Associated Press (Washington), "S & L Commits $11 Million to Correct Bias," *Dayton Daily News*, 23 August 1994, p. 8A.

23. Ibid.

24. Ibid.

25. Korean American Inter-Agency Council, "KAIAC Press Packet," 8 March 1993, p. 5.

26. Stephen Kurkjian, "Inner-city Businesses Go without Insurance," *Boston Globe*, 26 June 1995, p. 1:5.

27. Matt Schulz, "Regulators: CRA Strategic Plans Fall Short in Numbers, Detail," *American Banker*, 6 June 1996, p. 11:3.

28. Peter F. Drucker, *Managing for the Future: The 1990s and Beyond* (Dutton: Truman Talley Books, 1992).

29. Blant Hurt, "In Defense of Arkansas," *Wall Street Journal*, 13 April 1994, p. A:12.

30. Bernard Sanders, "Whither American Democracy?" *Los Angeles Times*, 16 January 1994, p. M:5.

31. David Hamilton, "Says a Japanese Maverick: They've Got Some of It Right," *Wall Street Journal*, 8 June 1995, p. A:9; Eisuke Sakakibara, *Beyond Capitalism: The Japanese Model of Market Economics* (Lanham, MD: University Press of America, 1993).

32. Ivan Light and Edna Bonacich, *Immigrant Entrepreneurs: Koreans in Los Angeles* (Berkeley: University of California Press, 1988). I agree with them except on the point that most Korean immigrants to the United States were not laborers in Korea; many were professionals with college degrees.

33. Noam Chomsky, "The Masters of Mankind," *The Nation*, 29 March 1993, p. 412.

34. Ibid.

35. Lori Ioannou, "Capitalizing on Global Surplus Labor," *International Business* (April 1995), pp. 32-42.

36. Chomsky, "The Masters of Mankind," p. 412.

37. Ibid.

38. Ibid., p. 414.

39. Ernest F. Hollings, "Thumbs Down on Mexico Pact," *Christian Science Monitor*, 6 July 1993, p. 20:3.

40. David Pace, "Job Losses Spur New Look at NAFTA," *Atlanta Journal Constitution*, 26 November 1995, p. B:2. On the sixth stop of a twenty-city barnstorming tour (1 December 1995) state and national leaders charged that NAFTA has failed and has cost the United States as many as 350,000 jobs (Chance Conner, "NAFTA Job Losses Decried, *Denver Post*, 2 December 1995, D:1).

41. Hubert M. Blalock, Jr., *Toward a Theory of Minority-Group Relations* (1975).

42. Light and Bonacich, *Immigrant Entrepreneurs*, p. 17.

43. Ibid., pp. 17-18.

44. In 1990 Mr. Chang's Red Apple store was boycotted by the Brooklyn African-American community because a Haitian woman claimed that she was thrown to the floor by Chang's family members. Latasha Harlins was fatally shot in Los Angeles by Korean-American shopkeeper Soon Ja Du over a bottle of orange juice in 1991.

45. U.S. Bureau of the Census, *1980 Census of Population*, vol. 2, Subject Reports, *Asian and Pacific Islander Population in the United States: 1980*, table 45A.

46. Light and Bonacich, *Immigrant Entrepreneurs*, pp. 243-72.

47. Susan Moffat, "Shopkeepers Fight Back," *Los Angeles Times*, 15 May 1992, cited by Sumi K. Cho, "Korean Americans *vs.* African Americans: Conflict and Construction," in *Reading Rodney King Reading Urban Uprising*, ed. Robert Gooding-Williams (New York: Routledge, 1993), p. 200.

48. Peter Kwong, "The First Multicultural Riots," *Inside the L.A. Riots* (Los Angeles: The Institute for Alternative Journalism, 1992), p. 90.

49. Ibid. Cf. Robert Famighetti, ed., *The World Almanac and Book of Facts 1996* (Mahwah, NJ: World Almanac Books, 1996), p. 394.

50. Famighetti, *The World Almanac and Book of Facts 1996*, p. 383.

51. Troy Segal, "The Riots: 'Just As Much about Class As about Race,'" *Business Week*, 18 May 1992, p. 47.

52. Cedric J. Robinson, "Race, Capitalism, and Antidemocracy," in Gooding-Williams, *Reading Rodney King Reading Urban Uprising*, p. 75.

53. Sylvia Nasar, "The 1980's: A Very Good Time for the Very Rich," *The New York Times*, 5 March 1992.

54. Otto Johnson, ed., *Information Please Almanac 1995*, 48th ed. (Boston: Houghton Mifflin Co., 1995), p. 63.

55. Paul Kyusup Lee, "An Approach to the Ministry for Juvenile Delinquency in the Context of the *Koamerican* Immigration," D.Min. dissertation, School of Theology at Claremont, Claremont, CA, 1990, p. 33.

56. Paul Nagano, "The Japanese Americans' Search for Identity, Ethnic Pluralism and a Christian Basis of Permanent Identity," Rel.D. dissertation, School of Theology at Claremont, Claremont, CA, 1970, p. 79.

57. Erik H. Erikson, *Childhood and Society* (New York: W. W. Norton & Co., 1963), p. 261.

58. Ibid., p. 262.

3 The Sin of Korean-American Communities

1. Robert C. Toh, "Blacks Pressing Japanese to Halt Slurs, Prejudice," *Los Angeles Times*, 13 December 1990. Charles Murray and Richard Herrnstein recently argued that the evidence of an African- and Euro-American IQ gap is overwhelming and that intellectuals and policymakers have largely overlooked the role IQ plays in determining wealth and social status (Richard Herrnstein and Charles Murray, *The Bell Curve: Intelligence and Class Structure in American Life* [New York: Free Press, 1994]). They concentrated in their research only on genetic factors.

2. Sandra Scarr, "IQ Correlations in Transracial Adoptive Families," *Intelligence* (October 1993), pp. 541-55.

3. Eui Hang Shin and Hyung Park, "An Analysis of Causes of Schisms in Ethnic Churches: The Case of KA Churches," *Sociological Analysis* 49 (1988), pp. 234-35.

4. Ibid.

5. Mark R. Pogrebin and Eric D. Poole, "South Korean Immigrants and Crime: A Case Study," *Journal of Ethnic Studies* (Fall 1989), p. 60.

6. Hurh and Kim, *Korean Immigrants in America: A Structural Analysis of Ethnic Confinement and Adhesive Adaptation* (Madison, NJ: Fairleigh Dickinson University Press, 1984), p. 124.

7. Rebecca Stafford, Elaine Buchman, and Pamela Dibona, "The Division of Labor among Cohabiting and Married Couples," *Journal of Marriage and the Family* 39, pp. 43-57, cited by Kim and Hurh, *Korean Immigrants in America*, p. 126.

8. Nancy Abelmann and John Lie, *Blue Dreams: Korean Americans and the Los Angeles Riots* (Cambridge: Harvard University Press, 1995), p. 170.

9. Ibid., p. 213.

10. See Alice Yun Chai, "The Struggle of Asian and Asian American Women toward a Total Liberation," *Spirituality and Social Responsibility: Vocational Vision of Women in the United Methodist Tradition*, ed. Rosemary Skinner Keller (Nashville: Abingdon Press, 1993), pp. 249-328.

11. In addition to the committee system, Korean-American United Methodist churches adopted an elder-deacon system for laity.

12. John Dart, "Korean Congregations May Break with Church," *Los Angeles Times*, 21 August 1993, p. B4.

13. David Hilley, "Koreatown Suffering Growing Pains," *Los Angeles Times*, 8 December 1984.

14. Ivan Light and Edna Bonacich, *Immigrant Entrepreneurs* (Berkeley: University of California Press, 1988), p. 355.

15. Ibid.

16. Ibid., pp. 359-60.

17. Ibid., p. 365.

18. Hurh and Kim, *Korean Immigrants in America*, p. 108.

4 A Vision for Society

1. Thomas Kuhn, *The Structure of Scientific Revolutions*, 2d ed. (Chicago: The University of Chicago Press, 1970), p. 12.

2. Sallie McFague, *Models of God: Theology for an Ecological, Nuclear Age* (Philadelphia: Fortress Press, 1987), p. xi.

3. Muzafer Sherif, et al., *Intergroup Conflict and Cooperation: The Robbers' Cave Experiment* (Norman: Institute of Group Relations, University of Oklahoma, 1961), p. 151.

4. Richard T. Schaefer, *Racial and Ethnic Groups*, 4th ed. (New York: HarperCollins Publishers, 1990), pp. 82-83.

5. Sherif, et al., *Intergroup Conflict and Cooperation*, p. 159.

6. Ibid., p. 182.

7. James E. Blake and Jane S. Mouton, "The Inter-group Dynamics of Win-Lose Conflict and Problem-Solving Collaboration in Union-Management Relations," in Muzafer Sherif, *Inter-group Relations and Leadership* (New York: Wiley, 1987), pp. 94-100. Marian R. Yarrow, John D. Campbell, and Leon J. Yarrow, "Acquisition of New Norms: A Study of Racial Desegregation," *Journal of Social Issues* 1 (1958), pp. 8-28.

8. Martin E. Marty poignantly depicts David's story in "Christmas: Power in Weakness," *The Christian Century*, 1 December 1988, p. 1167.

9. His father, Cornish Rogers, was an associate editor of *The Christian Century* and has been a professor at the School of Theology at Claremont since 1985.

10. Ibid.

11. Ibid.

12. Dennis Hunt, "Crips and Bloods 'Bangin' on Wax,' Not on the Street," *Los Angeles Times*, 27 February 1993, p. F1.

13. Vivek Chaudhary, "'Do What We Say, Not What We Used to Do,' LA's Urban Warriors Warn Any Potential British Wannabes," *Guardian*, 31 October 1994, p. 1:20.

14. Robert N. Bellah and Christopher Freeman Adams, "Strong Institutions, Good City," *The Christian Century*, 15-22 June 1994, pp. 604-7.

15. Ibid., p. 605.

16. *Korea Times: Monthly English Edition*, March 1994, p. 2.

17. DongWoo Kim, "Martyr of Love," *Korea Times*, 25 December 1993, p. A3.

18. Yong-Soo Hyun, "On Why Crime Is the Real Enemy in L.A.," *Los Angeles Times*, 7 February 1994, p. B4. Also, Yong-Soo Hyun, "Is It Ethnic Conflicts or Crime?" *Korea Times: Monthly English Edition*, March 1994, p. 6.

19. Ibid.

20. R. D. Bullard, *Dumping in Dixie: Race, Class, and Environmental Quality* (Boulder, CO: Westview Press, 1990).

21. P. Costner and J. Thornton, *Playing with Fire* (Washington, D.C.: Greenpeace, 1990).

22. *The Korea Times*, 30 June 1994, p. A16.

23. "Home Street, USA: Living with Pollution," *Greenpeace Magazine* (October/November/December 1991), pp. 8-13.

24. Robert D. Bullard, "Anatomy of Environmental Racism and the Environmental Justice Movement," in *Confronting Environmental Racism: Voices from the Grassroots*, ed. R. D. Bullard (Boston: South End Press, 1993), p. 29.

25. Associated Press (Washington), "Minorities More Likely to Live near Waste Sites," *Dayton Daily News*, 25 August 1994, p. 6A.

26. Ibid.

27. Sandra Postel, "Denial in the Decisive Decade," in *State of the World 1992*, ed. Lester R. Brown, et al. (New York: W. W. Norton & Co., 1992), p. 4.

28. United Nations Development Program, *Human Development Report 1992* (New York: Oxford University Press, 1992), cited by Sandra Postel, "Carrying Capacity: Earth's Bottom Line," in *State of the World 1994*, ed. Lester Brown, et al. (New York: W. W. Norton & Co. 1994), p. 5.

29. Lester Brown, "Facing Food Insecurity," in Brown, et al., *State of the World 1994*, p. 181.

30. Postel, "Carrying Capacity," p. 5.

31. Earth has constantly harbored life for over four billion years in spite of collisions with comets, changes in solar energy, and land, sea, and air catastrophes. One hundred million years ago Earth was a hothouse with no icecaps at the South and the North poles. The atmosphere was filled with CO_2, creating the greenhouse effect (6-12°C warmer than today). Dinosaurs ranged over Greenland. Eighteen thousand years ago, Earth was frozen, covered by glaciers (5°C cooler than today). Atmospheric CO_2 was about 60 percent of modern levels. For the past ten thousand years, we have enjoyed the relative stability of the latest interglacial age (Miller, *Living in the Environment: Principles, Connections, and Solutions*, 8th ed. [Belmont: Wadsworth Pub. Co., 1995], pp. 291-95).

32. Ibid., p. 298.

33. Raymond C. Van Leeuwen, "Christ's Resurrection and the Creation's Vindication," in *The Environment and the Christian: What Can We Learn from the New Testament*, ed. Calvin Dewitt (Grand Rapids: Baker Book House, 1991), p. 69.

34. Martine Lee and Norman Solomon, *Unreliable Sources* (New York: Lyle Stuart, 1990), pp. 246-47, cited by Michael Parenti, *Inventing Reality: The Politics of News Media* (New York: St. Martin's, 1993), p. 16.

35. Parenti, *Inventing Reality*, p. 11.

36. Ibid., p. 30.

37. E. Baskakov, "Empire of Lies and Deception," *Democratic Journalist* (October 1987), pp. 25-26.

38. Ibid.

39. Marguerite Michaels, "Walter Wants the News to Say a Lot More," *Parade*, 23 March 1980, p. 4, cited by Parenti, *Inventing Reality*, p. 5.

40. Ben Bagdikian, *The Media Monopoly*, 3d ed. (Boston: Beacon Press, 1990), p. 36.

41. Newspaper editors and radio and television program producers can edit or kill any story they choose, yet the final version is contingent upon review by their top executives. Executives regularly convene with editors and producers to retain tabs on story selection. In spite of their veto or overriding rights over their editors, most executives abstain from exerting such power on a daily basis. However, anticipatory self-censorship plays the role of daily censorship. Freedom of the press is circumscribed by the power of money.

42. It was approved on the condition that the influence of cable giant Tele-Communications Incorporation in the combined company should be limited. Bryan Gruley and Eben Shapiro, "Time, FTC Staff Agree on Turner Deal," *The Wall Street Journal*, 18 July 1996, p. A3-4; Farrell Kramer, "Mergers Could Spur Clicking," *Dayton Daily News*, 18 July 1996, p. A3.

43. Kramer, "Mergers Could Spur Clicking," p. A3.

44. Leo Bogart, *Commercial Culture* (New York: Oxford University Press, 1995), p. 308.

45. Frances Moore Lappé and Paul Martin Du Bois, *The Quickening of America* (San Francisco: Jossey-Bass, 1994), pp. 119-20.

46. ACORN is a well-grounded national organization with five hundred chapters and 100,000 members, mostly in low-income communities, developing the power of information and knowledge.

47. Lappé and Du Bois, *The Quickening of America*, p. 121.

48. Ibid.

49. Ibid., pp. 129-30.

50. Leo Bogart, *Commercial Culture* (New York: Oxford University Press, 1995), pp. 320-21. Bogart is a sociologist specializing in mass communications.

51. See Lappé and Du Bois, *The Quickening of America*, p. 120.

52. Bogart, *Commercial Culture*, pp. 320-21.

53. Ibid.

54. Eileen Klineman, "Nine Petaluma Schools Join TV Turn-off," *The Press Democrat* (Santa Rosa, CA), 2 March 1994.

55. Cal Thomas, "Cultural Pollutants," *Dayton Daily News*, 7 June 1995, p. 9A.

56. Lappé and Du Bois, *The Quickening of America*, pp. 121-22.

5   A Vision for the Church

1. Helmer Ringgren, *The Messiah in the Old Testament* (Philadelphia: Fortress Press, 1956), pp. 23ff.

2. Rudolf Otto, *The Kingdom of God and the Son of Man* (London: The Lutterworth Press, 1938), p. 35.

3. Ringgren, *The Messiah in the Old Testament*, pp. 25-38.

4. Arthur L. Moore, *The Parousia in the New Testament* (Leiden: E. J. Brill, 1966), p. 10.

5. Christopher R. North, *The Suffering Servant in Deutero-Isaiah: An Historical and Critical Study* (London: Oxford University Press, 1956), pp. 6-116.

6. Harold H. Rowley, *The Faith of Israel* (London: SCM Press, 1956), p. 197.

7. Except in Ezekiel, there are some sporadic uses of the title as a synonym for *man*.

8. A. Bentzen, *King and Messiah* (London: Lutterworth Press, 1955), p. 75.

9. Moore, *The Parousia in the New Testament*, p. 13.

10. T. W. Manson, "The Son of Man in Daniel, Enoch and the Gospels," in *Bulletin of the John Ryland Library* 32 (1949), pp. 174ff.

11. C. H. Dodd, *According to the Scriptures: The Sub-structure of New Testament Theology* (London: Nisbet, 1952), p. 117.

12. Jürgen Moltmann criticizes process theologians who believe in God's becoming. For him, God is coming.

13. *Minjung* theologians believe that the Son of Man in Daniel refers to the collective concept, the *minjung* (the suffering majority). Byung Mu Ahn, "The Subject of History in the Perspective of Mark," in *Minjung kwa HanKuk Shinhak* (*Minjung and Korean Theology*) (Seoul: HanKuk Shinhak Yonguso, 1982), pp.177-80.

6   A Vision for the Self

1. Robert N. Bellah, et al., *Habits of the Heart: Individualism and Commitment in American Life* (Berkeley: University of California Press, 1985).

2. Ibid., p. viii.

3. Ibid., p. 143.

4. Hebertus G. Hubbeling, "Some Remarks on the Concept of Person in Western Philosophy," in *Concepts of Person in Religion and Thought*, ed. Hans G. Kippenberg, Yme B. Kuiper, and Andy F. Sanders (New York: Mouton de Gruyter, 1990), p. 10.

5. Ibid., p. 10.

6. Paul Ricoeur, *Oneself as Another*, trans. Kathleen Blamey (Chicago: The University of Chicago Press, 1992), pp. 4-5.

7. Ibid.

8. *Categorical imperative* means that our action should be capable of serving as the basis of a universal law.

9. Hubbeling, "Some Remarks on the Concept of Person in Western Philosophy," p. 12.

10. See Nona R. Bolin, "Kierkegaard's Theological Suspension of the Self," in *God the Self and Nothingness: Reflections Eastern and Western*, ed. Robert E. Carter (New York: Paragon House, 1990), pp. 107-20.

11. Sigmund Freud, *New Introductory Lectures on Psycho-analysis*, in *The Standard Edition of the Complete Psychological Works of Sigmund Freud*, vol. 22, ed. James Strachey (London: Hogarth Press, 1953-1966), p. 73.

12. Ibid., p. 74.

13. Ibid., p. 67.

14. George Herbert Mead, *Mind, Self, and Society* (Chicago: University of Chicago Press, 1934).

15. Anselm Strauss, ed., *George Herbert Mead on Social Psychology* (Chicago: University of Chicago Press, 1956), p. 207.

16. Ricoeur, *Oneself as Another*, p. 355.

17. Ibid., pp. 317-55.

18. Frank Johnson, "The Western Concept of Self," in *Culture and Self: Asian and Western Perspectives*, ed. Anthony J. Marsella, George DeVos, and Francis L. K. Hsu (New York: Tavistock Publications, 1985), pp. 128-30.

19. Ibid.

20. Julia Ching, *Confucianism and Christianity: A Comparative Study* (New York: Kodansha International, 1977), p. 97.

21. Lin Yutang, ed., *The Wisdom of Confucius*, trans. Lin Yutang (New York: The Modern Library, 1938), p. 121.

22. Ibid., p. 124.

23. Confucianist Scriptures, "The Book of Filial Piety," in *The Bible of the World*, ed. Robert O. Ballou (New York: The Viking Press, 1939), p. 463.

24. *Nien-pu*, 1:4, Hung-chih 15, cited in Wm. Theodore de Bary, *Learning for One's Self: Essays on the Individual in Neo-Confucian Thought* (New York: Columbia University Press, 1991), p. 131.

25. Confucianist Scriptures, "The Book of Filial Piety," p. 463.

26. *Ihn* and *inn* are pronounced the same. For the sake of distinction, I spell them differently.

27. Tu Wei-ming, *Humanity and Self-Cultivation: Essays in Confucian Thought* (Berkeley: Asian Humanities Press, 1979), pp. 5-6.

28. Ibid., p. 9.

29. Ibid., p. 10.

30. Ibid., p. 12.

31. Ibid.

32. *The Analects of Confucius*, trans. and annotated Arthur Waley (New York: Macmillan, 1939), I.2. Inserts are mine.

33. Sung Bum Yun, *Ethics East and West*, trans. Michael C. Kalton (Seoul: Christian Literature Society, 1973), p. 87.

34. Mencius, *The Chinese Classics*, 5 vols., trans. James Legge (Hong Kong: Hong Kong University, 1960), II:I,i,2.

35. There are exceptional cases. Some abused children are entitled not to love their parents in a normal sense. They need a parental substitute to restore their relationship with their parents.

36. *The Hsiao ching* (*The Classic of Filial Piety*), ed. Paul K. T. Sih, trans. Mary Lelia Makra (New York: St. John's University, 1961), IX.

37. Mencius, *The Chinese Classics*, II:IV,i,27,1. The insert is mine.

38. Ibid., VII,i,45.

39. See Yu-Wei Hsieh, "Filial Piety and Chinese Society," in *The Chinese Mind: Essentials of Chinese Philosophy and Culture*, ed. Charles A. Moore (Honolulu: University of Hawaii Press, 1967), p. 173.

40. In the case of incest, the victim cannot love the parental offender. Incest, a distortion of authentic love, is so narcissistic and cannibalistic that it does not allow space for filial respect and affection. Incest victims suffer the utter destruction of their threefold self and withdraw into isolated selfhood. They desperately need the restoration of the threefold self brought about by making creative space for themselves set apart from their parents. Blind filial piety in the midst of incestuous relations is dangerous and idolatrous. Authentic filiality rectifies such abuse of power and love. To resolve the *han* of incest, victims need to participate in challenging their parents with care and need to be involved in helping other incest victims (see Andrew Sung Park, *The Wounded Heart of God* [Nashville: Abingdon Press, 1993], chap. 9).

41. Tu Wei-ming, "Selfhood and Otherness in Confucian Thought," in Marsella, DeVos, and Hsu, *Culture and Self: Asian and Western Perspectives*, pp. 238-43.

42. Marc S. Mullinax and Hwain Chang Lee, "Does Confucius Yet Live?: Answers from Korean American Churches" (Chicago: American Academy of Religion, 1994), unpublished article, p. 12. Marc S. Mullinax teaches religion at Iona College, and Hwain Chang Lee is a doctoral student at Drew University. Their data are based on the questionnaires they distributed to four hundred Korean-American Christians in the New York metropolitan area. Three hundred twelve (78%) were returned.

43. Ibid., p. 13.

44. Hans Küng and Julia Ching, *Christianity and Chinese Religions* (New York: Doubleday, 1989), p. 82.

45. See Sung Bum Yun, *Ethics East and West: Western Secular, Christian, and Confucian Traditions in Comparative Perspective*, trans. Michael C. Kalton (Seoul: Christian Literature Society, 1977), p. 16, n. 4, the translator's comment.

46. Ibid.

47. De Bary, *Learning for One's Self*, p. 2.

48. *The Analects of Confucius*, VI:28.

49. De Bary, *Learning for One's Self*, pp. 4-5.

50. Ibid., p. 2.

51. Ibid., p. 4.

52. Ibid., p. 4.

53. There is no equivalent term that can translate the Eastern *self* (in Chinese *ko-jen*, in Korean *Gah-inn*) into English. *Gah-inn* consists of two words: *each* and *person*. It means each person, where *each* presupposes the context of a group. The term *individual* derives from Medieval Latin *individualis*, whose meaning is indivisible, indicating its smallest unit as a being. While *Ga-inn* signifies the interdependence of a being, *individualis* refers to the independence of a being.

54. Tu Wei-ming depicts the self as a center of relationship and as a dynamic process of becoming. However, the self is inseparable from parents. "My relationship to my father is vitally important for my own salvation, because if it is ignored, I can no longer face up to the reality of who I am in a holistic sense" ("Selfhood and Otherness in Confucian Thought," p. 247). The self is a continuing part of a family lineage.

7 Sociological Theories

1. Stewart G. Cole and Mildred W. Cole, *Minorities and the American Promise* (New York: Harper and Brothers, 1954), chap. 6, cited in Milton M. Gordon, *Assimilation in American Life: The Role of Race, Religion, and National Origins* (New York: Oxford University Press, 1964), p. 85.

2. Robert E. Park and Ernest W. Burgess, *Introduction to the Science of Sociology* (Chicago: University of Chicago Press, 1991), p. 735.

3. Robert E. Park, *Race and Culture* (Glencoe, IL: Free Press, 1950), p. 150.

4. Gordon, *Assimilation in American Life*, p. 70.

5. Ibid., p. 81.

6. Ibid.

7. Ibid., p. 111. There are some exceptions, of course. Jay Kim, a Korean immigrant, was elected a congressman in southern California in 1992. Hae Chong Kim, a Korean immigrant, was elected a bishop of the United Methodist church in the New York area in the same year. Neither identified himself with the dominant culture by losing his Korean-American identity.

8. Charles B. Keely, "Immigration: Considerations on Trends, Prospects, and Policy," in *Demographic and Social Aspects of Population Growth*, ed. Charles R. Westoff and Robert Parke, Jr. (Washington, D.C.: U.S. Government Printing Office, 1972), p. 184.

9. Richard T. Schaefer, *Racial and Ethnic Groups*, 4th ed. (HarperCollins Publisher, 1990), p. 121.

10. J. Hector St. John Crèvecoeur, *Letters from an American Farmer* (New York: Albert and Charles Boni, 1925; reprinted from the original edition, London, 1782), pp. 54-55, cited by Gordon, *Assimilation in American Life*, p. 116.

11. Frederick Jackson Turner, *The Frontier in American History* (New York: Henry Holt and Co., 1920), pp. 22-23.

12. Israel Zangwill, *The Melting Pot* (New York: Macmillan, 1925), p. 33.

13. William M. Newman, *American Pluralism: A Study of Minority Groups and Social Theory* (New York: Harper & Row, 1973), pp. 66-67.

14. Horace M. Kallen, "Democracy *Versus* the Melting-Pot," *The Nation* (February 18 and 25, 1915).

15. Horace M. Kallen, *Culture and Democracy in the United States* (New York: Boni and Liveright, 1924), p. 116.

16. Horace M. Kallen, *Americanism and Its Makers* (Bureau of Jewish Education, 1944), p. 8.

17. Kallen, *Culture and Democracy in the United States*, pp. 209-10.

18. Kallen, *Americanism and Its Makers*, p. 13.

19. Ruby Jo Reeves Kennedy, "Single or Triple Melting Pot? Intermarriage Trends in New Haven, 1870-1940," *American Journal of Sociology* 49 (January 1944), pp. 331-39; idem, "Single or Triple Melting Pot? Intermarriage Trends in New Haven, 1870-1950," *American Journal of Sociology* 58 (1952), pp. 56-59.

20. Newman, *American Pluralism*, p. 76.

21. Will Herberg, *Protestant-Catholic-Jew* (Garden City, NY: Doubleday, 1955).

22. Ibid., p. 43.

23. Ibid.

24. Newman, *American Pluralism*, pp. 105-7.

8   Current Korean-American Models

1. H. Richard Niebuhr, *Christ and Culture* (New York: Harper & Row, 1951). His five models are Christ against Culture, the Christ of Culture, Christ above Culture, Christ and Culture in Paradox, and Christ the Transformer of Culture. In his last model, he sharply criticizes a perverted culture based on the distortion of human nature and suggests the mission of Christ for the transformation of the culture.

2. Won Moo Hurh and Kwang Chung Kim, "Religious Participation of Korean Immigrants in the United States," in *Korean Immigrants in the United States*, comp. Kwang C. Kim (Chicago, 1992), p. 20.

3. Joseph H. Fichter, *Sociology* (Chicago: University of Chicago Press, 1957), p. 229.

4. Michael Novak, *The Rise of the Unmeltable Ethnics* (New York: Macmillan, 1971).

5. Dr. Lee is professor of systematic theology at Princeton Theological Seminary.

6. Sang Hyun Lee, "Called to Be Pilgrims," in *Korean American Ministry: A Resource Book*, ed. Sang Hyun Lee (Princeton: The Consulting Committee on Korean American Ministry, Presbyterian Church [U.S.A], 1987), p. 97.

7. Ibid., p. 92.

8. Ibid., p. 107.

9   Embodying the Community of God

1. H. Richard Niebuhr, *Christ and Culture* (New York: Harper Torchbooks, 1956), p. 32.

2. Lao Tzu, *Tao Teh King*, interpreted by Archie J. Bahm (New York: F. Ungar, 1958), LXIII, p. 56.

3. I use the term *community of Christ* to describe a concrete, historical community of God where the intense presence of God is noticeable. A Christic community is a community of economic, cultural, and political democracy, growing further toward a community of tolerance, equity, affection, appreciation, gusto, and peace.

4. Karl Popper, *The Open Society and its Enemies*, 2 vols. (Princeton: Princeton University Press, 1966). Popper was professor of logic and sci-

entific method at the University of London and taught at the London School of Economics and Political Science.

10 Koreanness

1. Many Korean scholars transliterate this term *han*. To avoid confusion between the *han* of woundedness and the *han* of greatness, I use *hahn* for the latter. In Korean, they are the same word, although *hahn* is pronounced longer than *han*.

2. Tongshik Ryu, *Hanguk Chonggyo wa Kidoggyo* (*The Christian Faith Encounters the Religions of Korea*) (Seoul: The Christian Literature Society, 1965). *Minsok Chonggyo wa Hanguk Munhwa* (*Folk Religion and Korean Culture*) (Seoul: Hyundae Sasangsa, 1978). *To wa Logos* (*Tao and Logos*) (Seoul: The Korean Christian Publishing Co., 1978). *Hanguk Shinhak ui Kwangmaek* (*The Treasure Vein of Korean Theology*) (Seoul: Chunmangsa, 1982). Ryu is professor emititus of Religion at Yonsei University in Seoul, Korea.

3. Sang Yil Kim, *Han Chulhak* (*Han Philosophy*) (Seoul: Chunmangsa, 1983). *Segye Chulhak kwa Han* (*World Philosophy and Han*) (Seoul: Chunmangsa, 1989). *Fuzy wa Hanguk Munhwa* (*Fuzy and Korean Culture*) (Seoul: Chunja Shinmunsa, 1992). Kim is professor of philosophy at Hanshin University.

4. Charles A. Clark, *Religions of Old Korea* (New York: Fleming H. Revell, 1932), p. 196.

5. Some Korean terms describe its supremacy: *hahn-duh-we* (intense heat), *hahn-chang* (the peak), *hahn-notz* (midday).

6. Ryu, *Hanguk Shinhak ui Kwangmaek* (*The Treasure Vein of Korean Theology*), p. 18. *Chunbugyong* is a scripture of the *Tangun* religion, a sect of *Chundogyo*.

7. Min-Hong Choi, *A Modern History of Korean Philosophy* (Seoul: Seong Moon Sa, 1978), pp. 238-39.

8. Ibid.

9. Min-Hong Choi, *A Modern History of Korean Philosophy*, p. 14. Cf. Kang Nam Oh, "Hanism as a Catalyst for Religious Pluralism in Korea," in *Hanism as Korean Mind*, ed. Sang Yil Kim and Young Chan Ro (Los Angeles: The Eastern Academy of Human Sciences, 1984), p. 83.

10. Lao Tzu, *Tao Teh King*, interpreted by Archie J. Bahm (New York: F. Ungar, 1958), LI, p. 48.

11. Ibid., pp. 78-79.

12. Cf. Sang Yil Kim, "What Is Han?" in Kim and Ro, *Hanism as Korean Mind*, p. 22.

13. Ibid., pp. 23-24.

14. Ibid., p. 29.

15. Ryu, *Hanguk Chonggyo was Kidoggyo* (*The Christian Faith Encounters the Religions of Korea*), p. 218.

16. Chu-Hsi's philosophy played a great role in the intellectual life of the Yi dynasty. Its study reached its peak during the sixteenth century.

17. Choi, *A Modern History of Korean Philosophy*, p. 86. For further study, see Young Chan Ro, "Han Philosophy and Korean Neo-Confucianism," in Kim and Ro, *Hanism as Korean Mind*, pp. 62-74.

18. Suun Choe founded the *Donghak* (Eastern learning or Eastern philosophy) movement in 1860.

19. Yong Choon Kim, *The Chondogyo Concept of Man: An Essence of Korean Thought* (Seoul: Pan Korea Book Corporation, 1978), p. 41.

20. Ibid.

21. Ibid., pp. 75-83.

22. Soon-Woo Choi, "The Beauty of *Jung-da-um*," *Sam-Tuh* (February 1973), pp. 55-57.

23. Jung-Soon Jun, "*Ihn-jung*," *Sam-Tuh* (January 1972), pp. 114-15.

24. So-Wol Kim, "Azalea," in Hee Bo Kim, *Hankuk ui Myongshi* (Seoul: Chongrho Suhjuk, 1988), p. 50. The translation is mine.

25. Sung Bum Yun was president of Seoul Methodist Theological Seminary. He was one of the pioneers who identified *mut* as the Korean mind. See *Kidoggyo wa Hanguk Sasang (Christianity and Korean Thought)* (Seoul: The Christian Literature Society of Korea, 1964). Tongshik Ryu, professor emeritus of religion at Yonsei University, significantly contributed to the development of *mut*. For him, Korean thought can be epitomized in three concepts: *hahn, mut,* and *sarm* (living). See *Hanguk Shinhak ui Kwangmaek (The Treasure Vein of Korean Theology)*, pp. 13-32. Since *sarm* is a universal concept compared with the two others, I exclude it from our discussion.

26. Young Hoon Shin, "Woo-ri Moon-hwa wa E-oot Moon-hwa" (Our Culture and Neighbor Culture), *The Chosun Daily*, 28 October 1995, p. 8.

27. See Ryu, *Hanguk Shinhak ui Kwangmaek (The Treasure Vein of Korean Theology)*, pp. 24-25.

28. Ibid.

29. William Henthorn, *A History of Korea* (New York: The Free Press, 1971), p. 45.

30. See Ryu, *Hanguk Shinhak ui Kwangmaek (The Treasure Vein of Korean Theology)*, pp. 24-25. According to Ryu, play is a dimension of *hahn*.

31. Ibid., pp. 19-25.

11 The Extended Family

1. Otto Johnson, ed., *1995 Information Please Almanac*, 48th ed. (Boston: Houghton Mifflin Co., 1995), p. 435.

2. Johnson, *1995 Information Please Almanac*, p. 841.

3. Moynihan was interviewed on "Adam Smith," a PBS program, on 15 July 1994.

4. Alexis de Tocqueville, *Democracy in America*, trans. George Lawrence, ed. J. P. Mayer (New York: Doubleday, Anchor Books, 1969).

5. Robert N. Bellah, et al., *Habits of the Heart: Individualism and Commitment in American Life* (Berkeley: University of California Press, 1985), p. 112.

6. In Korea, since industrialization, many Korean families working in urban areas and tending toward the Western lifestyle of efficiency and convenience have adopted the nuclear family system.

7. Kwang Chung Kim and Won Moo Hurh, "Family-Kinship System of Asian Immigrants: A Case Study of Korean Immigrants' Extended Conju-

gal Family," in *Korean Immigrants in the United States: A Reader*, comp. Kwang C. Kim (Chicago: Dept. of Sociology and Anthropology, Western Illinois University, 1992), p. 12.

8. Ibid., in *Abstract.*

9. Ibid.

10. Colleen L. Johnson, "Interdependence, Reciprocity and Indebtedness: An Analysis of Japanese Kinship Relations," *Journal of Marriage and the Family* 39 (May 1977), pp. 351-63, cited by Kim and Hurh, "Family-Kinship System of Asian Immigrants," p. 22.

11. This is in contrast to the modified extended family, which is nonhierarchical and without the norm of filial piety. Ibid., pp. 18-23.

12. Eugene Litwak, "Occupational Mobility and Extended Family Cohesion," *American Sociological Review* 25 (1960), pp. 9-21,.

13. Johnson, "Interdependence, Reciprocity and Indebtedness," p. 351.

14. Litwak, "Occupational Mobility and Extended Family Cohension," p. 10.

15. Ibid., p. 9

16. Eugene Litwak, "Geographical Mobility and Extended Family Cohesion," *American Sociological Review* 25 (1960), pp. 385-94.

17. Leonard Felson, "Reach Out for a Sense of Community," *New York Times*, 7 August 1994, p. CN13.

18. Cf. Kim and Hurh, "Family-Kinship System of Asian Immigrants," p. 21.

19. Xiaoying Wang, "Derrida, Husserl, and the Structural Affinity between the 'Text' and the Market," *New Literary History* (Spring 1995), pp. 261-82.

20. Barbara D. Whitehead, "The New Family Values," *UTNE Reader* (May 1993), pp. 61-66.

21. James Kerwin, "Area Kids Adopt 'Grandparents for a Day,'" *Detroit News*, 6 June 1990, p. BWW3.

22. Theresa Tighe, "Youngsters Take a Look at Aging," *St. Louis Post-Dispatch*, 10 April 1995, p. B1.

23. Franklyn Crawford, "The Grand Tour," *USA Today*, 23 June 1989, p. USW10. Korean-American churches usually involve a group *Hyo-do Kwankwang* (a filial piety tour, a travel of retired parents organized by children as an expression of filial piety). Children, of course, pay or subsidize the travel costs. Emphasizing this virtue can be a great endowment to this society.

24. "Seniors Making a Difference in the Lives of Teen Mothers," *Michigan Chronicle*, 5 June 1991, p. A5.

25. Barbara Vobejda, "Single Parents' Double Bind," *Washington Post*, 26 April 1992, p. A3.

26. Steven Mintz and Susan Kellogg, *Domestic Revolutions: A Social History of American Family Life* (New York: The Free Press, 1988), pp. 208-9.

27. Steven Mintz and Susan Kellogg, "Recent Trends in American Family History: Dimensions of Demographic and Cultural Change," *Houston Law Review* 21 (1984), pp. 790-91.

28. Mintz and Kellogg, *Domestic Revolutions*, p. 223.

29. Julia Lawlor, "Busters Have Work Ethic All Their Own," *USA Today*, 20 July 1993, p. B1.

30. Steven Mintz, "New Rules: Postwar Families (1955-Present)," in *American Families: A Research Guide and Historical Handbook*, ed. Joseph M. Hawes and Elizabeth I. Nybakken (New York: Greenwood Press, 1991), p. 190.

31. Mintz and Kellogg, *Domestic Revolutions*, pp. 233-25.

32. "Contract with America—The Family Reinforcement Act," *Inside Politics* (a CNN Television program), 22 December 1994.

33. Mintz and Kellogg, *Domestic Revolutions*, pp. 237, 240-41.

34. Selma Berrol, "Immigrant Working-Class Families," in Hawes and Nybakken, *American Families*, p. 322.

35. C. Caverno, "Family," in *The International Standard Bible Encyclopaedia*, ed. James Orr, 5 vols. (Grand Rapids: Eerdmans, 1960), II:1094-96.

36. Those who were neglected or abused as children by their parents need to resolve the *han* of abuse before trusting in their parents. The process of resolution will be treated in Chapter 14.

37. John A. Hutchison, *Paths of Faith* (New York: McGraw-Hill, 1975), p. 219.

38. Sallie McFague, *Models of God: Theology for an Ecological, Nuclear Age* (Philadelphia: Fortress Press, 1987).

39. Ibid., p. 87.

40. On this point, Christianity needs further dialogue with Asian Confucianism.

12 Theology of Seeing

1. Cornel West, *Race Matters* (Boston: Beacon Press, 1993).

2. Alfons Weiser, *Die Apostelgeschichte* I, II (Gütersloh and Würzburg: ÖTK 5, 1981), p. 84, cited by Gerd Lüdemann, *Early Christianity according to the Traditions in Acts*, trans. John Bowden (Minneapolis: Fortress Press, 1989), p. 41.

3. Ernst Haenchen, *The Acts of the Apostles* (Philadelphia: The Westminster Press, 1971), pp. 173-74.

4. Ibid., p. 173.

5. Lüdemann, *Early Christianity according to the Traditions in Acts*, p. 41.

6. Joachim Jeremias, *Eucharistic Words of Jesus* (London: SCM Press, 1966), pp. 109, 174f.

7. C. F. Evans, *Saint Luke* (Philadelphia: Trinity Press International), pp. 912-13.

8. Jeremias, *Eucharistic Words of Jesus*, p. 120, 120 n.3.

9. Arthur A. Just, Jr., *The Ongoing Feast: Table Fellowship and Eschatology at Emmaus* (Collegeville, MN: The Liturgical Press, 1993), pp. 260-61.

10. Eduard Schweizer, *The Good News According to Luke*, trans. David E. Green (Atlanta: John Knox Press, 1984), p. 373.

11. Cf. Jeremias, *Eucharistic Words of Jesus*, p. 120 n.3.

12. J. E. Alsup, *Post-Resurrection Appearance Stories* (Stuttgart: Colwer-Verlag, 1975), pp. 197-98.

13. A. R. C. Leaney, *The Gospel according to St. Luke* (London: A. & C. Black, 1966), p. 293.

14. Traditionally, there are two ways to know Jesus as the Christ: through the word and through the sacraments. In this Lukan tradition, a shared-meal tradition is emphasized in *seeing* (recognizing) Jesus.

15. Cf. Just, *The Ongoing Feast*, pp. 256-57.

16. Chi-ha Kim, *Chang Il-dam*, cited in Nam Dong Suh, "Towards a Theology of Han," in Yong Bock Kim, *Minjung Theology* (Singapore: The Christian Conference of Asia, CTA, 1981), p. 64. I changed "food" to "rice" in this quotation because Chi-ha Kim used the term for rice in the original.

17. Just, *The Ongoing Feast*, pp. 260-61.

18. See Mark Taylor, *Erring: A Postmodern A/theology* (Chicago: The University of Chicago Press, 1984), p. 103. For Taylor, the disciples recognized Jesus' presence in absence and absence in presence. His radical Christology is "*thoroughly* incarnational—the divine '*is*' the incarnate word." The incarnational Jesus denotes the death of God, the sacrifice of the transcendent Creator. In the theology of *seeing*, this either-or thinking is rejected. Incarnational Christology and the presence of God mutually underpin each other: absence means absence *and* full presence, and presence indicates presence *and* absence.

19. Evans, *Saint Luke*, pp. 469-70.

20. Ibid.

21. On this theme, see, for example, Henri J. M. Nouwen, *The Wounded Healer: Ministry in Contemporary Society* (Garden City, NY: Doubleday, 1972).

22. Christian hope is crucial and *seeing* elicits *hope*. When we see Christ in spite of all our troubles, Christian hope transpires. Without *seeing*, there can be no hope.

13 Seeing Others Well

1. "Pigs in the Eyes of a Pig: Moohahk," *Modern Buddhism* (December 1995), p. 47.

2. My conversation with Professor Young-chan Ro of George Mason University was helpful on this subject.

3. *Se Kwang 450 Songs* (Seoul: Se Kwang Music Publishing Co., 1971), p. 267. We do not know the meaning of "Ari-rang Hill" in this song, but it might mean the hill of love, the consummation of their relationship.

4. D. T. Suzuki, *On Indian Mahayana Buddhism*, ed. Edward Conze (New York: Harper Torchbooks, 1968), p. 235.

5. Ibid., pp. 49-50, 172.

6. Ibid., p. 228.

7. Lao Tzu, *The Tao-Te-King* in *The Bible of the World*, ed. Robert O. Ballou (New York: The Viking Press, 1939), X, p. 474.

8. Lao Tzu, *Tao Teh King*, interpreted by Archie J. Bahm (New York: F. Ungar, 1958), XLVIII, p. 46.

9. Alan Sponberg, "Wonhyo on Maitreya Visualization," in *Maitreya, the Future Buddha*, ed. Alan Sponberg and Helen Hardacre (Cambridge: Cambridge University Press, 1988), p. 101.

10. Ibid.

11. The practice (*hang*) is threefold. First is hearing the name Great Benevolence (i.e., Maitreya, the future Buddha) and repenting with reverent

mind the transgressions formerly committed. Second is hearing the name Benevolent One and respectfully having faith in the virtues of the name. Third is undertaking the practice of the ritual acts (ibid., p. 98).

12. Ibid., pp. 101-2. Buddhist cosmology is divided into three interconnected spheres: the desire realm, the realm of form, and the formless realm. *Tusita* Heaven is only the fourth of six heavens in the desire realm—still very close to the level of human existence. It is surpassed by over twenty higher heavens in the other two realms.

13. Ibid.

14. Fred Alan Wolf, *Taking the Quantum Leap* (San Francisco: Harper & Row, 1981), pp. 3-6. Rushworth M. Kidder, "Living Proof of the Strange Quantum Ways," *Christian Science Monitor*, 15 June 1988, p. B2.

15. Fritjof Capra, *The Tao of Physics*, rev. and updated ed. (New York: Bantam Books, 1984), p. 127.

16. Albert Einstein, quoted in Rushworth Kidder, "Living Proof of the Strange Quantum Ways," *Christian Science Monitor*, 15 June 1988, p. B3.

17. H. P. Stapp, "S-Matrix Interpretation of Quantum Theory," *Physical Review* D3 (15 March 1971), p. 1310.

18. Capra, *The Tao of Physics*, p. 127.

19. Andrew Sung Park, *The Wounded Heart of God* (Nashville: Abingdon Press, 1993), pp. 138-47.

14 Balm for Healing

1. The word *hermeneutics* is a technical term for the science of interpreting a text. I use it here to mean the story-telling method of interpreting a context.

2. Pierre Teilhard de Chardin, *Christianity and Evolution* (New York: Harcourt Brace Jovanovich, 1971), p. 101.

3. Hugh of Saint-Victor, *Hugh of Saint-Victor: Selected Spiritual Writings*, trans. A Religious of C.S.M.V. (New York: Harper & Row, 1962).

4. Ibid., p. 183.

5. Ibid., p. 184.

6. Ibid.

7. People of obtuse seeing judge others only through their appearance and judge things only through phenomena. They see instrumental value in others or things, but overlook their intrinsic value. They see others' suffering, but understand little of their pain. Isaiah sighed for such people: "Keep listening, but do not comprehend; keep looking, but do not understand" (Is 6:9-10).

8. The term *hermeneutics of suspicion* has been used in theology and philosophy. I avoid the term because *suspicion* implies distrust before an initial examination. The term *questioning* implies an investigation of reality without a preconceived suspicion.

9. Leonardo Boff and Clodovis Boff, *Introducing Liberation Theology*, trans. Paul Burns (Maryknoll, NY: Orbis Books, 1987), pp. 1-2.

10. On the distinction between anger and hatred, see Robert M. Brown, *Elie Wiesel: Messenger to All Humanity*, rev. ed. (Notre Dame, IN: University of Notre Dame Press, 1989), pp. 200-3.

11. While deconstructionist theologians eliminate the transcendental God, the hermeneutics of questioning removes the gods of oppressive principalities.

12. The recognition of *han* initiates the healing process. At the same time, this seeing helps us to see our own wrongdoing, which caused *han* in others, and to repent our misconduct. Intellectual seeing heals our own and others' *han* on the one hand and our sins on the other.

13. In contrast to a phenomenon, *noumenon* refers to reality inaccessible to experience.

14. Paul Tillich, *Systematic Theology*, 3 vols. (Chicago: The University of Chicago Press, 1951-63), I: 239.

15. D. T. Suzuki, *Essays in Zen Buddhism* (London: Rider & Company, 1958), p. 13. Cf. C. S. Song, *Third-Eye Theology*, rev. ed. (Maryknoll, NY: Orbis Books, 1979), pp. 26-27.

16. Suzuki, *Essays in Zen Buddhism*, p. 13.

17. Swami Sivananda Radha, *Kundalini Yoga for the West* (Boulder: Shambhala, 1978).

18. The Buddhist understanding of karma (the law of rewards and punishments) can be interpreted as self-causing *han*, for karma views all suffering as punishment for one's own previous work.

19. This is equivalent to Wonhyo's *Kuan-hang* (visualization and practice).

20. *Spirit* is derived from the Latin *spiritus* ("breathing"). *Soul* comes form the Old English *sawl*, related to "sea" (John Ayto, *Dictionary of Word Origins* [New York: Arcade Publishing, 1990], p. 490).

21. The divine Soul is divine unconsciousness, whereas the divine Mind is divine consciousness.

22. Superconsciousness as the state of consummation is comparable with John Wesley's Christian perfection, in which love rules over our heart and action.

23. R. N. Vyas, *From Consciousness to Superconsciousness* (New Delhi: Cosmos Publications, 1984), p. 140.

24. I use *ego* as a negative component to be transcended, whereas *self* is a positive entity to be formed.

25. Ken Wilbur, *Eye to Eye: The Quest for the New Paradigm*, exp. ed. (Boston: Shambhala, 1990), pp. 264-65.

26. Both *spiritual* and *soul* include our consciousness, although they transcend it.

27. Cf. St. Teresa of Avila, *The Complete Works of Saint Teresa of Jesus*, ed. E. Allison Peers (New York: Sheed & Ward, 1946), p. 65. To explain the four degrees of prayer, she uses the metaphors of a water bucket, a windlass, a stream, and heavy rain.

28. Ha-Tae Kim, *Dong-Suh Chul-hahk ui Man-Nam (The Encounter of Eastern and Western Philosophy)* (Seoul: Chong-Rho Suh-Juck, 1985), pp. 137-52.

29. J. Gould, *The Development of Plato's Ethics* (Massachusetts: Cambridge, 1955), pp. 5f.

30. While the third eye envisages what we deeply yearn for, the fourth eye sees what the divine yearns for us.

31. The *mut eye* is comparable with the seventh *chakra*, *sahasrara-chakra*, whose physical correspondent is the brain. This *chakra* signifies cosmic consciousness. The person in the seventh *chakra* experiences superconsciousness, supreme knowledge, and supreme bliss (Swami Sivananda Radha, *Kundalini Yoga for the West* [Boulder, CO: Shambhala, 1978]).

The *mut eye* chiefly operates in superconsciousness along with consciousness and unconsciousness, while the seventh *chakra* concentrates on superconsciousness. They are similar in terms of reaching universal consciousness.

32. *Intasy* is a phenomenon in Korean shamanism. While Tungus shamans fly away to join spirits (*ecstasy*), Korean shamans experience spirits moving into them (*intasy*).

33. Tillich, *Systematic Theology*, I: 238.

34. If images identify themselves with actuality, they turn into idols. But if an image identifies with reality, the image can embody the actuality of the reality.

35. The world of the *mut* eye engages with soul images and arche-patterns. *Archepatterns* (images) are the roots of *archetypes* (symbols). If archetypes are compared to dresses (symbols), arche-patterns can be like their designs (images) (Taegon Kim, *Hankuk Mingahn Shinang Yongu* (*A Study of Folk Religion in Korea*), vol. 6, 2d ed. [Seoul: Jip Moon Dang, 1987], pp. 369-76).

Bibliography

Abelmann, Nancy, and John Lie. *Blue Dreams: Korean Americans and the Los Angeles Riots.* Cambridge: Harvard University Press, 1995.

Ahn, Byung Mu. "The Subject of History in the Perspective of Mark." *Minjung kwa HanKuk Shinhak (Minjung and Korean Theology).* In Korean. Seoul: HanKuk Shinhak Yonguso, 1982.

Alsup, John. E. *Post-Resurrection Appearance Stories.* Stuttgart: Calwer-Verlag, 1975.

Ayto, John. *Dictionary of Word Origins.* New York: Arcade Publishing, 1990.

Bagdikian, Ben. *The Media Monopoly.* 3d edition. Boston: Beacon Press, 1990.

"Bank of America, Security Pacific Continue to Ignore Minorities." *Los Angeles Sentinel,* 16 January 1992.

Barclay, William. *The Gospel of Matthew.* Philadelphia: The Westminster Press, 1975.

de Bary, William Theodore. *Learning for One's Self: Essays on the Individual in Neo-Confucian Thought.* New York: Columbia University Press, 1991.

Baskakov, E. "Empire of Lies and Deception." *Democratic Journalist,* October 1987.

Bates, Timothy, and William Bradford. *Financing Black Economic Development.* New York: Academic Press, 1979.

Bellah, Robert N. *Beyond Belief: Essays on Religion in a Post-Traditional World.* New York: Harper & Row, 1970.

Bellah, Robert N., et al. *Habits of the Heart: Individualism and Commitment in American Life.* Berkeley: University of California Press, 1985.

Bellah, Robert N., and Christopher Freeman Adams. "Strong Institutions, Good City." *The Christian Century,* 15-22 June 1994.

Bentzen, A. *King and Messiah.* London: Lutterworth Press, 1955.

Berrol, Selma. "Immigrant Working-Class Families." *American Families: A Reserach Guide and Historical handbook.* Edited by Joseph M. Hawes and Elizabeth I. Nybakken. New York: Greenwood Press, 1991.

Blackett, Patrick M. S. *Fear, War, and the Bomb.* New York: Whitley House, 1948.

Blalock, Hubert M., Jr. *Toward a Theory of Minority-Group Relations.* New York: Wiley, 1975.

Bloom, Leonard, and Ruth Riemer. *Removal and Return: The Socio-economic Effects of the War on Japanese Americans.* Berkeley: University of California Press, 1949.

Boff, Leonardo, and Clodovis Boff. *Introducing Liberation Theology.* Translated by Paul Burns. Maryknoll, NY: Orbis Books, 1987.

Bogardus, Emory S. "Comparing Racial Distance in Ethiopia, South Africa, and the United States." *Sociology and Social Research* 52 (January 1968).

Bogart, Leo. *Commercial Culture*. New York: Oxford University Press, 1995.

Bolin, Nona R. "Kierkegaard's Theological Suspension of the Self." In *God, the Self, and Nothingness: Reflections Eastern and Western*. Edited by Robert E. Carter. New York: Paragon House, 1990.

Brown, Lester. "Facing Food Insecurity." In *State of the World 1994*, pp. 177-97. Edited by Lester Brown, et al. New York: W. W. Norton & Co., 1994.

Brown, Robert McAfee. *Elie Wiesel: Messenger to All Humanity*. Revised Edition. Notre Dame, IN: University of Notre Dame Press, 1989.

_____. *Unexpected News*. Philadelphia: The Westminster Press, 1984.

Browne, Zamgba. "Justice Dept. Rules in Favor of Black Bank Loan Applicants." *Amsterdam News*, 10 June 1995.

Bullard, Robert D. *Dumping in Dixie: Race, Class, and Environmental Quality*. Boulder, CO: Westview Press, 1990.

_____. "Anatomy of Environmental Racism and the Environmental Justice Movement." In *Confronting Environmental Racism: Voices from the Grassroots*. Edited by R. D. Bullard. Boston: South End Press, 1993.

Bullard, Robert D. "Overcoming Racism in Environmental Decision-making." *Environment*, May 1994.

Canfield, Jack, and Frank Siccone. *101 Ways to Develop Student Self-Esteem and Responsibility*. 2 vols. Boston: Allyn and Bacon, 1993.

Capra, Fritjof. *The Tao of Physics*. Revised and updated edition. New York: Bantam Books, 1984.

Caverno, C. "Family," In *The International Standard Bible Encyclopaedia*. 5 vols. Edited by James Orr. Grand Rapids: Wm. B. Eerdmans, 1960.

Chai, Alice Yun. "The Struggle of Asian and Asian American Women toward a Total Liberation." In *Spirituality and Social Responsibility: Vocational Vision of Women in the United Methodist Tradition*. Edited by Rosemary Skinner Keller. Nashville: Abingdon Press, 1993.

Chang, Jeff. "Race, Class, Conflict and Empowerment." *Amerasia Journal* 19, no. 2 (1993): 87-107.

Chaudhary, Vivek. "'Do What We Say, Not What We Used to Do,' LA's Urban Warriors Warn Any Potential British Wannabes." *Guardian*, 31 October 1994.

Ching, Julia. *Confucianism and Christianity: A Comparative Study*. New York: Kodansha International, 1977.

Cho, Sumi K. "Korean Americans *vs*. African Americans: Conflict and Construction." In *Reading Rodney King Reading Urban Uprising*. Edited by Robert Gooding-Williams. New York: Routledge, 1993.

Chomsky, Noam. "The Masters of Mankind." *The Nation*, 29 March 1993.

Choi, Min-Hong. *A Modern History of Korean Philosophy*. Seoul: Seong Moon Sa, 1978.

Choi, Soon-Woo. "The Beauty of *Jung-da-um*." In Korean. *Sam-Tuh*, February 1973.

The Chosun Daily, In Korean. 5 January 1996.

Clark, Charles A. *Religions of Old Korea*. New York: Fleming H. Revell, 1932.

Cobb, John B., Jr. *Sustainability: Economics, Ecology, and Justice*. Maryknoll, NY: Orbis Books, 1992.

Cole, Stewart G., and Mildred W. Cole. *Minorities and the American Promise*. New York: Harper & Brothers, 1954.

Confucius, *The Analects of Confucius*. Translated and annotated by Arthur Waley. New York: Vintage Books, 1939.

Confucianist Scriptures. "The Book of Filial Piety," In *The Bible of the World*. Edited by Robert O. Ballou. New York: The Viking Press, 1939.

"Contract with America—The Family Reinforcement Act." *Inside Politics*, a CNN Television program, 22 December 1994.

Convergence [a magazine of the Christic Institute], Summer 1991.

Costner, P., and J. Thornton. *Playing with Fire*. Washington, DC: Greenpeace, 1990.

Crawford, Franklyn. "The Grand Tour." *USA Today*, 23 June 1989.

Crèvecoeur, J. Hector St. John. *Letters from an American Farmer*. New York: Albert and Charles Boni, 1925.

Cumings, Bruce. "The Division of Korea." In *Two Koreas—One Future?* Edited by John Sullivan and Roberta Foss. Lanham, MD: University Press of America, 1987.

Cummings, Charles. *Eco-Spirituality: Toward a Reverent Life*. New York: Paulist Press, 1991.

Daly, Herman E., and John B. Cobb, Jr. *For the Common Good: Redirecting the Economy toward Community, the Environment, and a Sustainable Future*. Boston: Beacon Press, 1989.

Dart, John. "Korean Congregations May Break with Church." *Los Angeles Times*, 21 August 1993.

Davis, Mike. "Burning All Illusions in LA." *Inside the L.A. Riots: What Really Happened, and Why It Will Happen Again*. New York: The Institute for Alternative Journalism, 1992.

Dennett, Tyler. "Roosevelt and the Russo-Japanese War." Ph.D. dissertation. Johns Hopkins University, 1924.

Didsbury, Howard F., Jr., ed. *The Years Ahead*. Bethesda, MD: World Future Society, 1993.

Dodd, C. H. *According to the Scriptures: The Sub-structure of New Testament Theology*. London: Nisbet, 1952.

Drucker, Peter F. *Managing for the Future: The 1990s and Beyond*. Dutton: Truman Talley Books, 1992.

Erikson, Erik H. *Childhood and Society*. New York: W. W. Norton & Co., 1963.

Evans, C. F. *Saint Luke*. Philadelphia: Trinity Press International, 1990.

Fadiman, James, and Robert Frager. *Personality and Personal Growth*. New York: Harper & Row, 1976.

Famighetti, Robert, ed. *The World Almanac and Book of Facts 1996*. Mahwah, NJ: World Almanac Books, 1996.

Feagin, Joe R. *Racial and Ethnic Relations*. 2d edition. Englewood Cliffs, NJ: Prentice-Hall, 1984.

Felson, Leonard. "Reach Out for a Sense of Community." *New York Times*, 7 August 1994.

Fichter, Joseph H. *Sociology*. Chicago: University of Chicago Press, 1957.

Freud, Sigmund. *New Introductory Lectures on Psycho-analysis*. In *The*

Standard Edition of the Complete Psychological Works of Sigmund Freud. Edited by James Strachey. Vol. 22. London: Hogarth Press, 1953-66.

Gitlin, Todd. *The Whole World Is Watching.* Berkeley: University of California Press, 1980.

Gooding-Williams, Robert, ed. *Reading Rodney King Reading Urban Uprising.* New York: Routledge, 1993.

Gordon, Milton M. *Assimilation in American Life: The Role of Race, Religion, and National Origins.* New York: Oxford University Press, 1964.

Gould, J. *The Development of Plato's Ethics.* Massachusetts: Cambridge, 1955.

Haenchen, Ernst. *The Acts of the Apostles.* Philadelphia: The Westminster Press, 1971.

Hamilton, David. "Says a Japanese Maverick: They've Got Some of It Right." *Wall Street Journal,* 8 June 1995.

Han, Woo-Keun. *The History of Korea.* Translated by Kyung-shik Lee. Seoul: The Eul-Yoo Publishing Co., 1970.

Happold, F. C. *Mysticism.* New York: Penguin Books, 1963.

Henthorn, William. *A History of Korea.* New York: The Free Press, 1971.

Herberg, Will. *Protestant-Catholic-Jew.* Garden City, NY: Doubleday, 1955.

Herrnstein, Richard, and Charles Murray. *The Bell Curve: Intelligence and Class Structure in American Life.* New York: Free Press, 1994.

Hill, Herbert. "The Racial Practices of Organized Labor—The Age of Gompers and After." In *Employment, Race, and Poverty.* Edited by Arthur M. Ross and Herbert Hill. New York: Harcourt, Brace, and World, 1967.

Hill-Holzman, Nancy, and Mathis Chaznov. "Police Credited for Heading Off Spread of Riots." *Los Angeles Times,* 7 May 1992.

Hilley, David. "Koreatown Suffering Growing Pains." *Los Angeles Times,* 8 December 1984.

Hollings, Ernest F. "Thumbs Down on Mexico Pact." *Christian Science Monitor,* 6 July 1993.

"Home Street, USA: Living with Pollution," *Greenpeace Magazine,* October/November/December 1991.

The Hsiao Ching (The Classic of Filial Piety). Edited by Paul K. T. Sih. Translated by Mary Lelia Makra. New York: St. John's University Press, 1961.

Hsieh, Yu-Wei. "Filial Piety and Chinese Society." In *The Chinese Mind: Essentials of Chinese Philosophy and Culture.* Edited by Charles A. Moore. Honolulu: University of Hawaii Press, 1967.

Hubbeling, Hebertus G. "Some Remarks on the Concept of Person in Western Philosophy." In *Concepts of Person in Religion and Thought.* Edited by Hans G. Kippenberg, Yme B. Kuiper, and Andy F. Sanders. New York: Mouton de Gruyter, 1990.

Hugh of Saint-Victor. *Hugh of Saint-Victor: Selected Spiritual Writings.* Translated by A Religious of C.S.M.V. New York: Harper & Row, Publishers, 1962.

Hunt, Dennis. "Crips and Bloods 'Bangin' on Wax', Not on the Street." *Los Angeles Times,* 27 February 1993.

Hurh, Won Moo, and Kwang Chung Kim. "Religious Participation of Korean Immigrants in the United States." In *Korean Immigrants in the United States*. Compiled by Kwang C. Kim. Chicago: Dept. of Sociology and Anthropology, Western Illinois University, 1992.

_____ . *Korean Immigrants in America: A Structural Analysis of Ethnic Confinement and Adhesive Adaptation*. Madison, NJ: Fairleigh Dickinson University Press, 1984.

Hurh, Won Moo. "The 1.5 Generation: A Cornerstone of the Korean-American Ethnic Community." In *Korean Immigrants in the United States*. Compiled by Kwang C. Kim. Chicago: Dept. of Sociology and Anthropology, Western Illinois University, 1992.

Hurt, Blant. "In Defense of Arkansas." *Wall Street Journal*, 13 April 1994.

Hutchinson, John A. *Paths of Faith*. New York: McGraw-Hill, 1969.

Hyun, Young-Hak. "Minjung the Suffering Servant and Hope." Unpublished paper presented at Union Theological Seminary in New York, 13 April 1982.

Ioannou, Lori. "Capitalizing on Global Surplus Labor." *International Business*, April 1995.

Jefferson's First Inaugural Address (1801). Reprinted in Paul Angle, *By These Words*. New York: Rand McNally, 1954.

Jeremias, Joachim. *Eucharistic Words of Jesus*. London: SCM Press, 1966.

Johnson, Colleen Leahy. "Interdependence, Reciprocity and Indebtedness: An Analysis of Japanese Kinship Relations." *Journal of Marriage and the Family* 39, May 1977.

Johnson, Frank. "The Western Concept of Self." In *Culture and Self: Asian and Western Perspectives*. Edited by Anthony J. Marsella, George DeVos, and Francis L. K. Hsu. New York: Tavistock Publications, 1985.

Johnson, Otto, ed. *1995 Information Please Almanac*. 48th edition. Boston: Houghton Mifflin Co., 1995.

Jun, Jung-Soon. "*Ihn-jung*." In Korean. *Sam-Tuh*, January 1972.

Jung, Carl. *Letters*. Edited by G. Adler. Princeton: Princeton University Press, 1973.

Jung, Carl. "Individual Dream Symbolism in Relation to Alchemy." In *Collected Works*. Vol. 12. Edited by R. M. Fordham and G. Adler. London: Routledge, 1934.

Just Jr., Arthur A. *The Ongoing Feast: Table Fellowship and Eschatology at Emmaus*. Collegeville, MN: The Liturgical Press, 1993.

Kallen, Horace M. *Culture and Democracy in the United States*. New York: Boni and Liveright, 1924.

_____ . *Americanism and Its Makers*. Bureau of Jewish Education, 1944.

Keely, Charles B. "Immigration: Considerations on Trends, Prospects, and Policy." In *Demographic and Social Aspects of Population Growth*. Edited by Charles R. Westoff and Robert Parke, Jr. Washington, DC: U.S. Government Printing Office, 1972.

Kennedy, Ruby Jo Reeves. "Single or Triple Melting Pot? Intermarriage Trends in New Haven, 1870-1940." *American Journal of Sociology* 49, January 1944.

Kerwin, James. "Area Kids Adopt 'Grandparents for a Day.'" *Detroit News*, 6 June 1990.

Kidder, Rushworth M. "Living Proof of the Strange Quantum Ways." *Christian Science Monitor* 15 June 1988.

Kidder, Rushworth. "How Might Quantum Thinking Change Us?" *Christian Science Monitor*, 17 June 1988.

Kim, Chung Ha. "The Plea of the Rejected Woman." In Korean. *The Chosun Daily*, 27 June 1994.

Kim, Ha-Tae. *Dong Suh Chul-hahk ui Man Nam (The Encounter of Eastern and Western Philosophy)*. Seoul: Chong-Rho Suh-Juck, 1985.

Kim, Kwang Chung, and Won Moo Hurh. "Family-Kinship System of Asian Immigrants: A Case Study of Korean Immigrants' Extended Conjugal Family." In *Korean Immigrants in the United States: A Reader*. Compiled by Kwang C. Kim. Chicago: Dept. of Sociology and Anthropology in Western Illinois University, 1992.

Kim, Sang Yil. *Fuzy wa Hanguk Munhwa (Fuzy and Korean Culture)*. In Korean. Seoul: Chunja Shinmunsa, 1992.

Kim, Sang Yil. *Segye Chulhak kwa Han (World Philosophy and Han)*. In Korean. Seoul: Chunmangsa, 1989.

Kim, Sang Yil. "What Is Han?" In *Hanism As Korean Mind*. Edited by Sang Yil Kim and Young Chan Ro. Los Angeles: The Eastern Academy of Human Sciences, 1984.

_____. *Han Chulhak (Han Philosophy)*. In Korean. Seoul: Chunmangsa, 1983.

Kim, So Wol. "Azalea." In *Hankuk ui Myongshi*. Edited by Hee Bo Kim. In Korean. Seoul: Chongrho Suhjuk, 1988.

Kim, Taegon. *Hankuk Mingahn Shinang Yongu (A Study of Folk Religion in Korea)*. In Korean. Vol. 6. 2d edition. Seoul: Jip Moon Dang, 1987.

Kim, Yong Bock, ed. *Minjung Theology*. Singapore: The Christian Conference of Asia, 1981. A revised edition of this book, edited by the Commission on Theological Concerns of the Christian Conference of Asia, was published in 1983 by Orbis Books (Maryknoll, NY), Zed Press (London); and The Christian Conference of Asia (Singapore).

Kim, Yong Choon. *The Chondogyo Concept of Man: An Essence of Korean Thought*. Seoul: Pan Korea Book Corporation, 1978.

Klineman, Eileen. "Nine Petaluma Schools Join TV Turn-off." *The Press Democrat* (Santa Rosa, CA), 2 March 1994.

Ko, Eun. "*Han ui Kuek-Bok ul We-Ha-Yuh*," (*For Overcoming Han*). In *Han ui Yi Yah Ki (The Story of Han)*. Edited by David Kwang-sun Suh. In Korean. Seoul: Borhee, 1988.

The Korea Times, In Korean. 15 January 1992, 16 January 1992, 17 January 1992, 23 April 1994, 30 June 1994

Korea Times: Monthly English Edition, 7 September 1994.

Korean American Inter-Agency Council. "KAIAC Press Packet." Unpublished data, 8 March 1993.

"The Korean Christian Church in Japan: Appendix I, Introduction to the Problems in the Korean Community in Japan." A Proposal for Human Rights and Community Development Project, Osaka, Japan, 1981.

Koyama, Kosuke. "'Building the House by Righteousness': The Ecumenical Horizons of Minjung Theology." In *An Emerging Theology in World Perspective*. Edited by Jung Young Lee. Mystic, CT: Twenty-Third Publications, 1988.

Kuhn, Thomas. *The Structure of Scientific Revolutions.* 2d edition. Chicago: University of Chicago Press, 1970.

Küng, Hans, and Julia Ching. *Christianity and Chinese Religions.* NewYork: Doubleday, 1989.

Kurkjian, Stephen. "Inner-city Businesses Go without Insurance." *Boston Globe*, 26 June 1995.

Kwong, Peter. "The First Multicultural Riots." *Inside the L.A. Riots.* Los Angeles: The Institute for Alternative Journalism, 1992.

Lao Tzu. *The Tao Teh King.* Interpreted by Archie J. Bahm. New York: F. Ungar, 1958.

_____. *The Tao-Te-King.* In *The Bible of the World.* Edited by Robert O. Ballou. New York: The Viking Press, 1939.

Lappé, Frances Moore, and Paul Martin Du Bois. *The Quickening of America.* San Francisco: Jossey-Bass, Inc., 1994.

Lawlor, Julia. "Busters Have Work Ethic All Their Own." *USA Today*, 20 July 1993.

Leaney, A. R. C. *The Gospel according to St. Luke.* London: A. & C. Black, 1966.

Lee, Jin Sook. "The Case of Korean 'Comfort Women.'" *Korea Report* (Spring 1992):18.

Lee, Martine, and Norman Solomon. *Unreliable Sources.* New York: Lyle Stuart, 1990.

Lee, Paul Kyusup. "An Approach to the Ministry for Juvenile Delinquency in the Context of the *Koamerican* Immigration." D.Min. dissertation. Claremont, CA: School of Theology at Claremont, 1990.

Lee, Sang Hyun. "Called to Be Pilgrims." In *Korean American Ministry: A Resource Book.* Edited by Sang Hyun Lee. Princeton: The Consulting Committee on Korean American Ministry, Presbyterian Church (U.S.A), 1987.

Lee, Warren W. *A Dream for South Central: The Autobiography of an Afro-Americanized Korean Christian Minister.* A self-published book, 1993.

Light, Ivan and Edna Bonacich. *Immigrant Entrepreneurs.* Berkeley: University of California Press, 1988.

Litwak, Eugene. "Occupational Mobility and Extended Family Cohesion." *American Sociological Review* 25, 1960.

Loeb, Penny. "The New Redlining." *U.S. News & World Report*, 17 April 1995.

Lüdemann, Gerd. *Early Christianity according to the Traditions in Acts.* Translated by John Bowden. Minneapolis: Fortress Press, 1989.

Manson, T. W. "The Son of Man in Daniel, Enoch and the Gospels." *Bulletin of the John Ryland Library* 32, 1949.

Marty, Martin E. "Christmas: Power in Weakness." *The Christian Century*, 1 December 1988.

Marx, Karl, and Frederick Engels. *The German Ideology: Part One.* Edited by C. J. Arthur. New York: International Publishers, 1970.

Matthew's Chinese-English Dictionary. Cambridge: Harvard University Press, 1963.

McFague, Sallie. *Models of God: Theology for an Ecological, Nuclear Age.* Philadelphia: Fortress Press, 1987.

McNamee, Mike. "Color-Blind Credit: How the Banks Can Do Better." *Business Week*, 29 June 1992.

Mead, George Herbert. *Mind, Self, and Society.* Chicago: University of Chicago Press, 1934.

Meier, John P. *The Vision of Matthew: Christ, Church, and Morality in the First Gospel.* New York: Paulist Press, 1979.

Mencius. *The Chinese Classics.* 5 vols. Translated by James Legge. Hong Kong: Hong Kong University, 1960.

Meyer, Richard, and Barry Bearak. "Poverty: Toll Grows amid Aid Cutbacks." *Los Angeles Times,* 28 July 1985.

Michaels, Marguerite. "Walter Wants the News to Say a Lot More." *Parade,* 23 March 1980.

Miller, G. Tyler. *Living in the Environment: Principles, Connections, and Solutions.* 8th edition. Belmont: Wadsworth Pub. Co., 1995.

Min, Kyung Bae. *The Church History of Korea.* In Korean. Seoul: The Christian Literature Society, 1972.

"Minorities More Likely to Live near Waste Sites." *Dayton Daily News,* 25 August 1994.

Mintz, Steven. "New Rules: Postwar Families (1955-Present)." In *American Families: A Research Guide and Historical Handbook.* Edited by Joseph M. Hawes and Elizabeth I. Nybakken. New York: Greenwood Press, 1991.

Mintz, Steven, and Susan Kellogg. *Domestic Revolutions: A Social History of American Family Life.* New York: The Free Press, 1988.

_____. "Recent Trends in American Family History: Dimensions of Demographic and Cultural Change." *Houston Law Review* 21 (1984): 790-91.

Moffat, Susan. "Shopkeepers Fight Back." *Los Angeles Times,* 15 May 1992.

Moore, Arthur L. *The Parousia in the New Testament.* Leiden: E. J. Brill, 1966.

Moore, Michael. "Scapegoats Again." *The Progressive* 52, February 1988.

Mullinax, Marc S., and Hwain Chang Lee. "Does Confucius Yet Live?: Answers from Korean American Churches." Chicago: American Academy of Religion, 1994. An unpublished article.

Nagano, Paul. "The Japanese Americans' Search for Identity, Ethnic Pluralism and a Christian Basis of Permanent Identity." Rel.D. dissertation. Claremont, CA: School of Theology at Claremont, 1970.

Nasar, Sylvia. "The 1980's: A Very Good Time for the Very Rich." *The New York Times,* 5 March 1992.

Nelson, Andrew N. *The Modern Reader's Japanese-English Character Dictionary.* Tokyo: Charles E. Tuttle, 1962.

Newby, I. A. *Challenge to the Court.* Louisiana: Louisiana State University, 1967.

Newman, William M. *American Pluralism: A Study of Minority Groups and Social Theory.* New York: Harper & Row, 1973.

Niebuhr, H. Richard. *Christ and Culture.* New York: Harper & Row, 1951.

North, Christopher R. *The Suffering Servant in Deutero-Isaiah: An Historical and Critical Study.* London: Oxford University Press, 1956.

Novak, Michael. *The Rise of the Unmeltable Ethnics.* New York: Macmillan, 1971.

Oh, Kang Nam. "Hanism as a Catalyst for Religious Pluralism in Korea." In *Hanism as Korean Mind.* Edited by Sang Yil Kim and Young Chan Ro.

Los Angeles: The Eastern Academy of Human Sciences, 1984.

Otto, Rudolf. *The Kingdom of God and the Son of Man*. London: Lutterworth Press, 1938.

Owen, Carolyn, Howard Eisner, and Thomas McFaul. "A Half-Century of Social Distance Research: National Replication of the Bogardus Studies." *Sociology and Social Research* 66 October 1981.

Parenti, Michael. *Democracy for the Few*. 5th edition. New York: St. Martin's Press, 1988.

_____ . *Inventing Reality: The Politics of the Mass Media*. New York: St. Martin's, 1987.

Park, Andrew Sung. "Theology of Han." *Quarterly Review*, Spring 1989.

_____ . *The Wounded Heart of God*. Nashville: Abingdon Press, 1993.

Park, Robert E., and Ernest W. Burgess. *Introduction to the Science of Sociology*. Chicago: University of Chicago Press, 1991.

Park, Robert E. *Race and Culture*. Glencoe, IL: Free Press, 1950.

Parrillo, Vincent N. *Strangers to These Shores*. 3d edition. New York: Macmillan, 1990.

"Pigs in the Eyes of a Pig: Moohahk." *Modern Buddhism*. In Korean. December 1995.

Pogrebin, Mark R., and Eric D. Poole. "South Korean Immigrants and Crime: A Case Study." *Journal of Ethnic Studies*, Fall 1989.

Popper, Karl. *The Open Society and Its Enemies*. 2 vols. Princeton: Princeton University Press, 1966.

Postel, Sandra. "Denial in the Decisive Decade." In *State of the World 1992*. Edited by Lester R. Brown, et al. New York: W. W. Norton & Co., 1992.

_____ . "Carrying Capacity: Earth's Bottom Line." In *State of the World 1994*. Edited by Lester R. Brown, et al. New York: W. W. Norton & Co., 1994.

Radha, Swami Sivananda. *Kundalini Yoga for the West*. Boulder, CO: Shambhala, 1978.

Rice, Yoshie N. "The Maternal Role in Japan: Cultural Values and Socioeconomic Conditions." Ed.D. dissertation, Harvard University, 1994.

Ricoeur, Paul. *Oneself As Another*. Translated by Kathleen Blamey. Chicago: University of Chicago Press, 1992.

Ringgren, Helmer. *The Messiah in the Old Testament*. Philadelphia: Fortress Press, 1956.

Robinson, Cedric J. "Race, Capitalism, and Antidemocracy." In *Reading Rodney King Reading Urban Uprising*. Edited by Robert Gooding-Williams. New York: Routledge, 1993.

Robinson, John A. T. *Jesus and His Coming: The Emergence of a Doctrine*. Nashville: Abingdon Press, 1957.

Rorty, Richard. *Contingency, Irony, and Solidarity*. Cambridge: Cambridge University Press, 1989.

Rowley, Harold H. *The Faith of Israel*. London: SCM Press, 1956.

Rue, David S. "Depression and Suicidal Behavior among Asian 'Whiz Kids.'" In *Korean Immigrants in the United States*. Compiled by Kwang C. Kim. Chicago: Dept. of Sociology and Anthropology in Western Illinois University, 1992.

Ryu, Tongshik. *Hanguk Shinhak ui Kwangmaek (The Treasure Vein of Korean Theology)*. In Korean. Seoul: Chunmangsa, 1982.

_____. *Minsok Chonggyo wa Hanguk Munhwa (Folk Religion and Korean Culture)*. In Korean. Seoul: Hyundae Sasangsa, 1978.

_____. *To wa Logos (Tao and Logos)*. In Korean. Seoul: The Korean Christian Publishing Co., 1978.

_____. *Hanguk Chonggyo wa Kidoggyo (The Christian Faith Encounters the Religions of Korea)*. In Korean. Seoul: The Christian Literature Society, 1965.

"S & L Commits $11 Million to Correct Bias." *Dayton Daily News*, 23 August 1994.

Sakakibara, Eisuke, *Beyond Capitalism: The Japanese Model of Market Economics*. Lanham, MD: University Press of America, 1993.

Sanders, Bernard. "Whither American Democracy?" *Los Angeles Times*, 16 January 1994.

Sauerzopf, Marty. "Minorities Turned Down at Twice the Rate for Whites." *Los Angeles Sentinel*, 14 November 1991.

Schaefer, Richard T. *Racial and Ethnic Groups*. 4th edition. HarperCollins Publishers, 1990.

Schweizer, Eduard. *The Good News according to Luke*. Translated by David E. Green. Atlanta: John Knox Press, 1984.

Segal, Troy. "The Riots: 'Just As Much about Class As about Race.'" *Business Week*, 18 May 1992.

"Seniors Making a Difference in the Lives of Teen Mothers," *Michigan Chronicle*, 5 June 1991.

Sherif, Muzafer, et al. *Intergroup Conflict and Cooperation: The Robbers Cave Experiment*. Norman, OK: Institute of Group Relations, University of Oklahoma, 1961.

Sherrill, Robert. "Buying His Way to a Media Empire." *The Nation*, 29 May 1995.

Shin, Eui Hang, and Park Hyung. "An Analysis of Causes of Schisms in Ethnic Churches: The Case of KA Churches." *Sociological Analysis* 49, 1988.

Shin, Sung-Ryu. *Hawaii Imin Yahksah (A Brief History of Hawaii Immigration)*. In Korean. Seoul: Korea University Press, 1988.

Shin, Young Hoon. "Woo-ri Moon-hwa wa E-oot Moon-hwa" ("Our Culture and Neighbor Culture"). *The Chosun Daily*, In Korean. 28 October 1995.

Sifry, Micah L. "Leaning on the F.C.C." *The Nation*, 29 May 1995.

Smith, Archie, Jr. *The Relational Self: Ethics and Therapy from a Black Church Perspective*. Nashville: Abingdon Press, 1982.

Song, C. S. *Third-Eye Theology*. Revised edition. Maryknoll, NY: Orbis Books, 1979.

Sponberg, Alan. "Wonhyo on Maitreya Visualization." In *Maitreya, the Future Buddha*. Edited by Alan Sponberg and Helen Hardacre. Cambridge: Cambridge University Press, 1988.

Stapp, H. P. "S-Matrix Interpretation of Quantum Theory." *Physical Review*, 15 March 1971, D3.

Strauss, Anselm, ed. *George Herbert Mead on Social Psychology*. Chicago: University of Chicago Press, 1956.

Suh, David Kwang-sun. "A Biographical Sketch of an Asian Theological Consultation." In *Minjung Theology.* Edited by The Christian Conference of Asia, 1981. Revised edition edited by the Commission on Theological Concerns of the Christian Conference of Asia. Maryknoll, NY: Orbis Books; London: Zed Press; Singapore: The Christian Conference of Asia, 1983.

_____ , ed. *Han ui Yi Yah Ki (The Story of Han).* In Korean. Seoul: Borhee, 1988.

Suzuki, D. T. *On Indian Mahayana Buddhism.* Edited by Edward Conze. New York: Harper Torchbooks, 1968.

_____ . *Essays in Zen Buddhism.* London: Rider & Company, 1958.

Taylor, Charles. *Sources of the Self: The Making of the Modern Identity.* Cambridge: Harvard University Press, 1989.

Taylor, Mark. *Erring: A Postmodern A/theology.* Chicago: University of Chicago Press, 1984.

Teilhard de Chardin, Pierre. *Christianity and Evolution.* New York: Harcourt, Brace, Jovanovich, 1971.

Teresa of Avila. *The Interior Castle.* Translated by Kieran Kavanaugh and Otilio Rodriguez. New York: Paulist Press, 1979.

_____ . *The Complete Works of Saint Teresa of Jesus.* Edited by E. Allison Peers. New York: Sheed & Ward, 1946.

Tidwell, Billy J., ed. *The State of Black America 1993.* New York: National Urban League, Inc., 1993.

Tighe, Theresa. "Youngsters Take a Look at Aging." *St Louis Post-Dispatch*, 10 April 1995.

Tillich, Paul. *Systematic Theology.* 3 vols. Chicago: University of Chicago Press, 1951-63.

Time, 14 November 1983.

de Tocqueville, Alexis. *Democracy in America.* Translated by George Lawrence. Edited by J. P. Mayer. New York: Doubleday, Anchor Books, 1969.

Toennies, Ferdinand. *Community and Society.* Translated by Charles P. Loomis. New York: Harper & Row, 1965.

Toh, Robert C. "Blacks Pressing Japanese to Halt Slurs, Prejudice." *Los Angeles Times*, 13 December 1990.

Tracy, David. *The Analogical Imagination: Christian Theology and the Culture of Pluralism.* New York: Crossroad, 1981.

Trumbull, H. Clay. *Seeing and Being or Perception and Character.* Philadelphia: John D. Wattles, 1889.

Tu Wei-ming. *Humanity and Self-Cultivation: Essays in Confucian Thought.* Berkeley: Asian Humanities Press, 1979.

_____ . "Selfhood and Otherness in Confucian Thought." In *Culture and Self: Asian and Western Perspectives.* Edited by Anthony Marsella, George DeVos, and Francis L. K. Hsu. New York: Tavistock Publications, 1985.

Turn, Frederick Jackson. *The Frontier in American History.* New York: Henry Holt and Co., 1920.

United Nations Development Program. *Human Development Report 1992.* New York: Oxford University Press, 1992.

U.S. Bureau of the Census. *1980 Census of Population.* Vol. 2, Subject Reports, *Asian and Pacific Islander Population in the United States: 1980.*

U.S. Commission on Civil Rights. *Statement on Metropolitan School Desegregation.* February 1977.

U.S. Commission on Civil Rights. *The State of Civil Rights, 1979.* 1980.

The U.S.–Japan Committee for Racial Justice. *Unmasking Racism at the Intersection of U.S. and Japan Racism: A Handbook for Analysis and Action.* A self-published booklet, 1994.

Van Leeuwen, Raymond C. "Christ's Resurrection and the Creation's Vindication." In *The Environment and the Christian: What Can We Learn from the New Testament.* Edited by Calvin Dewitt. Grand Rapids: Baker Book House, 1991.

Veroff, Joseph, Elizabeth Douvan, and Richard A. Kulka. *Inner American: A Self-Portrait from 1957 to 1976.* New York: Basic Books, 1981.

Vyas, R. N. *From Consciousness to Superconsciousness.* New Delhi: Cosmos Publications, 1984.

Wang, Xiaoying. "Derrida, Husserl, and the Structural Affinity between the 'Text' and the Market." *New Literary History,* Spring 1995.

Weiser, Alfons. *Die Apostelgeschichte* I, II (Gütersloh and Würzburg: ÖTK 5, 1981). Cited by Lüdemann, *Early Christianity according to the Traditions in Acts.*

West, Cornel. *Race Matters.* Boston: Beacon Press, 1993.

Whitehead, Barbara D. "The New Family Values." *UTNE Reader,* May 1993.

Wilbur, Ken. *Eye to Eye: The Quest for the New Paradigm.* Expanded edition. Boston: Shambhala, 1990.

Wolf, Fred Alan. *Taking the Quantum Leap.* San Francisco: Harper & Row, 1981.

Writht, James. "Gong, Meek Takes on GOP's Gingrich." *Afro-America,* 28 January 1995.

Yarrow, Marian R., John D. Campbell, and Leon J. Yarrow. "Acquisition of New Norms: A Study of Racial Desegregation." *Journal of Social Issues* 1, 1958.

Yu, Eui-Young. "We Saw Our Dreams Burn for No Reason." *San Francisco Examiner,* 24 May 1992.

Yun, Sung Bum. *Ethics East and West: Western Secular, Christian, and Confucian Traditions in Comparative Perspective.* Translated by Michael C. Kalton. Seoul: Christian Literature Society, 1977.

_____. *Kidoggyo wa Hanguk Sasang (Christianity and Korean Thought).* In Korean. Seoul: The Christian Literature Society of Korea, 1964.

Yutang, Lin, ed. *The Wisdom of Confucius.* Translated by Lin Yutang. New York: The Modern Library, 1938.

Zangwill, Israel. *The Melting Pot.* New York: Macmillan, 1925.

Index

African-Americans: discrimination
against Asian-Americans by, 20;
Korean employment of, 33–34,
36; Korean racism toward, 41–43,
139; media racism and, 23–24,
41; nihilism among, 129;
redlining and, 29–31; shared *han*
of, 154

Amalgamation model: defined, 2;
drawbacks of, 92, 102; history of,
87–88; vision of, 106

AM/FM (Affiliated Media Foundation Movement), 64

Anger, 147–48

Assimilation model: defined, 2, 85–
87; drawbacks of, 92, 102; for
Korean-Americans, 95–96; vision
of, 106

Association of Community Organizations for Reform Now (ACORN),
64

Augustine, 4

Bellah, Robert, 56, 72, 118, 123

Bentley, Helen, 17–18

Bible, the: coming of the messiah in,
68–71; real life interpretations of,
66; significance of seeing in, 6,
129–37

Bonacich, Edna, 33, 36, 45–46

Boston, Mass., redlining in, 32

Buddhism: *hahn* mind and, 109;
mut and, 113; seeing in, 141–42;
third eye in, 153

Bush, George, 34, 62

Capitalism: destructive aspects of,
33–34, 38, 59; individualism and,
72, 121

Chang, Won H., 43

Chardin, Teilhard de, 145

Che-myun, 46

Chicago, Ill.: environmental racism

in, 60; immigrant churchgoers in,
94; immigrant family structures
in, 119–20; Korean-owned
businesses in, 36; racially-
motivated violence in, 22;
redlining in, 29–30

Chin, Vincent, 16–18

Choi, Min-Hong, 107, 108

Christianity: cultural change and,
99, 101–6, 107, 115; ethnic
communities and, 26; filial piety
and, 79–80, 125–26; healing and,
24–25, 136–37; indispensability
and, 56–57; individualism and,
158; Japanese converts to, 91;
Koreanness and, 114–15; media
exposure of, 65–66; *parousia* and,
5, 67–71; Pentecost and, 130–32;
racism within, 20–21; strangers
and, 132–35. *See also* Churches

Chu Hsi, 77, 109

Chundogyo, 109–10

Churches: culture and, 93–98;
discrimination in, 21; family
renewal by, 125–26; focus on *han*
by, 4, 145; racially divided
societies and, ix, 43, 93, 99, 136;
redlining and, 32; sexism in, 44,
101–2; transmutation of, 101–2

Class divisions. *See* Racial conflict

Confrontation, 150

Confucianism, 76–81, 109, 125

Corporations, transnational, 32–35,
59

Cross, the, 103–5

Cultural change: models of, 93, 99–
106, 107; religion and, 3, 158

Cultural pluralism model: defined,
2; drawbacks of, 92, 102; history
of, 88–90; vision of, 106

Descartes, René, 73, 81